THE GREAT SCHISM 1378

Photo: Alinari, Florence

GREGORY XI RETURNS TO ROME IN TRIUMPH FROM AVIGNON.
ST. CATHERINE OF SIENA, HOLDING A LILY,
IS IN THE LEFT FOREGROUND.

A detail from the fresco by Matteo di Giovanni Bartolo in the Hospice of S Maria della Scala, Siena

TURNING POINTS IN HISTORY

General Editor: SIR DENIS BROGAN

THE GREAT SCHISM

1378

BY

JOHN HOLLAND SMITH

HAMISH HAMILTON

LONDON

First published in Great Britain, 1970
by Hamish Hamilton Ltd
90 *Great Russell Street London WC*1
Copyright © 1970 *by John Holland Smith*

SBN 241 01520 0

Printed in Great Britain by
Western Printing Services Ltd
Bristol

CONTENTS

PART I
INTRODUCTION

PART II
THE SWORD OF THE LORD: THE GROWTH OF PAPAL POWER

PART III
THE CHURCH DIVIDED

PART IV
AUTHORITY AFTER THE SCHISM

LIST OF ILLUSTRATIONS

PART ONE

INTRODUCTION

Chapter I

EUROPE 1378

FOR ALMOST nine hundred years after the flight from Rome of the Emperor Romulus 'Augustulus' in A.D. 476, the foundation-stone of European civilization was the papacy, the Rock of Peter.

Its stability was visible to everyone. Its spiritual authority was rarely challenged west of Hungary. Its political authority grew continually and although often challenged was never long withstood. In 1300, when Pope Boniface VIII proclaimed a year of jubilee at Rome, it seemed to the common people, who flocked there in hundreds of thousands, that the Kingdom of God and its glory had at last become visible upon earth.

In fact, however, the rock of the papacy was already being shaken. Philip the Fair, King of France, was refusing to pay his taxes. Soon his soldiers were to arrest and abuse the pope himself, and bring about his death. In less than a decade, the popes were to leave Italy and rule the church, French puppets in the eyes of many, from Avignon.

The migration of the papal court from Rome was almost as disastrous as the flight of the imperial court had been. Less than seventy years later, the rock of Peter split and the Great Schism began.

The 'Babylonian Captivity' of the papacy at Avignon lasted from 1309 to 1376. During that period, seven popes ruled the church. They were all Frenchmen. Only one of them visited Italy. Because of its dependence upon France in a period when nationalism was growing stronger all over Europe, the influence of the papacy on the political life of the continent was weakened and almost destroyed. England would not accept it, because England was intermittently at war with France, and papal envoys from Avignon were barely distinguishable from French propagandists. Germany found it hard to accept, because the rulers of Germany, the Holy Roman Emperors, were used to exerting a direct influence on the popes at Rome. While

3

the papacy was at Avignon, the Germans decreed that German imperial elections should no longer be subject to papal approval and ruled that the Emperor had no superior in the political sphere. The spiritual power of the popes was not yet denied except by a few extremists who had suffered under it, but scholars at the new universities springing up in every country began to argue about where it began and ended. While the pope was his own man, ruling from Rome, it was relatively easy to give assent to the proposition that he stood above all secular rulers. But when he became apparently the mouthpiece of the French king, directing the church from Avignon, these new men of the Renaissance began to ask on what grounds he wielded any power at all.

Yet despite the scandals of the fourteenth century, the weaknesses of the popes, the growing nationalism of the peoples and the widening speculations of the scholars, Peter's rock still seemed firm enough to withstand any shocks when, in 1376, Pope Gregory XI led the papal court back to Rome. The journey itself was something of a triumph. It was begun unwillingly, after pressures on the pope at Avignon had become intolerable. It ended gloriously, with the pope mobbed by cheering crowds of Romans. The senate and the people presented Gregory XI with the keys of the city and its gates, bridges and fortresses. Convinced that a new era had begun in the life of their church and their city, they were willing for the time being to overlook the fact that he was a foreigner—although only a few months earlier they had offered his throne to the Italian Abbot of Monte Cassino, and he had expressed himself willing to accept it with the words, pregnant with menace for the future, 'I am a citizen of Rome, and my first law is the voice of my country.' He was not the only nationalist whose ambitions were extinguished by Rome's warm welcome to Gregory in 1376. Despite the French pope's manifest shortcomings, while he continued to live and rule from Rome, no one in Italy could successfully dispute his apostolic authority.

Unfortunately, Gregory XI lived only fourteen months after arriving in Rome. It could be argued that when he died, the Middle Ages died with him. Yet at the time skilled observers of the political and religious scene missed the significance of his death. The first diplomatic reports of the election of his successor gave no hint of trouble to come. Typical of them was the despatch which Christofero of Piacenza, the envoy at the papal court of the Duke of Mantua, sent to his master on April 9, 1378:

Most Magnificent My Lord—
Commending myself once more to you, I write to inform Your
Sovereignty that, as I wrote earlier, the Lord Pope Gregory left this
world on the twenty-seventh day of March, and that on the eighth day
of April the Lord Cardinals . . . elected to the papacy the Lord
Bartholomeo, Archbishop of Bari, a man of Neapolitan descent, a person both learned in the law and well versed in the usages of the world,
and one who will assuredly be advantageous to the Holy Church of
God . . .

The facts recorded in this despatch were correct; but the circumstances in which the election had taken place were so fantastic that
their omission from it amounted to a deliberate suppression of the
truth.

Almost before Gregory XI was dead, it became clear that only the
lustre of his office had protected him; there was no love in Rome for
Frenchmen. Before his body was buried, the mobs were out in the
streets demanding an Italian pope. Within a day of his death, all the
members of the Sacred College of Cardinals then in Rome knew that
if a foreigner were elected to succeed him, he would probably not
live to rule. The cardinals themselves were threatened. The French
Cardinal Jean de Cros was warned, 'Give us an Italian or a Roman
pope, or all the cardinals from beyond the Alps will be knifed.'

Almost all the cardinals were from beyond the Alps. Five of the
total of twenty-two were still living there, at Avignon, having refused
to accompany Gregory XI. Of the sixteen who were in Rome, eleven
were French—enough, if they were united, to give any candidate
with French backing the two-thirds majority he needed for election.
There was one Spaniard, Cardinal Peter de Luna, and the remaining
four were Italians.* The rules drawn up for papal elections by
Alexander III a century and a half earlier required these sixteen men
to wait ten days after the death of the pope before entering into a
secret conclave to choose his successor. If the citizens of Rome were
to nullify the French advantage in numbers, their move had to be
made during those ten days.

In the fourteenth century the tradition of the church taught—as it
still does today—that popes were elected by the Holy Spirit of God

---

* They were the Romans Francesco Tebaldeschi and Giacomo Orsini (the
favourite of the Roman mob), the Milanese Simone da Brassano, and the
Florentine Pietro Corsini. The Cardinal of Amiens was at Sarzena on papal
business, and unable to return to Rome for the election.

operating through the minds and wills of the cardinals. The Romans of 1378, however, had good reason to know that the electors were open to the influence of other forces not at once obviously spiritual. Emperors and kings had for centuries guided the church in its choice of earthly rulers. Even those Romans who knew no history except that of their own times, realized that until recently Rome had been poverty-stricken simply because the popes, the Bishops of Rome, were living at Avignon—and that they had lived at Avignon because the kings of France had willed it. Moreover, Gregory XI had threatened more than once to return himself to Avignon. The idea that the papal court might once again desert Rome was intolerable. The Holy Spirit, who had so often manifested his will through the kings of France, must also be made to reveal it through the people of Rome.

The threat made to Cardinal Jean de Cros within a few hours of Pope Gregory's death was not an isolated occurrence. During the ten days before the conclave, the Romans spared themselves no effort to win what they wanted. Between March 28 and April 7, Rome was a place of terror to the French cardinals' servants. Citizens took over the functions of the papal guard, made themselves masters of the whole district known as the Borgo San Pietro, and expelled the nobles whose duty it was to protect the cardinals. Fearing that these might attempt to flee from the city and elect one of themselves elsewhere—irregular but quite legal in this period of interregnum, for wherever the cardinals were, there was the electoral power of the church—the Romans blocked the roads out of the city and confiscated the oars and rudders of all the boats on the Tiber. When news of these disturbing events spread into the Campagna, bands of armed men swarmed in from the countryside and hills and skirmishing in the streets broke out between them and the retinues of the cardinals. Noble Romans and wary visitors made ready for worse to come. Some sent their possessions into the country. Others—like Cardinal Peter de Luna—made their wills. Most of the cardinals, however, seem not to have taken the threats very seriously at this stage. They continued to live in the city, taking few extra precautions for their own safety, until the time came for them to surrender to the officers of the conclave and allow themselves to be locked in the Vatican Palace, with one servant-adviser each, until after the election.

The majority of the sixteen who surrendered to the guard on April 7 were later to allege that the election was invalid, because it was not free. Ecclesiastical canon law stipulated that to assume validity a papal election had to be freely made by cardinals not under the constraint of fear. There can be no doubt that by April 7 the pressure on them to elect an Italian was extreme, but not one protested at the time or for some weeks afterwards. Yet as they entered the conclave they were given the message from the twelve governors of the districts of Rome, 'Name an Italian or a Roman pope, otherwise your lives and ours are in danger'—and their message was strongly emphasized by a riotous mob demonstrating outside the palace throughout the night of April 7 to 8. Three days after the conclave ended, Cardinal de Luna's servant wrote of this disturbed night, 'One hour after we were shut up, there arose from outside an uproar from the mob which grew until the cardinals could hardly make themselves intelligible to one another.' Towards morning, the crowd grew so threatening that the alarm was sounded, and the three priors appointed to direct the affairs of the conclave went out intending to parley with the leading demonstrators. The guard turned them back with the warning, 'You run the risk of being torn to pieces. . . . We are outside and can judge the danger better than you can.'

Ominously, the shout was now, 'Death—or an Italian pope!' Bonfires, ready to burn the cardinals if they made a mistake, were being heaped up on the corners of the narrow streets leading to the Vatican. When the first official scrutiny was called, after a Mass of the Holy Spirit had been sung on the morning of April 8, the cardinals were in very real, but not immediate danger. At this last moment, one of them—or so it was said later—refused to take any part in an election held under such conditions. He was Cardinal Orsini, the Roman whom most Romans wanted as their pope. His protest (if in fact he made it: the records show that all sixteen cardinals recorded their votes) was not strong enough to delay the count. When the voting papers were read, the cardinals' choice was found to have fallen unanimously upon Bartholomeo Prignano, the Archbishop of Bari and chancellor of the papal curia under Gregory XI.

Ever since 1378, opinions have been divided over both the election and the character of Prignano. At the scrutiny, it appeared that some of the cardinals had tried to put their own doubts to rest by the form of words in which they expressed their choice. 'I freely name Bari,' one of them wrote, and another, 'I name the Archbishop of Bari with the intention that he shall be undeniably pope.'

As the Archbishop of Bari was not a cardinal, and therefore not actually present at the scrutiny, the cardinals had to delay the announcement of the election until his consent could be obtained. They waited, but the people of Rome would not. Cardinal de Luna's servant was an eye-witness of what happened: 'There arose an even more powerful howl from the devil-possessed mob: "We want a Roman!" With this cry on their lips and bloody swords in their hands, they finally broke into the chapel.'

While the guards were fighting to hold them back, some of the cardinals hastily dressed the aged Roman Cardinal Tebaldeschi in pontifical robes, put him on the throne, and left him to his fate. But he refused to continue with the masquerade telling the people, 'I am not the pope. They have elected a better one, the Archbishop of Bari.' The delay was, however, long enough for the French cardinals to get away. They climbed over roofs and dropped out of windows to escape the swords. It was an ignominious end to an undignified night's work. Within a short time, several of them had barricaded themselves for safety in the Castel Sant' Angelo, Hadrian's mausoleum on the west bank of the Tiber. Others hid in odd corners of the city. But some merely went to their rooms in the Vatican and waited for the noise to die down. None of them was actually harmed in any way.

Whatever doubts the original sixteen who elected Prignano may privately have felt at this stage, not one of the twelve who could be found the next day declared himself unwilling to take part in the solemn enthronement of the new pope on Easter Sunday, April 18. The letters sent out by the cardinals during the next few days announcing the election to the princes of Europe indicated no doubts about the validity of the proceedings. One of the most interesting as seen in the light of later events, that written on April 14 by Cardinal Robert of Geneva, the French king's cousin, to the Emperor Charles IV of Germany, reveals slight uneasiness at the brevity of the conclave, but does not question its outcome:

> Most serene Highness and beloved Lord and Cousin, after first reminding you of the death of our Lord Pope Gregory XI, which I announced to Your Serenity in an earlier letter, I would inform you that the ten days after the death required by canon law having passed, my lords the other cardinals and I were shut up in conclave, and the name of the Archbishop of Bari, as he then was (but now the Supreme Pontiff), a man of the nation of the Neapolitans, having been suggested

to us . . . the cardinals and I unanimously gave our votes to him on the eighth day of this month, in solemn conclave, one night's delay having passed, because the Romans would not consent to any more time being spent in the said conclave . . .

In fact, the announcement of Prignano's election seems to have been greeted with general applause, both in Rome itself and beyond. Before his election he had been regarded as a model papal courtier, serving loyally at Avignon as Neapolitan vice-chancellor to Gregory XI. That remarkable woman Catherine of Siena, who had made a journey to Avignon to persuade Gregory to come to Italy, and had said after Gregory's death that the Archbishop of Bari was the only man at court fit to be pope, rejoiced at the news of his election. Christofero of Piacenza wrote again to the Duke of Mantua:

I write to inform your Lordship that since I wrote to you last on the ninth day of the present month, saying that we had an Italian pope, on that same day, at about the twenty-second hour, the Lord Cardinals gave him a name, and he was proclaimed Urban VI . . . and I truly believe that we have a pope to please you, and am convinced that the church of God will be well governed, and will even go so far as to say that for a hundred years or more the Holy Church of God has not had a pastor like him . . .

To the general dismay, this last sentiment all too quickly proved to be true. So unparallelled was Urban VI's behaviour towards all who opposed him that it has even been suggested that the shock of being elected was too much for his mind. He may or may not have been mad. He certainly appears to have been an idealist who during all the years of his vice-chancellorship had nursed dreams of a remodelled and revitalized church. As soon as he had been crowned and enthroned, he set in motion a general reform.

The particular crimes against which he set his face were clerical ostentation and simony, the selling of ecclesiastical offices. Extravagance under Gregory XI had reduced the papacy to the expedient of borrowing money on a large scale. Simony, although long forbidden, had for centuries been bringing obloquy on the church and making it impossible for popes and bishops effectively to denounce financial corruption in the secular world. But if Urban's intended reform was necessary, the methods he used in attempting to achieve it were deplorable. Soon Catherine of Siena was writing to him 'Justice without mercy may well seem more like injustice' and 'Go about your work with moderation and benevolence and a tranquil heart.

For the love of Jesus Crucified, Holy Father, soften a little the sudden movements of your temper'.

The sudden movements of Urban's newly revealed temper were ultimately to bring five cardinals to the rack. During the first months of his pontificate, he did no more than shout gross insults and try to strike anyone who annoyed him. He made enemies of the cardinals and of the papacy's closest allies, but for some time no overt move was made against him. None of the Christian rulers of Europe denounced the election. Even Charles V of France, who had obviously lost most as a result, raised no objection that year. Opposition, however, existed, and was growing.

By ones and twos the cardinals began to leave Rome. The excuse they gave was that it was now summer, and the city was too hot. First to go were the French. They retired to Anagni, a small city some forty miles south-east of Rome, on the road to Monte Cassino. By June, the papal court was severely depleted. Urban, instead of creating enough Italian cardinals to outvote the French (as Catherine of Siena urged him to do), appealed to the Frenchmen to return. Their reply was that they doubted if he had any right to ask them to do so: they had elected him when in fear for their lives, and it was quite possible that he was not really pope at all.

On July 26, three of the four Italian cardinals left Rome for an undisclosed destination. The fourth, Francesco Tebaldeschi, Urban's only remaining supporter in Rome, lay on his deathbed. A few days later, the three Italians appeared at Anagni. By August, thirteen of Urban's sixteen electors were together there, one was dead, and the other two were in France. On August 9, the French cardinals issued a proclamation from Anagni, declaring that Urban VI was not the pope, that the church had no ruler, that the election of the Archbishop of Bari had been invalid, and that he himself was to be regarded as excommunicate and anathema. Another conclave would be held in a place of peace and safety, and a true pope elected to rule the church.

The place they chose for the conclave was Fondi, a city on the Via Appia almost midway between Rome and Naples, within the jurisdiction of Queen Joanna I of Naples and her fourth husband Otto of Brunswick. Although Joanna's natural sympathies lay with Urban as a native of her kingdom, she had fought all her life to preserve the frontiers of her territory for her successors, and saw the pope ruling in Rome, and by his presence there strengthening the Papal States, as a definite threat. Moreover, Urban VI had already succeeded in personally antagonizing Joanna and her husband, and also her vassal, Count Gaetani of Fondi. While the cardinals remained at Fondi, therefore, they were as safe as her army could make them. Urban never forgave Joanna for protecting his enemies. He ensured that within a few years it should cost her first her throne and then her life.

The new conclave was not held immediately the cardinals arrived at Fondi. They waited for international reactions to their August Declaration before taking what was certain to be an irrevocable step; in particular, they wanted to be sure of the support of Charles V of France. It reached them on September 18, in the form of a letter promising not immediate recognition for a new pope but a subsidy of 20,000 francs and an army to protect them against Urban. Charles also wrote to the Queen of Naples, urging her to do her utmost to protect 'his faithful friends' the cardinals. On the following day, the thirteen cardinals—French, Spanish and Italian—entered into conclave at Fondi. All the rules were observed. On the 20th, they announced that they had elected a true pope, Cardinal Robert of Geneva, who would be known as Clement VII.

The rock of Peter had split. Catherine of Siena, when she heard of this second election, wrote to her friend Urban: 'In my opinion, these devils incarnate have not elected a Christ on earth, but have brought into being an antichrist against you, who are Christ on earth.' This is still the orthodox Catholic reaction to the election at Fondi.

Robert of Geneva, Clement VII, was not obviously an antichrist. Like Bartholomeo Prignano, he was an official of the church, tried by long and exacting service. Prignano had been a political and legal officer, the vice-chancellor at Avignon. Robert of Geneva had been an executive, Gregory XI's legate in Italy and the commander of the military forces of the Papal states. Like most military commanders, he had been forced during his career to order some unsavoury actions. But he had never been accused of disloyalty.

In modern Catholic lists of the popes, published under authority, Robert of Geneva is named as the first antipope of the Great Schism which lasted until 1417 and beyond. The second election at Fondi is condemned and Urban VI, although almost no one defends him as an estimable person, is declared to have been the true ruler of the church, duly elected and confirmed. The authors of these lists owe their certitude to much later events. The validity of Prignano's election was demonstrated long after 1378 by men anxious to restore papal authority after the schism. At the time of Robert of Geneva's counter-election, the issue was by no means so clear.

Even Charles V of France seems to have been in two minds about the situation. Although he had a vested interest in the election of his cousin and the return of the papal court to Avignon which could be confidently expected to follow it, he made no direct move either for Clement VII or against Urban VI until a month after the election at Fondi. He then called an assembly of the clergy of France to hear Clement's case from his envoys, and debate the matter. The clergy met at Vincennes, on November 16, and sought the advice of those French cardinals who, because they were absent from Italy, had taken part in neither election. Perhaps not surprisingly, they expressed themselves opposed to Urban, the new cardinals he was reported to be creating to fill posts in his empty court, and everyone who supported him in every way.

Charles V agreed, but not all his clergy were convinced. Normandy and Provence proved especially difficult. Still moving cautiously, in January Charles consulted the University of Paris. The doctors proved to be as puzzled as everyone else. It was not until May 30 that the delegates of the university reported to the king, quite untruthfully, that 'from the beginning the University has adhered to Clement VII as the true pope'. Lie or otherwise, it was all that was needed. From then on, Clement was never without French royal protection, open and declared.

He would soon need it, for Urban had meanwhile decided that action must be taken against Clement's other supporter, the Queen of Naples. Knowing that as a Neapolitan he could command some support among the people of Naples, he denounced the queen as a schismatic and declared her throne forfeit. Fortunately—as it must have seemed to him at that moment—there was at hand a politically acceptable claimant to Naples, Charles of Durazzo, a great-nephew of Joanna's grandfather, King Robert 'the Wise', who had willed his throne to her. On June 1, 1378, Urban named him King of Naples and the next day solemnly crowned him in St. Peter's. Unfortunately for Joanna, Clement, having been defeated in battle by Italian mercenaries fighting for Urban, was on the point of returning to France, and the man whom she had named as her heir, Charles V of France's younger brother, Louis, Duke of Anjou, had not yet arrived in Naples. There was no soldier in Joanna's kingdom capable of defeating Charles of Durazzo in battle and by July 26 he had taken the whole kingdom except the Castel d'Uovo at Naples itself. Joanna took refuge there, but shortly afterwards she was driven out. Urban appeared to control Southern Italy.

Soon, however, Charles of Durazzo discovered the difficulty of remaining Urban's ally. Part of the agreement between them had been based on the promise that as soon as Charles ruled in Naples, he would give a number of cities, including Capua, Amalfi, Caserta and Fondi, to the pope's nephew and make him a duke. But he did not keep his word, and when Urban pressed him, offered his allegiance to Clement. He remained loyal to his new master even when, in 1382, an expeditionary force from France landed in Naples with the object of seizing both his kingdom and the Papal States for the benefit of Louis of Anjou. He defeated the French army and continued to follow the French pope. Even after he died in 1385 during an attempt to add the throne of Hungary to his dominions, the regents of his son Ladislas continued to support Clement until Urban's death.

If, however, political considerations left the rulers of France and Naples few real hesitations over which of the rival popes they would support, the rest of Europe generally found itself in greater difficulties. In the far west of Catholic Europe, Portugal decided for Clement, England for Urban. There seems little doubt that the ministers of England's eleven-year-old Richard II made their choice because France was the traditional enemy, and as recently as 1377 had shown her hostility by mounting a series of attacks on the coast of Sussex, the Isle of Wight and the Thames Estuary. Indeed the English refused to meet Clement's envoys and within three years had forced the King of Portugal to renounce his own first adherence and opt for Urban. Robert II of Scotland, on the other hand, chose Clement and the continuation of the French alliance, and even when France herself repudiated Clement's successor, Scotland remained loyal to him.

In Germany, the Emperor Charles IV to whom Robert of Geneva had sent his announcement of Urban's election lived only until the end of 1378. He accepted its validity and, when he heard of the counter-election at Fondi shortly before his death, announced that he had no doubts that Urban was nevertheless the true pope. He was succeeded by his son, Wenceslas IV of Bohemia, and the new emperor-elect also chose Urban, partly from conviction, partly from filial piety, partly from antagonism towards France, and partly because his election entitled him to be called King of the Romans and it was politically expedient for him to have living within his dominions an amenable—that is, a non-French—pope. His example was not followed by all the dukes, princes, bishops and kings of his empire. Some at first supported Clement, but gradually Urban, and pan-German interests, claimed the majority.

The nations of south-western Europe, apart from Portugal, were exceedingly scrupulous over their decision. The Kings of Castile, Aragon and Navarre all remained neutral until it became quite clear that the schism would not heal itself. The King of Castile had careful enquiries made in Italy and France, and the reports of his commissioners were debated until 1381 before at last he acknowledged Clement as the true pope. It was eight years after the beginning of the schism before Aragon and its overseas dependencies gave allegiance to Clement, and four more before Charles III of Navarre decided against Rome and in favour of Avignon. By that time, Urban and Clement were dead, and the schism had been given every appearance of permanency by the election of successors to them both.

In Italy itself, the other small states were, like Naples in the first months, inclined towards Urban until one by one he alienated them. His violence in his own domains drove Umbria and Tuscany into a hostile alliance. Florence, Bologna and all the northern territories under the Viscontis of Milan initially received Urban's ambassadors, but finally gave their support to Clement. The rulers of Sicily corresponded with both popes; subjects of Aragon until 1410, they appear to have been personally more inclined towards Avignon, although the native nobility and peasantry favoured Rome.

Far to the east, from the island kingdom of Cyprus, Charles V of Lusignan, a nobleman of French extraction, also gave his support to Clement.

What emerges from this brief survey of allegiances after the schism became an established fact of European life, is that the question 'Who is the true pope?' was by no means as easy to answer in the 1380s as some later propagandists have suggested that it should have been. The argument raged over all Europe. The hesitancies of so many to make a firm decision give a clear indication that the schism was a very real moral problem, and not merely a political gamble among unscrupulous adventurers interested only in power. The King of Navarre left his decision between Rome and Avignon until as late as 1390, twelve years after the schism began, not because it did not matter to him who ruled the church, but because it mattered supremely. The position of the papacy in the late fourteenth century was unique. For both political and religious reasons, it was impossible that there should be two popes, since only one of the two claimants could be the true ruler of Catholic Christendom. It was, therefore, vitally important to know whether the true line ran through Rome or through Avignon, and even more imperative to decide how one of the lines, preferably the false one, could be eliminated.

It is difficult for us, brought up in the post-Great-Schism tradition of national independence, to realize how pressing this latter problem was nearly six centuries ago. Something of the pain and confusion that intelligent men felt in this period of chaos can be felt in an extract from a letter sent by the professor of law at Bologna, John of Spoleto, to his fellow-scholar James of Altovitis, about the year 1394:

> The longer this schism lasts, the more it appears to be costing, and the more harm it does: scandal, massacres, ruination, agitations, troubles and disturbances ... this dissension is the root of everything: divers tumults, quarrels between kings, seditions, extortions, assassinations, acts of violence, wars, rising tyranny, decreasing freedom, the impunity of villains, grudges, error, disgrace, the madness of steel and of fire given license.

Significantly, when he wrote these lines John was joining in a debate about the need for what might nowadays be called a round table conference between all interested parties to cure the ills of the time. The suggestion that such a conference might be held was a revolutionary one. For centuries, popes and bishops alone had ruled the Western church. To recommend, as John of Spoleto and his contemporaries at the universities now began to do with ever-increasing conviction, that scholars and lawyers, simple priests and laymen, should play an active part in shaping the future of the church, horrified traditionalists in a way that can only be appreciated in the light of the origins and development of papal authority in the West. John and his fellow-lawyers invented the system of national voting on international affairs, but it was not forced on Europe without a struggle. The first time it was tried, during a Council at Pisa set up to end the schism, it failed; the second time it was used, at the 1415 Council of Constance, its results were ambiguous, but the schism was ended.

The Council of Constance was quite unlike most earlier Western church councils, such as the Third Council of the Lateran which in 1215 accepted Pope Alexander III's proposals for solving the problems of papal elections. Its origins were different. It was called—as the first general councils of the church had been—not by a pope, but by an emperor, Sigismund, the German King of the Romans. Its procedure was different. It demanded the resignation of the rival claimants to the papal throne—there were three living, one of whom must have been the true pope—as a preliminary to most of its real work. It debated not the fulfilment of the will of the successor to St. Peter, but the question of whether that will ought to be fulfilled at all if it had not first been discussed and voted the will of the whole church. Only its climax was predictable. It ended in a reactionary movement, a swing of the pendulum against those who, while the Great Schism lasted, had argued for the total subjection of future popes to the authority of general councils. Martin V, the pope who emerged from the debate as ruler of the church, would accept domination by nobody. Nor would his successors, the popes of the Renaissance and the Reformation. By the time of his election, however, the pattern of the life of the church and of the continent of Europe had been subtly yet permanently changed.

For the inescapable fact was that a council of subordinates had successfully brought pressure on the most absolute of authorities. The popes claimed to be the plenipotentiary representatives of God in the world, the sole source of all secular power and spiritual authority, but at Constance their claims had been not openly derided but practically ignored. Basic assumptions about the nature of the framework of the civilized world had been called into question. A moment before the final eclipse of the concept of a universal Roman Empire, the power of the King of the Romans had once again changed the course of history. The Great Schism and the Council of Constance which ended it determined the pattern of the Reformation and Counter-reformation. More remotely, they helped to lay the foundation both for the development of modern Western political thinking on the distribution of power and for the construction of nineteenth- and twentieth-century concepts of authority in the church—concepts ranging from those enshrined in the dogma of papal infallibility promulgated at the First Council of the Vatican in 1870 to those hinted at in the liberalizing decrees of the Second Vatican Council and still being elaborated by discussions among Christians today.

PART TWO

*THF SWORD OF THE LORD: THE
GROWTH OF PAPAL POWER*

Chapter I

THE CHURCH AND THE EMPIRE

'THE FIRST foundation of salvation', Pope Hormisdas wrote in the year 517 to the bishops of Spain, 'is to preserve the rule of true faith and deviate not at all from the constitutions of the fathers. Hence it is impossible to disregard the ruling made by our Lord Jesus Christ when he said, "Thou art Peter and upon this rock I will build my church" . . . I trust therefore that when the apostolic see recommends something in a communication to you, it will be heeded.'

Throughout the Middle Ages, from the time of Pope Hormisdas to the era of the Great Schism and beyond, no ordinary Christian doubted that the Gospels preserved the actual words of Jesus in the context in which they had been spoken. Few men in the West questioned the doctrine that Jesus had founded a hierarchical church and given Peter authority in it with the very words 'Thou art Peter and upon this rock I will build my church' and that the Bishops of Rome had inherited Peter's authority over the whole church—although it was denied in Greece and Asia Minor, where supreme power under Christ was attributed to oecumenical, or universal, councils of the church, and the Bishop of Rome was regarded only as the patriarch of the West, comparable in authority to the patriarchs of Antioch, Alexandria, Constantinople and Jerusalem. From Italy to Britain, wherever there were orthodox Christians, the promise to Peter was quoted to prove papal authority and the rock-like immutability of the church.

— Puritan view

The earliest Christians drew their ideas of the form their society should take from the patterns provided by the civilizations with which they were already acquainted. In the Near East in the first and second centuries of the Christian era, all societies were hierarchical and patriarchal. Christianity first appeared in the setting of Judaism, quickly spread into the non-Jewish world and grew up in a niche it found for itself in the realm of ideas, midway between Judaism and the hellenized Roman Empire. Both these dominant cultures were monarchical and rigid in structure. Although the Lord Yahweh and the Emperors of Rome differed in almost every other respect, they had this much in common, that they both ruled absolutely through a hierarchy of subordinate officers.

If the picture of the earliest Christian community at Jerusalem drawn in the first part of the Acts of the Apostles is to be trusted— and although it poses some historical problems there is no good reason seriously to question its broad outlines—the Christian *ecclesia* was to some degree hierarchical from the beginning. Converts were taught that 'Jesus is Lord'. The 'apostles' led 'the brethren'. They appointed 'servants' or 'ministers', the deacons, to distribute charity. They settled disputes, laid down rules for future action and, as the church began to spread to new centres, set up new communities with leaders called 'elders' (presbyters) and 'overseers' (*episkopoi*). The precise nature of the relationship in the new communities between the leaders and the led is not altogether clear from the New Testament itself. It is debatable, for instance, whether the 'elders' and the 'overseers' held the same rank and whether the leadership in a new community was an individual or a corporate office. The structure of early communities probably varied from place to place within the limits set on the one hand by the simple form of the Jewish synagogue and on the other by the more complex organization of the Roman province. Certainly the apostles themselves, and in later years Paul, were recognized to have special credentials as chosen eye-witnesses, and there is no evidence of any attempt to perpetuate their particular kind of authority after their deaths, although some successful missionaries were honorifically remembered as the apostles of those whom they had converted.

Inevitably, however, given the climate of the times, once the apostles were prevented by death or incapacity from exercising their own special kind of authority, new men took over the functions of leadership, and within a hundred years or so of the Crucifixion the principle was well established throughout the Greek-speaking world that, on the death of a community-leader, another was elected by those who had worked with and under the dead man, and confirmed in his position by an act of consecration performed by leaders from other communities generally recognized as orthodox.

In second-century documents the leader of a local Christian group symbolizes and guarantees the orthodoxy and continuity of that group. It was the boast of the oldest communities that they had been founded by apostles, and name-lists of bishops, *episkopoi*, were compiled to prove the authority of community-leaders and the antiquity of their churches. Although it is still not possible to prove beyond all doubt that Peter ever visited Rome or that he and Paul were martyred there in the sixties of the first century, their names were certainly venerated there from very early times, and Rome prided herself on being the only diocese with two founding fathers, both killed on her own soil. The destruction of Jerusalem by the legions in A.D.70 and A.D.135 ensured that the old Holy City would not rival the imperial capital as the main centre of early Christianity. It was perhaps inevitable that Rome should soon begin to claim for herself a leading role in the affairs of the church: whether she was 'right' to do so, in a moral or theological sense, is a question of conscience rather than of history.

In his *Against the Heresies*, written during the reign of Pope Eleutherius (?175–189), Irenaeus of Lyons gave Rome a unique position among the churches, calling it 'the greatest and most ancient church, familiar to everybody, founded and established at Rome by the two most glorious apostles Peter and Paul' and declaring that 'with this church, by reason of the authority of its origin, every church— that is to say, the faithful everywhere—should agree. For in it the apostolic tradition has been continually preserved by faithful men'.

He listed the 'faithful men' from Peter and Paul to his own times: 'Linus . . . Anacletus . . . Clement . . . Evarestus . . . Alexander . . . Xystus . . . Telesphoros . . . Hyginus . . . Pius . . . Anicetus . . . Soter . . . Eleutheros', not merely to prove that the list was known but also that the tradition was secure and trustworthy. Rome's was the authentic voice of tradition, and anyone teaching differently from Rome must be regarded with suspicion. When, probably less than ten years later, however, Eleutheros's successor, Victor, found himself in dispute with the bishops of Asia Minor over the date of the Easter festival, Irenaeus (himself a native of Asia Minor, although a bishop in Gaul) boldly supported the Eastern bishops, reminding Victor that different parts of the church had been observing different customs for a very long time, and that none of his predecessors had tried to impose Roman customs on the East, nor had they made differences of practice 'a ground for rejecting anyone'. If Irenaeus's advice on toleration had been accepted, subsequent Christian history would have been very different.

Polycrates of Ephesus, the leader of the Eastern bishops in this dispute, set a precedent that was long to be observed by flatly refusing to obey Rome: he wrote to Victor, 'We shall continue scrupulously in our own Easter observances, adding nothing and taking nothing away'.

The fact should not be overlooked that before the end of the period of persecution by the Roman Empire, the Christians of the West were a relatively unimportant and uninfluential body, probably forming a majority in no centre of population west of Asia Minor. The various honours and powers granted to different bishops by Christians themselves had little effect on the life of the majority of the citizens of the empire, which persecuted them as members of a secret society menacing the stability of the state. The church was strongest in the most hellenized parts of the empire: in the East, and at Rome itself, where according to an ancient tradition, the language of worship was Greek until the reign of Pope Damasus (366–84). It was after the Emperor Constantine first tolerated and then began to favour the Christian faith that the stream of converts became a flood and the control of Christianity a matter of daily concern to the bureaucrats of the empire. The Christian emperors used the oecumenical council as their chief instrument for handling their Christian subjects, and the 'political' history of the church for more than a thousand years after the publication of the Edict of Toleration in A.D.313 was the complicated story of the changing relationships between emperors, popes, patriarchs and councils.

Constantine first became involved in an ecclesiastical dispute within months of the publication of the Edict. Toleration followed what had perhaps been the most bitter of all persecutions in Africa, that under Diocletian. As often happened, the time of trial had a bitter aftermath. In 312, an African synod declared the recent election of a bishop of Carthage invalid, because he had received ordination at the hands of Felix, Bishop of Aptunga, who during the persecution had been a *traditor*, one who had surrendered the scriptures and other sacred objects to imperial officers for destruction in accordance with the law. The synod elected a new bishop, Donatus, and the ensuing controversy did not die down for more than a century.

To Donatus and his supporters, it seemed obvious that a sacrament such as ordination could be effective only if both its minister and its recipient were morally fit, the one to give, the other to receive. To the rest of the church, it was equally obvious that the power of God was not limited by his servants. Even a bad bishop was still a bishop, and could still validly ordain priests.

The problem was a very real one, and has often recurred since. At the time of the Great Schism it was to be the authority of unworthy popes that concerned the church. In Carthage, nearly a thousand years earlier, the problem was a traitorous bishop: soon there were two bishops, one 'Catholic', the other 'Donatist', in many of the dioceses which had suffered severe persecution and where feelings naturally ran highest against the *traditores*. Constantine was involved in the conflict because, as a tolerated religion after 313, Christianity was entitled to the protection of the law. His letters to Christian leaders, explaining the privileges of toleration, had referred only to advantages to be granted to Catholic bishops—the right to own property, especially cemeteries, and to reclaim property sequestered during the persecutions being the most important among them. The letters took no account of possible divisions in the church, and the Catholics of Africa used them to subdue the Donatists. The latter appealed to Constantine's proconsul in Africa, asking that judges from Gaul—where the church was not involved in the dispute—should be appointed to settle the question of who should be tolerated and who not. The proconsul passed their request to Constantine he in turn appointed three Gallic bishops to review the case and decreed that they should present the evidence they collected to Melitiades, the Bishop of Rome, for his judgment.

Melitiades slightly changed the commission by calling a full synod at Rome to hear the evidence, thus in effect taking the matter out of the Gauls' hands. In October 313, nineteen bishops assembled at the Lateran condemned Donatus on several grounds, including that of re-baptizing Christians coming to him from other churches, but in order to avoid making the schism in Africa permanent refused to condemn those who had supported his campaign.

The opinion of the Roman synod was not, however, accepted as the final word on the question. Neither Catholics nor Donatists were satisfied by it. The case was re-examined at a Council at Arles in 314 —the first at which British bishops are known to have participated— and final judgment given by Constantine himself in November 316:

> I see clearly that Caecilian [the Catholic Bishop of Carthage] is a wholly innocent man, who observes all the duties of his religion and serves it in a fitting manner. It seems to me fully proven that no one has

been able to bring any proof of any fault in his conduct, contrary to the accusations made against him in his absence by the hypocrisy of his adversaries . . .

On the basis of this judgment, Constantine—who was not yet baptized—issued a severe decree against the Donatists, unleashing the army against them. Many were killed, defending their churches: few were converted. The decree was not repealed until May 321, when a special edict of toleration was issued in respect of the sect.

Neither repression nor toleration put an end to Donatism, but the appeal to Constantine and his reaction had established a dangerous set of precedents. Emperors claimed authority over every aspect of life in the empire, and it was not long before Constantine and his successors began to look on it as their right to intervene in Christian affairs whenever they chose and to attempt to bend the direction of Christian evolution to suit imperial policies. Eventually, the Western church countered by claiming that all power, even the imperial, was derived from God through the Bishop of Rome. But at the time of Constantine, general acceptance of that theory in the West lay nine hundred years in the future and before it was finally agreed to there were to be many battles between emperors and bishops. The pattern of the future was set for the imperial side by Constantine's handling of the Donatist affair and confirmed by his action in taking it on himself, in 325, to summon the first oecumenical council, the Council of Nicaea.

By then, Christians had become so numerous throughout the empire that any dispute among them threatened peace and stability. When Arius, a presbyter of Alexandria, began to teach that the Son was subordinate to the Father, there were many new converts to the church ready to believe that this was common Christian teaching. Soon the bishops of the newly-Christian world were engaged in a war of pamphlets and sermons. Their untheological converts went much further and carried the dispute into the streets. Constantine, who prided himself on his grasp of theology and Christian politics although he was still nominally a pagan, summoned all the bishops of the empire to travel at his expense to Nicaea in Asia Minor, close to his new capital of Constantinople, and debate the truth with him there. Early church historians record that three hundred and eighteen bishops answered his summons. The Bishop of Rome, Sylvester I, was not among them, but was represented by two priests. The Western position—that the Son is equal to the Father—was ably put by

Bishop Hosius of Cordoba, who persuaded Constantine himself to speak in defence of the same view. It is difficult to judge how much weight the emperor's influence carried, but Arius's teaching was condemned. For good or evil, politicians had begun to speak on church affairs. The Donatist controversy and the Council of Nicaea saw the birth of a new kind of relationship between church and state, one which in the East was to grow through the centuries until the church became dependent on the state, and the state, to a lesser extent, on the church. The effects of caesaro-papism—the doctrine, crudely defined, that the secular ruler is the natural head of the church within his dominions—have been far-reaching in the lands which once belonged to the Eastern empire or, like Russia, were evangelized from them.

Roman claims to universal jurisdiction were forged in the fires of controversy as weapons to be used in combating the presumption, as Rome saw it, of emperors, Eastern patriarchs, and heretics. Traditional rights of judgment were claimed by Pope Julius I as early as 340 in a haughty letter to the Eastern bishops, asking, 'Do you not know that it is customary to write to us at the outset [of a dispute], so that justice may be done from here?' Three years later, at the Western Synod of Sardica, it was ruled that no bishop could be deposed anywhere in the world 'unless the case has been judicially decided by the Bishop of Rome'. The effect of this canon was to make the Bishop of Rome the 'emperor' of the church, the final judge in the appeals court of the City of God. In later times, the right of prelates to appeal to Rome was to be steadfastly upheld by the papacy and was to become a frequent cause of dispute between the ecclesiastical and secular authorities of Europe. The pope's imperial juridical rights inevitably appeared to national rulers to deny them their full powers in their own kingdoms. But during the controversies of the fourth and following centuries they were at one moment admitted and at another denied, according to the exigencies of the situation. Thus, in 379, the Eastern emperor issued a decree to the effect that 'any doctrine differing from the faith clearly taught by the Pontiff Damasus [of Rome] and by Peter, the Bishop of Alexandria' was to be rigorously suppressed; and two years later the first general council of Constantinople adopted the Roman and Alexandrian creed as the sole official statement of faith, ruling also that 'the Bishop of Constantinople is to have primacy of honour next after the Bishop of Rome, because Constantinople is the new Rome', but forbidding bishops to interfere in the affairs of one another's dioceses, so effectively rejecting Roman claims to juridical rights throughout the world.

In fact, those claims were not yet admitted everywhere even in Italy. The common attitude to Rome was one of respect but not subservience. Thus at the end of the century Ambrose of Milan, although he taught his catechumens that it was fitting to follow the practice of the Roman Church in all things, nevertheless insisted on the autonomy of his own diocese, even going so far on one occasion as to call a council of his own to re-try the case of a suspected heretic already condemned by Rome 'to remain outside the church . . . eternally'. It was the welfare of the church as a whole, and not the authority of the church of Rome, that concerned Ambrose and most of his contemporaries, even including the most authoritarian and influential of them all, Augustine of Hippo, the model for whose 'City of God' was not the Holy City of Peter and the saints, but the imperial city of Augustus and the Caesars.

Imperial Rome was dying, but to Augustine there was something about the old city and its empire that seemed to presage the celestial city where God would rule for ever. The Roman Empire had been a political concept whose success had been due to intellectual as much as to physical accomplishment. Men had believed in the empire, therefore the empire had come into being and had endured. It seemed to Augustine that the church must inherit this vision and faith. Rome had been the city of the divine emperor: the church would be the City of God. Rome had flourished for centuries on earth, but was dying because it was purely terrestrial: the City of God would last for ever, because it existed both on earth and in heaven, and Christ was its eternal emperor. Just as all kinds of men, sinners as well as saints, had lived under the protection of Rome, so all kinds of men could live in the City of God upon earth, the church in its visible aspect. But the City of God had a new dimension, the heavenly, not shared by the old city; its glories would be enjoyed only by the elect who, tried and proved by life, showed themselves worthy of the reward of eternal citizenship.

Neither in his *City of God* itself, nor in his other writings, however, did Augustine of Hippo indicate that the Bishops of Rome were to play a special, divinely-ordained part in the new world order. During the controversies of the early fifth century, both Innocent I and Zozimus claimed universal jurisdiction on the imperial pattern for the See of Peter, the latter writing quite explicitly, 'as Peter is the head of all authority, so all authority belongs to us, and no one can force the right of judgment out of our hands'.

These were brave words to come out of Italy in that decade. In 406, the frontiers of the empire had collapsed at last, and a flood of Goths and their kinsfolk had swept through Gaul and into the Iberian Peninsula. In 409, they had invaded Italy herself and bypassing Ravenna, where the Western emperor had established his capital, had driven on southwards to sack Rome. The old Provinces of Gaul and Spain had become confederations of Visigothic kingdoms owing only a shadowy allegiance to the empire. Britain had been lost entirely, given up for the sake of reinforcements. To hold on to any authority whatsoever, the popes had to assert their position in the strongest possible terms—the more so because the Goths were Arians.

Still more disastrously from the pope's point of view, so also were the next wave of invaders, the Vandals, who swept through the already established Visigothic kingdoms on their way to destroy Africa in the twenties of the fifth century; it was during their siege of Carthage that Augustine died. For a century after their invasion the popes, while endeavouring to assert their authority in the East in the face of growing defiance from Constantinople, were also energetically engaged in trying to convert these new Western Arians to Catholicism as a prelude to sending fresh missions to the still pagan lands of the North—a task which became even more pressing after a third invasion, that by Attila's Huns, reached the West in 450.

By then, the emperor of the West had become a shadowy figure, disappearing altogether before the century ended, and Rome had sunk to the status of a provincial city. Nonetheless, it was of Rome that the barbarians dreamed. To them it remained the capital of the world and they longed to become not Byzantines but Romans. The ruler of Rome was therefore a crucial figure in the new West, and after the collapse of imperial power, the most important person in Rome was her bishop, the only man in the administration whose name was influential outside the bureaus of the remaining Graeco-Roman clerks. While the patriarchs of the East struggled for power in a world that was still apparently stable, the patriarch of the West was learning to dominate a manifestly unstable world, where he had to play the roles of magistrate, ambassador and, soon, independent king.

Growing papal independence was no more welcome to the emperors of the East than papal assumption of juridical rights was to Eastern patriarchs. Seen from the East, independence looked like arrogance. Arriving at Ephesus in 431 for a council called by the Eastern emperor to settle the Nestorian controversy, the legates of Pope Celestine not only ignored the fact that the emperor's council had already started and convened another, but also demanded that everyone should accept their master's ruling on the points at issue. When there was next a council at Ephesus, in 449, and Celestine's successor, Leo I, sent representatives with a statement of Roman theology—the 'Tome of Leo'—to be imposed on the delegates, the council fathers refused to listen and the emperor ruled that the Bishops of Rome had no jurisdiction in the Eastern empire. But the situation changed with the accession of a Catholic to the throne the following year, and in 451 Leo's Tome, introduced into the debates of the Council of Chalcedon under the watchful eyes of imperial guards, was welcomed with cries of 'Peter has spoken through Leo!'; but the bishops, although willing to grant Leo's orthodoxy, would not admit his jurisdictional primacy. In the canons of the council, Rome is said to rule the church 'as a head over limbs' but Constantinople is named as the final court of appeal for the East.

Leo's Tome and the theological rulings based on it were the indirect cause of the first major schism between the Eastern and Western churches. The monks of Egypt rejected their teaching and fought so hard for their own interpretations that there were soon two churches in the East, one following the faith of Chalcedon, the other monophysitism, the doctrine that Christ was so dominated by the will of God that his human mind and will were extinguished. By 482, the situation had become so dangerous that the Emperor Zeno was driven to prepare what he hoped would be an acceptable compromise formula—the *Henotikon*—and decree that no one who opposed it could be accepted as a bishop. The patriarch of Constantinople approved the compromise, but the pope, Felix III, refused to subscribe to it, condemned the patriarch, and finally excommunicated both him and the Emperor Zeno himself. For thirty-five years, the orthodox churches remained divided, while monophysitism spread throughout the East and infected the West. This quarrel was only a foretaste of what was to come.

But the prestige of the Roman church rose in Italy during this troubled period. Already in the year 445, an edict of the Western emperor had named Leo I, the author of the Tome, as the highest authority in the church. Just over forty years later, with the Western empire little more than a memory, Theodoric of the Ostrogoths the most powerful king in Italy, the Eastern church split by the monophysite controversy, and most of the West still either Arian or pagan, Pope Gelasius repeated and strengthened Roman claims in the first official decretals, which set out the decrees of the Roman church on matters such as the canon of scripture and the hierarchy of authority within the church. 'Although the universal church diffused throughout the whole world is all of the one vinestock of Christ,' he wrote,

> the holy Roman church is by general agreement set before all other churches whatsoever, having been given primacy by the word of the Lord and Saviour in the Gospels, when he said, 'Thou art Peter . . . (*Matthew XVI*, 18*f.*)
>
> Moreover, with this was associated the presence [at Rome] of the most blessed apostle Paul, the vessel of election, who on one and the same day—and not, as the heretics gabble, at a different time—suffered and was crowned with a glorious death with Peter in the city of Rome under the Caesar Nero: and together they consecrated the abovementioned holy Roman church to Christ the Lord, giving it precedence before all other cities in the world by their presence and venerable triumph there.

Dominance over the whole church was, Gelasius believed, the right of the Roman see. Neither he nor any other early pope found it necessary to try and prove that the power of jurisdiction given to Peter in the Gospel passed to his successors: they assumed that it had, as imperial power passed from emperor to emperor. Peter's authority was inherited with his 'chair' at Rome.

Gelasius's claims actually went still further. Without setting out a detailed argument, he extended his powers to include authority over kings. 'There are,' he said, 'two things by which the world is primarily ruled, the authority of the holy pontificate, and the power of the king.' There was no doubt which Gelasius considered the more permanent and juridically important.

The right of the new barbarian kings to intervene in church affairs as soon as they became Catholic Christians was, however, claimed and admitted in Gaul within a few years of Gelasius's death in 496. In Gaul that same year, Clovis, King of the Franks was baptized by the Catholic Bishop St. Regimus and was soon followed into the church by many of his people. Already at the time of his baptism the most powerful of the barbarian kings ruling in the old province of Gaul, after this crucial event he carried his Catholicism with him as he extended the frontiers of his kingdom year by year into the lands of his neighbours. Catholicism became indeed one of the instruments of Frankish policy, and the bishops important figures in Frankish administration, part allies, part kings' officers. Obviously, though, they could not be allowed complete freedom. At a synod of the Frankish church at Orleans in 511, the court demanded and was granted the right to veto any episcopal appointment, and the kings soon demonstrated that they took this privilege to mean that they could appoint whom they chose, priest or layman, saint or sinner, to any vacant bishopric. Retired war-leaders, younger sons, royal favourites, all became bishops, receiving the income from their sees, even if they could not sign the receipts for it themselves, in exchange for an oath of fealty to the king couched in similar terms to that imposed on secular land-holders. Thus the church became involved at the very outset in what was to develop as the feudal system of land tenure in France, and did so in a way that could only cause trouble in the future.

Hope for a wider recognition of the authority of Rome in the East revived with the accession of the Emperor Justin I at Constantinople in 518. The new emperor was a Catholic, and Catholicism soon became the religion of the mob. Crowds rioted in Constantinople, demanding the deposition of those monophysites in power throughout the empire and the restoration of the faith of Leo the Great. Justin naturally agreed to these requests. He called a synod which deposed the patriarch of Constantinople, recognized the Council of Chalcedon as orthodox, and recommended that the emperor should write to Rome and restore unity between the churches.

Hormisdas, the reigning pope, welcomed these approaches and appointed legates to journey to Constantinople and establish papal authority there. On their arrival the following year they immediately made public a document which all the bishops of the East were to be asked to sign. Now known as the *Formula of Pope Hormisdas*, it was a remarkable expression of papal claims, ascribing absolute primacy to the popes on the ground that papal orthodoxy had never failed:

> We wish to continue in all circumstances in communion with the apostolic see, in which resides the perfect and true stability of the Christian faith, [and] by which religion has always been preserved immaculate . . .

so the bishops were made to swear, at the same time condemning all those who had at any time been anathematized by Rome and foreswearing communion with those 'separated from the communion of the Catholic church—that is, those who do not submit to the holy see'.

Traditionally, the 'Catholic church' had been the church of the orthodox in faith, those who followed the tradition of the apostles, adding nothing new. Now Catholic orthodoxy was identified with Roman authority and orthodoxy. The change was one of emphasis rather than of fundamental teaching, but its effects, if it were accepted, would be enormous.

At Constantinople, the bishops reacted favourably to this formula, but in the East generally there was much opposition. Forty bishops in the patriarchate of Constantinople refused to sign, and their lead was followed by most of the Egyptians and many in Asia Minor and Greece. Worse still, very few of the monks—of whom there were thousands in the East—agreed with it. They made their objections very clear and finally Justin closed their monasteries. It was an act of despair, ill-judged and ill-timed. The displaced monks swarmed all over the East, carrying monophysitism with them wherever they went, forcing out bishops who had submitted to Rome and setting up a rival church organization that was to be a source of trouble for many years to come.

Less than a decade after the introduction of the *Formula*, Justin's successor, the Emperor Justinian (527–65), inherited an empire so divided within itself between monophysites and Catholics that violence was liable to explode at any moment. Justinian's first edict on his accession revealed a passion for absolute—and so unattainable —justice. He was one of those dangerous men, a dreamer with most of the energy required to make his dreams come true. His ambition was to reconquer Africa from the Vandals and Europe from the Goths, Huns and Franks, and so see the Roman Empire restored in all its glory, both military and intellectual. As part of his work of restoration, he ordered a complete codification of the law, the effects of which can still be traced in the legal codes of many countries today. His attempts to restore the geographical empire were less successful. His laws show that he saw the whole empire as a rigid and unchanging structure, with himself at the head, ruling both state and church. Although they did not deny the spiritual authority of the bishops, they reveal that in imperial eyes bishops were not primarily teachers or sources of grace, but judges, permitted even to sit as magistrates in civil cases. The code called the pope 'the chief of all the holy priests of God' and Rome 'the fount of all priesthood', but in practice Justinian made it plain that all authority must be regarded as flowing from himself. But, since at least the time of Gelasius's *Decretals*, the Roman Pontiff had regarded himself as the source of all authority. A clash was inevitable as soon as Justinian moved to unify the church in the empire. It came in 543.

As the Emperor Zeno had done in somewhat similar circumstances, Justinian produced a compromise formula which he hoped would reunite the Christians of the empire. It was known that the monophysites would not accept the orthodoxy of the Council of Chalcedon at which Pope Leo's *Tome* had been so warmly received by the Catholics, however cleverly disguised acceptance was: nor would Catholics agree to any suggestion that the council had been wrong in its conclusions. Justinian's suggested compromise therefore ignored the council altogether, going back beyond it and inviting everyone to condemn three extremist teachers whose views could be considered to lie behind the whole problem. Their teachings were set out in three chapters, each of which the bishops were asked to condemn, and the document consequently became known in the West as *Tria Capitula*, the Three Chapters.

When the Three Chapters were presented to Pope Vigilius, he refused to recognize them as a valid compromise, because no mention was made in the document of the Council of Chalcedon and Leo's *Tome*. It was a bold gesture, for Vigilius owed a great deal to the royal family. Justinian's reaction was swift and harsh. He ordered the imperial general Belisarius, who was at that time trying to reconquer Italy for the empire, to march to Rome, arrest the pope, and bring him to Constantinople under guard. Vigilius lay in prison for three years before he was at last brought to sign a modified condemnation of the long-dead theologians.

His surrender provoked an immediate and violent reaction throughout the empire. A synod hastily convoked in Africa excommunicated him. Vigilius withdrew his condemnation, but confusion reigned for five years, until the emperor, exercizing what he believed to be his imperial prerogative, summoned a general council. A hundred and fifty-one bishops attended—but not Vigilius, who was still in a cell under guard. From prison, he agreed to condemn one of the theologians as a Nestorian, but the council insisted on the condemnation of all three. Vigilius held out for another six months before finally accepting the council's version of the condemnation. Only then was he released, discredited on all sides, to return to Rome and die. Yet his fall from strict orthodoxy did not halt the Roman Church's march to power in the West.

The parts of Africa, Italy and Spain reconquered during Justinian's reign were not held for long. But the brief period of restored imperial rule allowed Catholic missionaries to work among the Arian Visigoths and Suevi of Spain and Portugal. The Suevi were brought under papal rule in the middle of the sixth century, the Visigoths some thirty years later, after a bloody civil war. Meanwhile, the continuing expansion of the Frankish kingdom in Gaul brought large, if morally unreliable, populations under papal control. In the north of Europe, the same period saw far-ranging missionary work by Irish monks under Columbanus, as the result of which monasteries were founded from the Vosges to the Dolomites. However, while missions were spreading the net of papal authority ever wider, at home in Italy the careful work of centuries was being destroyed by the latest wave of invaders, the Lombards, who swept into Italy from the northern forests which had been their home since the time of Tiberius or earlier, and destroyed not only the remaining imperial forces but also three Frankish armies sent against them between 582 and 585. Only the greatest cities held out. Rome was one of them.

Rome survived because in 590 Gregory I was elected to the throne of Peter. Gregory was a Benedictine monk, a diplomat who had worked for several years at the court of Constantinople, but a devout man, ascetic and charitable as well as able. At different stages in his career as pope, he wrote books—two of which, the *Moralia in Job* and *On Pastoral Care*, were almost as influential in the later Middle Ages as Augustine of Hippo's *City of God*—founded monasteries, organized the distribution of charities, gave dowries to needy girls, acted as ration officer during a siege, arranged truces, named tribunes and planned the disposition of troops. He is best remembered, perhaps, for his reorganization of Rome's music and the foundation of the Gregorian choir school, and for the missions he sent abroad, especially that to England. Historians trace the origins of the Papal States to his careful planning of the monasteries he founded in Italy and Sicily to control the estates willed to the church by wealthy Christians and farmed to provide an income for the papal *curia* and food for the poor of Rome. The whole of his reign set a standard for the papacy, in power and prestige as well as holiness. Gregory, seen in retrospect, was the saintly king-scholar, the archetype of the mediaeval pope: Gregory the Great.

In another way, too, he was remarkable, in that he never claimed more authority than he actually needed. In Italy, he was the supreme ruler of the church, appointing bishops and deposing those he thought unworthy with complete freedom of action. In Spain, Gaul and Illyria, however, he urged the need for frequent local synods to direct the day-to-day life of the church, while reserving the right to intervene in important matters. Thus, in the kingdom of the Franks, he fought long and hard for modification of the right of royal veto granted by the Council of Orleans, insisting that laymen should not be made bishops merely because the king willed their appointment and would accept no other. His instructions concerning the English mission under Augustine 'of Canterbury' make it plain that he envisaged dioceses as administrative units not unlike monastic foundations, with local bishops acting as 'abbots' in the secular world, freely exercizing their authority subject only to the overall, but fairly remote, control of the chief bishop, the 'abbot-general' as it were of their order.

Augustine, like Gregory himself a Benedictine monk, received the *pallium*, the stole of his authority as Bishop of London, from Gregory before the mission began. His instructions were to appoint twelve other bishops to rule southern England 'under your authority, except that the bishop of the city of London ought always hereafter to be consecrated by his own synod and receive the *pallium* from this holy and apostolic see. . . .' Similar arrangements were to be made to set up an independent synod at York. In fact, the mission did not prosper quickly enough for Augustine to be able to set up his chair in London, and he and his successors ruled from Canterbury. But the local synod, appointing its own archbishop subject to the confirmation of the holy see (and of the king, in imitation of Frankish custom), became a reality of church life in England.

In fact, probably as a result of his monastic training as well as of his appreciation of the difficulty of swift communications now that imperial armies no longer maintained the roads, Gregory showed more respect for local authority than his dominant position in the church demanded of him. He called himself Bishop of Rome, Patriarch of Italy and the West, 'servant of the servants of God', but refused the title Universal Bishop, even when his advisers urged him to adopt it in reply to the Patriarch of Constantinople's assumption of the title 'oecumenical patriarch'. Gregory objected to the patriarch's presumption, as he was bound to do, for Justinian's Code and the canons of the councils both made it clear that the patriarch had no claim to jurisdiction in the West. The patriarch, however, persisted in using the title until his death, and his successor also adopted it immediately upon his election. By the year 602, the debate had grown so acrimonious that Gregory felt compelled to withdraw his legate from Constantinople. Once again, the rivalry between the old Rome and the new had come close to splitting the church.

Chapter II

BUILDING THE CITY OF GOD

BY PLACING the emphasis on monastic foundations and local synods, while maintaining a strong central government and court of appeal at Rome, Gregory the Great made it possible for the church to continue to work in the West during the 'dark ages' when there was no other force strong enough to weld Europe together.

The success of the mission to Britain, despite the divisions between the English tribes, and between the ancient Celtic and new English churches, demonstrates how well his system was constructed. While Augustine was at work among the Angles and Saxons of the south and east, the Gospel was being preached in the north by Scottish monks from Iona. Although Celtic missions in England owed a measure of allegiance to the popes as patriarchs of the West, they kept the liturgical calendar of the East—a later form of that calendar about which Pope Victor had been so concerned in the second century. They also followed Eastern practice in respect of the form of the tonsure and the law of fasting. Such differences, and the fact that the Romano-British Christians of Cornwall and Wales remained very suspicious of the Saxons even after these barbarians had been converted to Christianity, made it imperative for the prosperity of the mission to bring the two sides together. They met at a Synod at Whitby in 664, and it was agreed that all the churches of Britain should follow Roman custom and accept the primacy of the Archbishop of Canterbury, who, of course, would continue to receive the *pallium* of his authority from the pope. The Synod of Whitby did not end the troubles between the Saxons and the Celts, but nine years later it was possible to hold a synod at Hertford for the unification of the customs of the whole English church on the basis of Roman disciplinary canons, and in 680 a similar synod held at Heathfield 'affirmed the Catholic Faith' (in Bede's words) in the presence of a legate appointed from Rome, John, the Abbot of St. Martin's at

Tours. Abbot John's instructions from Pope Agatho were to teach the monks of Wearmouth 'the chant for the liturgical year as it was sung at St. Peter's in Rome' and 'to make careful enquiries about the faith of the English church, and make a report on it upon his return to Rome'. The pattern revealed here, of local authority supported from and assessed by Rome, is exactly in accordance with that laid down by Gregory the Great.

In a world falling to pieces—as it appeared to Christians in the seventh century—the main grounds for hope lay in the success of these distant missions, to Britain first, and later to Frisia and Germany. In the south and east, difficulties were multiplying year by year. Despite the fact that the Byzantines still held some parts of Italy, including Rome itself, no agreement had yet been reached on the proper relationship between either the pope and the Emperor of Constantinople on the one hand or the pope and the Eastern patriarchs on the other. Before the end of the century, the differences between Rome and Constantinople were to be made yet more poignant by the virtual extinction of the other patriarchates and the loss of North Africa in the Islamic invasions. Syria, Palestine and Egypt had gone by the middle of the century. Numidia and Africa fell in 695. By 711, most of the Iberian Peninsula was lost and Mahommedans were making probing attacks into the southern districts of the Frankish kingdom.

Nor were the Mahommedans the only problem. After Justinian's death, barbarian raids on the north-western frontiers of the empire, in the Danube area, increased in intensity until they became a full-scale invasion. Avars, Bulgars and Slavs settled permanently in the Balkan peninsula and by the year 680 a strong kingdom of Bulgaria had come into being. That same year, the Emperor Constantine IV was forced to admit that the Lombards would have to be permitted to stay in Italy because the empire was no longer strong enough to expel them. By then, only Rome, the Exarchate of Ravenna, small districts around Bologna, Ancona and Naples, Sicily and the coastlands of Apulia and Calabria were still subject to Byzantine governors.

Relations between the churches in what remained of the empire were poisoned by the dying monophysite controversy. In 624–5, Patriarch Sergius of Constantinople tried to reunite the churches by proposing that Christ had only one source of mental energy and will. Pope Honorius's acceptance of this 'monothelite' doctrine provided the Western church with the only pope ever to be condemned by a general council of Eastern and Western bishops.

Sergius' compromise satisfied Honorius but did not bring peace to the East. Continuing controversy drove the Emperor Constans II to decree that all discussions of Christ's nature must cease. Despite this ruling, Pope Martin I called a council in 649, which condemned monothelitism and all those who supported it, including Pope Honorius. It also condemned the imperial decree. No emperor could tolerate so open an act of rebellion, and Constans II had the pope arrested and taken to Constantinople. But Martin refused to repudiate either his synod or his own judgment, and was exiled to the Chersonese, where he died in September 655.

His death in such circumstances kept Rome and the East apart not only during his exile but also through the reigns of the next four popes, and peace was not restored until the reign of Constantine IV, when Agatho was pope. At this juncture after a preliminary synod at Rome, the emperor convened a general council at his capital. It met in 680, the year of the foundation of the Bulgarian and Lombard kingdoms, and was presented with the decisions of the Roman synod condemning monothelitism in a letter from the pope which was received, according to tradition, amidst a scene recalling the reception of Leo's Tome at Chalcedon, with cries of 'Peter has spoken through Agatho'. The council had no hesitation in condemning monothelitism and, with it, Pope Honorius.

A hundred and seventy years earlier, Pope Hormisdas had argued for Roman primacy on the grounds that Roman orthodoxy had never wavered. Now Honorius and the Roman synod stood condemned. A thousand years later, at the First Vatican Council, those opposed to the dogma of papal infallibility were to use Honorius' condemnation in support of their case.

The peace secured by Agatho's letter did not last long. In 717 a brilliant autocratic soldier named Leo of Isauria seized the throne of Constantinople only just in time to beat off a Mahommedan attack which had brought Islam to the gates of the city. He was long remembered in the East as one of the greatest administrators ever to control Byzantine affairs. At Rome, he was remembered equally as long both for his heresy and for his seizure of the income from all the 'patrimony of Peter', the estates in Southern Italy and Sicily by which the papacy supported itself.

His 'heresy' was that of many later puritans. He believed that the use of pictures and statues in churches led people into idolatry, and ordered that they should be destroyed. The edict, issued in 715, commanding iconoclasm throughout the empire found general support at Eastern synods, but met with total condemnation in the West. Pope Gregory II denounced it on the grounds not only that images had been used from the earliest times, but also that emperors had no right to direct the forms of Christian worship. It was, he said, for popes to define both the forms of worship and the limits of imperial power. And he threatened open rebellion if Leo made further trouble.

'With the arrogance of a fool,' he wrote,

> you say that you will send orders to Rome to smash the image of St. Peter, and that Gregory, like Martin his predecessor, shall be carried off in chains to the foot of the throne and to exile. Would that God would grant that I might follow in the footsteps of the Holy Martin! . . . But it is our duty to live for the edification and support of the faithful. And we have only to withdraw a distance of twenty-four *stadia*, to the nearest Lombard fortress—and then you may chase the winds. . . . They revere as a god upon earth the Apostle Peter whose image you threaten to destroy. . . . The barbarians have submitted to the yoke of the Gospel, you alone remain deaf to the shepherd's voice. These pious barbarians are on fire with rage . . .

Gregory's strength lay in the validity of his claim to Lombard support. Newly converted to Christianity, they had accepted it in the form practised by the common people and soldiers of Italy, the religion of Rome. When the pope wrote to Leo, he also wrote pastoral letters to the Italians, warning them that their faith was under attack. Within a short time, all Italy was in arms. Locally recruited soldiers in the exarchate revolted against their Byzantine officers and killed the exarch. The emperor sent a fleet to subdue Italy and arrest the pope, but it was destroyed by a storm in the Adriatic, and devout papalists said that the very elements were fighting for St. Peter. When a few ships disembarked troops at Ravenna, a papal army took the field for the first time in history. The imperial force was defeated and withdrew. Gregory called a synod at Rome and excommunicated everyone in East or West who attacked the traditions of the fathers. There was even popular agitation for an assault on Constantinople to depose the emperor and crown a Catholic in his place, but Gregory refused to countenance the suggestion. Instead he acted with restraint, calming the people and urging that nothing should be done to destroy what little unity remained in the empire. A new exarch was appointed to Ravenna and for the time being it seemed that the pre-war situation had been restored.

In fact, however, everything had changed. From 728, the year of the Battle of Ravenna, onwards, Rome was independent of Constantinople in all but name. A semblance of the old senate was restored, but the real ruler was the pope. Byzantine authority in Italy gradually failed, drained away by the success of the Italian revolt and of new attacks on the frontiers of the exarchate from the Lombard kingdom to the north. By 751, the Lombard King Aistulf had swept the exarchate away. The following year, he began to fight his way towards Rome, in a bid to conquer all Italy.

Faced with this emergency, the reigning pope, Stephen III, who was already involved in Byzantine attempts to regain the exarchate by diplomacy, wrote urgent appeals for troops to both his emperor and his most loyal adherent in Europe, Pepin II, the King of the Franks. Pepin's reply was prompt and friendly, and the pope was encouraged to write to him again, proposing that they should meet beyond the Alps, where they would be able to negotiate without fear of either Aistulf or the emperor. Pepin agreed. The meeting, one of the most significant in European history, took place at the royal villa of Ponthion on January 6, 754.

Technically, Pepin was a usurper. The only title he could legally claim was 'Mayor of the Palace' to the Merovingian king. Three years earlier he had forced the king to retire to a monastery; now he wanted recognition of his royalty from the pope. Stephen duly granted it, consecrating him, the queen and the two princes Carloman and Charles (later to be Charlemagne) at a ceremony at St. Denis. In return, Pepin promised military help in Italy.

In 755, a Frankish army, accompanied by the pope, marched into Italy and defeated the Lombards at Pavia. Aistulf quickly agreed to give the land he had conquered from the Byzantines to the pope, and guaranteed peace. The Frankish army returned home but, as soon as it had left, the war began again. Stephen was besieged in Rome, but succeeded in sending three letters, written in the name of St. Peter himself, to his Frankish allies. In a second season in Italy, Pepin's soldiers won fresh victories, forcing Aistulf to disgorge the territory he had swallowed and to pay a large indemnity. Pepin settled the land taken from Aistulf on the papacy; claims made in the emperor's name were ignored, and his legate in Italy returned to Constantinople with the news that both Rome and Ravenna were finally lost to the empire.

So a new Rome came into being in 756: the independent Rome, capital of a group of Papal States, foreshadowed by the virtual freedom of the previous thirty years. The text of the document recording Pepin's gift, the so-called 'Donation of Pepin', has unfortunately been lost, but subsequent events demonstrate that it made the popes sovereign in Rome and in the Patrimony on the west Italian coast, Ravenna and the plains around it on the eastern coast, and a strip of land, joining them, following the old military road through Perugia. Lombard Tuscany lay to the north, and to the south, the Lombard duchies of Benevento and Spoleto.*

It might well be thought that here was a real chance to build the City of God, but Stephen's successor, Paul I, soon learned how difficult it was to be a just ruler in a world where the physical possession of land was the mark both of nobility and authority. He had to lean heavily on his Frankish allies in order to maintain his position, and even though Pepin undertook a general reform of morals and ecclesiastical discipline in all Frankish territories, it is obvious from the *Liber Pontificalis* and other chronicles of the time that standards of justice were no higher in the new papal state than in any other duchy or principality of the period. Paul I acted like a secular ruler: it was not surprising, therefore, that at his death an attempt was made by a 'layman' to usurp the Patrimony of Peter before a new pope could be elected. Under Byzantine rule, the war-leader had been chosen by the knights, the *dux* by the *exercitus*, but in those relatively normal times only the clergy of Rome had shared in the election of popes; now that the pope had become the war-leader, it seemed to the knights that they should have a voice in his election. When it was learned that Paul I was ill, four knights, all brothers, mounted a demonstration of military power in Rome which ended with Pope Paul's death, and the election of one of the brothers as 'Pope Constantine of Nepi' on June 27, 767. The following Sunday, protected by a strong cavalry escort, he rode to St. Peter's and was

---

* The reality of this Donation of 756 has sometimes been questioned by historians: lacking the documentation, we can only notice that in 774, Charlemagne is said to have 'renewed' the gift (*Liber Pontificalis*, Vita Hadriani I). Even if there was no formal agreement, the Papal States certainly came into being at this time, and were a very real factor in the history of later centuries.

consecrated bishop by the Bishops of Preneste, Albano and Porto. He played at being pope for almost a year, corresponding with Pepin and the Eastern patriarchs, before a popular rising drove him out, and a new pope, Stephen IV, was elected by the prelates and people (including some members of the *exercitus*) in the Forum. To ensure that his irregular election was generally recognized, Stephen sent a mission to Pepin asking him to send Frankish bishops to Rome to a council, and mounted a military expedition against 'Pope Constantine'. The council, meeting at the Lateran in April 769, tried to lay down rules to prevent the repetition of such a scandalous election: 'No one of the laity or any other order,' the prelates decreed, 'shall be advanced to the sacred order of the pontificate, unless he has first been made a cardinal deacon or priest, rising by clearly distinct degrees;' and, 'election to the pontificate will be made exclusively by the sacerdotal body.'*

Stephen IV lived only until 772, a few months after Charlemagne had become sole King of the Franks. He was succeeded by Hadrian I who, in conjunction with Charlemagne, created a new order in Western Europe—an order sealed by Charlemagne's coronation at Rome in the year 800 as 'the Most Holy Augustus, crowned by God, the great and peace-bringing King of the Romans'.

It is impossible in this context to trace in detail the events of those immensely significant years which once again brought the popes an imperial master. From the beginning Charlemagne and Hadrian adhered to the principle of mutual support laid down by Pepin II and Stephen IV; although Charlemagne took great care to show reverence to the popes in matters of faith, he surrendered little to them where secular power was concerned. Following renewed trouble between the Lombards and the sovereign Papacy in 773-4, he led into Italy a Frankish army which destroyed Lombard power, but far from handing over all the captured territory to his ally Hadrian, he made himself King of the Lombards. While on a pilgrimage to Rome in 774, he promised to increase the Papal State so as to include all Italy south and east of a line from La Spezia to Venice, but the actual 'Donation of Charlemagne' in that year seems to have been restricted to little more than the Duchy of

---

* The origins of the term 'cardinal' are obscure, but at the time of this decree a cardinal priest was one ordained to serve in one of several important parish churches in Rome, and a cardinal deacon one of the seven deacons attached to those churches but serving the pope.

Spoleto. Four years later, Hadrian was still pleading for what he believed should be his:

Just as in the days of blessed Sylvester, the most pious Constantine of holy memory, that great emperor, by his liberality raised and exalted the holy church of God, catholic and apostolic, and granted it sovereignty in these Hesperidean regions, so in these present happy times, shared by you and by Us, the blessed Apostle Peter's holy church should flower more fully and be more highly exulted from day to day. Then the nations seeing these things will be able to say: Lord save the king: hear us in the day when we call upon Thee, for behold, a new most Christian Emperor, a new Constantine has just arisen . . . Restore . . . those properties . . . in the districts of Tuscany, Spoleto, Benevento, Corsica and the Sabine Lands which in the course of time have been seized and ravaged by the damnable nation of the Lombards . . .

The claim made in this letter that Constantine had given 'these Hesperidean regions' to the Roman Church was, of course, a fiction, but it was a legend given wide credence in this and later centuries. Although not perhaps during the reign of Hadrian himself, at any rate approximately at this time, the tale of Constantine's legacy to the church of the whole of the Western empire in thanksgiving for his miraculous healing from an attack of leprosy was recorded in a 'history' known as *The Donation of Constantine*. In it the emperor was alleged to have decreed that the whole empire would 'venerate and honour' the 'most holy Roman Church' and that 'the sacred See of the Blessed Peter' would be 'gloriously exalted above our empire and earthly throne'.

Nor did forgery stop here. At some time in the early ninth century, the *Donation* was included in a large collection of wholly spurious laws and decrees, all tending to magnify the powers and influence of the papacy at the expense of the empire, and attributed—quite falsely—to the early Spanish theologian Isidore of Seville. The collection was put together so as to resemble the collections of valid canon laws already widely known, the Decretals of Gelasius, the *Dionysiana*, and the *Hispana*, and under the title *The Decretals of Isidore* coloured the thinking of popes, bishops and kings from the ninth century until the fifteenth. The spurious Decretals were probably produced not at Rome but in France, by canonists seeking to increase papal influence over the policies of the Carolingians. It has even been suggested that Alcuin of York, Charlemagne's closest adviser in religious affairs, may have had a hand in their compilation, but this cannot be proved, although he was undeniably a romanizer. It was he, for instance, who oversaw the preparation of a Frankish edition of the Roman missal used to 'romanize' the old Frankish liturgy, and guided Charlemagne through the many reforming synods held in his empire. He may also have played a part in the compilation of the *Caroline Books*, a series of vituperative texts against the Byzantines, devoted to proving the authority of Rome and demonstrating the relative unimportance of Constantinople, which played an important part in preparing the West for Charlemagne's coronation as Augustus in 800.

Obstacles arose on the path to this ceremony because Charlemagne had been flattered into thinking himself 'the Second Constantine' and master of the world not only in secular affairs, but also in religious. Like the Roman emperors before him, he was not content to leave decisions to the bishops in matters of faith. He converted the Saxons of northern Germany to christianity by giving them a simple choice between baptism and the sword—a proceeding which provoked cries of horror from the bishops even of that century. When the decree of a council held at Nicaea in 787 to end inconoclasm reached the West, nothing would satisfy Charlemagne but that there should be a similar council in his empire to examine it and lay down rules for its application. A suitable occasion did not arise for some years—years during which the *Caroline Books* were spreading contempt for the East throughout the Frankish lands. The Western council eventually met at Frankfurt in 794, ostensibly to examine the orthodoxy of certain Spanish bishops. Misreading the Greek texts, it condemned the wholly orthodox Council of Nicaea, and requested Pope Hadrian to excommunicate the Empress Irene. He refused—but he also refused to condemn Charlemagne's Council of Frankfurt. As King of the Lombards, King of the Franks and *Patricius*, Father of the Roman People, Charlemagne was too powerful to be put in his place.

Hadrian died in the following year. His successor, Leo III, immediately revealed how dependent on Charlemagne the papacy felt when he dispatched to him, together with the notice of his election, a promise of obedience and fidelity, the keys of the *confessio* of St. Peter, the most holy spot in Rome, and the city standard. In return, Charlemagne sent merely a promise that he would maintain good relations between them. The letters suggest that the pope was no longer sovereign in central Italy, but was militarily Charlemagne's subject ally there. The correspondence is preserved in Alcuin's *Letters*, which also include a copy of Charlemagne's charges to his legate in Rome. They are illuminating about the characters of both men, as well as their relationship:

> You will diligently guide the pope to behave with complete propriety in the course of his life, preserve the holy canons with jealous care, and govern the holy church devoutly. When the opportunity occurs you will remind him of life's brevity, and that the honours he presently enjoys will endure only for a season . . .

Early in the year 800, after an attempt on his life, Leo visited Charlemagne at Paderborn. Their conversations were secret. Alcuin himself said that he would have given much to know what passed 'between the eagle and the lion', but the outcome was the coronation of Charlemagne as Emperor of Rome. Having placed the crown on his head, Leo prostrated himself before him. For the time being, the attempt of the papacy to exist in total independence of all secular powers had ended. And less than a generation later, during the reign of Louis the Pious, even the freedom to elect a pope without imperial permission disappeared when a decree was formulated which, while forbidding everyone except 'the Romans to whom the privilege had been granted by the whole of antiquity' to play a part in the elections, gave the new emperors the right to oversee the proceedings.

It would, however, be a mistake to imagine that all the gains were on the Frankish side. In the course of the century from the coronation of Charlemagne to the collapse of the Frankish empire, the papacy built a powerful machine based on the influence of authoritarian bishops and abbots from the Atlantic to the heartlands of Europe. That it failed to build the City of God, or even an acceptable semblance of it, was due to the general moral turpitude of the popes themselves. In the whole period, only one man was outstanding for his devotion to the office he filled: Nicholas I 'the Great' who, as well as fighting to control the excesses of the barons in Italy, also upheld the dignity of Rome in the East. After his death, the barbarian tide washed around the Lateran Palace itself. John VIII (872–882) appealed to the Franks for help and, when none came, wrote desparingly: 'We were waiting for the light, and in its stead there is darkness. We have sought help, and we have not dared to go out beyond the walls of the city, for outside there reigns an intolerable storm of persecution, because neither our spiritual son the emperor, nor anyone else, has helped us.' No one had done so, because no one was strong enough to control the situation. Several bloody years later, after riots, revolutions and at least one schism in the papacy had served notice on Italy that the Iron Age of rule by the sword had begun, a synod at Rome tried to save the church from the worst evils by placing papal elections under imperial control: 'Observing that acts of great violence occur at papal elections when the imperial legates are not present, we ordain that in future the pope shall be elected by the bishops [of the city] and clergy in the presence of the Senate and people, but may be consecrated only in the presence of the delegates of the emperor.' But this decree overlooked the fact that there was no emperor worthy of the name. Rome was ruled by whoever could seize control.

In the early tenth century, the masters of the city were sexual licence with murder, treachery, bribery and war. Neither the church not Italy could long survive so intolerable a situation. The first of the moves which were to bring it to an end was taken by John XII in 961, when in fear of imminent assassination he made a desperate plea for help to Otto of Saxony, the King of Germany.

The German kingdom had been created out of the ruins of Frankish Austrasia by the energy of Henry I. His successor, Otto, had been crowned at Charlemagne's capital, Aachen, in a deliberate attempt to recall the image of Charlemagne's glory. After a series of victories had confirmed his hold on Germany, he was proclaimed 'Emperor' and 'Father of his Country' by his soldiers in the Roman style, and in 961 led his army into Italy to refound the Western empire. He had already received the Iron Crown of the Lombards at Pavia when Pope John offered him imperial coronation at Rome if he would accept the role of defender of the Holy See formerly played by the Frankish kings. He accepted, and was anointed and crowned by the pope in 962.

The parallel with the coronation of Charlemagne was not exact, but both pope and king did their best to make it appear so and the ceremony is now seen to have laid the foundations of the Holy Roman Empire. After the ceremony, they signed a concordat, the terms of which were summarized in a document called the *Privilegium Ottonis*, by which Otto guaranteed the permanence of the

Papal States in exchange for nominal overlordship as emperor of the West, and the right to confirm papal elections.

He first used his privileges in the very year they were defined, by deposing John as a rebel and replacing him with an antipope. John protested, but Otto had the power of a victorious army behind him, and with it he and his sons after him kept a strong hold on the church until the end of the century. Even so, there were many scandals, several schisms, and almost no reasons to hope for a better future until the accession to the imperial throne of Henry II, the first emperor to be canonized in the West, in 1002.

In fact the church was not wholly corrupt, simply most rotten at its Roman heart. Ninety years before the accession of Henry II, before the horror at Rome reached its climax, a monastic reform had begun at Cluny which was at last to bear fruit in the city itself.

Cluny was founded in 910 with the express purpose of restoring the full rigour of the original Benedictine rule. Its strength lay in the remarkable character of its first five abbots, and in its freedom from interference by either bishops or kings. Its rules declared that its only external superior was the pope himself—and, surprisingly, even the worst popes seem to have taken their obligations to Cluny and its daughter houses seriously. The particular evils that the reformers saw as the main sources of the church's weakness were simony (the buying and selling of ecclesiastical offices and the sacraments, forbidden from the earliest times), sexual irregularity in the lives of the clergy and luxury in clerical dress.

The records all make it clear that these were especially common evils in the ninth and tenth centuries when it had become customary for laymen with political power to appoint the clergy within their dominions and 'invest' them with the property from which their income would derive, usually claiming a tax, often a year's income, for the gift of the benefice. A bishopric was a valuable possession, bringing both power and financial advantages to its tenant for life. Even a parish, with its farmlands, had a market value. Both could be bought and sold and often were. Although pluralism was forbidden, it had become common for men to hold many parishes or even several bishoprics, although personally attending to the spiritual business of none of them. In such circumstances, standards naturally declined, although there were always some who fought to hold them at as high a level as possible. The pain caused to a good bishop by conditions during the years when popes were carousing is plain from such letters

as the one written by a Bishop of Verceil to his clergy in the middle
of the tenth century:

> I am ashamed to say it, but I believe it would be dangerous to remain
> silent: many of you are so much under the spell of carnal passion that
> they allow courtesans to live in their houses, share their food, and show
> themselves with them in public. Enslaved by their charms, they let
> them rule their homes and make their bastards their heirs . . . and so
> that these women may appear well dressed, churches are stripped and
> the poor suffer.

When the Cluniac reform spread from the monasteries to the
dioceses and parishes, often through the endeavours of schoolmaster-
monks, it needed the active support of a man of influence and power
to ensure success. It found its man in Henry II who, even before his
coronation at Rome in 1014 formally made him the church's
champion, worked for the reform of the church on Cluniac lines
throughout the empire. But, although in 1022 he wrote into the law
of the empire reforming canons which had been passed at a synod
held at Pavia, even he could not wipe out all the evils of lay investiture.

The canons of Pavia are of special interest, as they mark the
beginning of the first intensive campaign to impose on the secular
clergy of the West the celibacy which had always been part of the
rule of monastic life. They laid it down that to preserve the property
of the church as well as the propriety of its ministers, no priest or
deacon should marry or maintain a concubine. They forbade bishops
to permit women to live under their roofs and ruled that children
born to women kept by clerics should be classed as serfs throughout
their lives, incapable of inheriting any property from their father's
estates.

Earlier attempts to introduce similar legislation had all failed. The
canons of Pavia deserved a better fate, but did not find it for several
decades, for both Henry II and the pope he had encouraged to
introduce them, Benedict VIII, died within two years of the synod
which adopted them. The new emperor, Conrad of Franconia, was
no saint. Nor was the new pope, Benedict's brother, the second son of
the Duke of Tusculum. Ignoring the new canons, his father bought
the papal throne for him at the election. In the morning he was
Senator Romanus: by evening, he was John XIX. Under him,
simony was the main source of papal income, and the Patriarch

Eustatius of Constantinople wrote of his reign, 'Love of money might be called king of the world today, but nowhere has it made its nest more firmly than among the Romans.' John's reign was brief, but he was followed by another candidate from the house of Tusculum, who some annalists say was only about fourteen years of age when he became Benedict IX by bribery and terror. He was soon faced with a revolt in the Papal States, and when he died in the fifth year of the reign of the Emperor Conrad's son, Henry III, he left such confusion behind him that at least three popes of doubtful validity claimed the throne of Peter. The situation was not unlike that confronting the church some three hundred years later at the Great Schism. The key man in the situation was Henry III. He sensibly decided that the only thing to do was persuade them all to resign and start again. In 1046, he accepted the proposal made by the most reputable of the three, reigning as Gregory VI, that he should call a council to decide who actually was pope. The council sat at Sutri in December of that year.

The surviving accounts of this synod unfortunately contradict one another. Gregory's two rivals were certainly declared schismatics and excommunicated, but it is impossible to decide from the available evidence who took it upon himself to judge Gregory. By this time, both true and false decretals had firmly implanted the idea that 'the first See can be judged by no one', yet whether Gregory deposed himself—as his namesake Gregory XII was to do at the Great Schism—or the emperor forced deposition on him, he certainly was removed from the papal throne. By the end of the synod there was no pope. The emperor stood revealed as the sole arbiter of the future of the Western church and for the next four years, he ruled through three short-lived puppet-popes elected at his direction. But his fourth choice, Bruno of Toul, consecrated in 1049 as Leo IX, was not the man to allow himself to be ruled even by the emperor who had promoted him.

Trained for the priesthood in Lorraine, where monastic reform was allowing many energetic men to display their abilities, Leo IX had shown his zeal as a priest travelling in the suite of Conrad II. Later, as Bishop of Toul, he had both defended the see vigorously against attempts by the Counts of Champagne to seize its lands and revenues, and pressed on with religious reforms. At Rome, he began work immediately with a synod at the Lateran, at which the chief target was simony. From Rome he travelled to Rheims, to hold a synod there at which bishops were questioned individually about how they had obtained their sees. At Maintz, later in the same year, he again attacked simony, and for good measure also Nicolaitism* and the investiture of bishops with their sees by the emperor, who was present at the time. Conflict on this question had been brewing for many years, mainly because lay investiture of bishops and abbots with the 'temporalities' of their sees, symbolized by the giving of the episcopal ring by the monarch, involved the newly-appointed prelate in swearing an oath of fealty to a lay lord. It was understandable that emperors should want to be surrounded by men they could trust, but they had begun to charge high fees for investiture and to refuse to make certain appointments. Leo IX's objections were also comprehensible, although unacceptable to the emperor. The controversy stirred up at the Synod of Maintz involved two evenly balanced sides and was not to be laid to rest for many years.

If energy is a sign of a good pope, Leo IX was one of the best; he was always travelling, always trying to restore what earlier popes had allowed to decay. He inspired many young, devoted priests to take up the cause of reform. Among them was Hildebrand, who was later to win renown as Gregory VII. Many of Leo's endeavours were crowned with success, but in two fields he failed completely, in his dealings with the Normans, and with the Byzantines.

The Normans had reached Italy as pilgrim-knights from the Holy Land in 1016, and had stayed to fight, first for the Byzantines, then against them. By 1051, under Drogo de Hauteville and his brother Robert Guiscard, they were ruling large stretches of Apulia and Calabria with terror and the sword. The people of Calabria appealed to Leo IX for protection and Benevento offered itself to him as a feudal fief. Leo accepted the charge and, assuming his duty as a feudal lord, raised an army to fight the Normans. On June 18, 1053, his forces were surrounded and cut to pieces at Civitate, a few miles from the Adriatic coast, and Leo himself was taken prisoner. The Normans carried him to his own city of Benevento and held him there throughout the coming winter, until at last he granted their demands: absolution from all censures against them, and a treaty guaranteeing their rights in the territories they had seized during the previous forty years.

* Nicolaitism: sexual promiscuity and breaches of the law of clerical celibacy, was so-called with reference to the traditional exegesis of Revelations ii, 6, with its reference to the abominable deeds of the Nicolaites.

It was during the winter that Leo was a prisoner at Benevento that the decisive dispute with the Eastern church reached its climax. Relations had been intermittently bad not merely for years, but for centuries. In 1052, however, there was talk in Italy of a rapprochement between the pope and the remaining Byzantines, against the Normans. Not everyone in Constantinople was pleased by the prospect. The patriarch, Michael Cerularius, ordered the closing of all the Latin churches in the city, and excommunicated the *capetan* of Byzantine Italy who was in Constantinople trying to persuade the emperor of the pope's sincerity. All these provocations weighed on Leo's mind during his imprisonment at Benevento, and if any further aggravation was needed, it was provided by the arrival of a copy of a letter—also, it seems, inspired by Cerularius—written by the Archbishop of Ochrida in Bulgaria to John of Trani and 'all Frankish bishops, monks and peoples, and the most reverend, the pope', renewing the Eastern attack on all those Latin customs of which Byzantines could not approve, from priestly celibacy to the inclusion of the *Filioque* clause in the creed.

The Western reply to Ochrida's letter was prepared by Humbert of Moyenmoutier, probably the only man at Benevento who could read and write Greek, and it was not designed to be pacific. It spoke with the voice of the False Decretals, demanding recognition of the papacy as superior to all other authorities whatsoever:

Holy Church was built upon a Rock, that is, Christ and Peter or Cephas, the son of John, who at first was called Simon. . . . And has it not been by the See of the leader of the apostles, this same Peter, and equally of his successors, that the fictions of all the heretics have been disproved, condemned and conquered, and have not the hearts of the brethren been strengthened by Peter's faith, which has never failed until now and shall not fail until the end? . . . The first see may be judged by nobody. . . .

News of the defeat at Civitate had reached Constantinople before this fiery epistle could do so and both the patriarch and the emperor had written moderate letters of commiseration to Leo, full of hope for a better future. Their arrival in Benevento led Leo to decide to send legates to the East. The men he chose were Humbert, Frederick of Lorraine (later to become Pope Stephen IX) and Peter of Amalfi. They took with them a new letter from the pope, hardly less bitter than the last, and seem to have expected immediate repentance from Michael Cerularius. He did not show any, however, and soon felt free to ignore the three-man embassy altogether, when he learned that Leo, after his release by the Normans, had died in Rome. The legates grew impatient. Cerularius refused to treat with them on the grounds that, their principle being dead, they had no authority. Better knights than diplomats, they lost what self-control impatience had left them, and on Saturday, July 16, 1054, marched the full length of Hagia Sophia during the celebration of the eucharist to place a bull of excommunication against the patriarch on the altar. On their way out of the church, they stopped at the door to shake the dust of the place from their feet and shout, 'May God see and judge!' The breach made that day has never been completely healed.

After Leo's death, the Romans accepted two more German popes before rebelling, during the minority of Henry III's successor, Henry IV, against the increasing Germanization of the Church. The aristocracy elected a Roman pope, who called himself Benedict X. Simultaneously the German faction appointed Nicholas II, the candidate of German birth proposed by Hildebrand. By 1059, there was not room in Rome for both of them and, threatened by Benedict's faction, Nicholas took the bold step of appealing for help to the old enemies of the papacy, the Normans in the south.

He was well received and succeeded in making a pact with them at Melfi, by which he recognized Robert Guiscard as Duke of Apulia and Lord of Sicily and the Isles (still, of course, in Saracen hands) in exchange for Robert's oath of fealty. The peace of Melfi brought an immediate reward: the Normans marched on Rome and drove Benedict X from the city. To prevent a recurrence of schism on the deaths of future popes, a council at Rome then decided to give the cardinal bishops sole responsibility in elections, and bound the rest of the clergy to accept their choice, although adding a rider preserving the right of Henry IV to exercise the imperial prerogative of veto, once he was old enough. When, at Nicholas's death, the Romans again tried to elect an antipope in opposition to the cardinals' choice, the new canons worked well, reducing support for the schismatic to a minimum.

In April 1073, just as Henry IV became old enough to exercise his prerogative and intervene in elections, Hildebrand was elected under these new canons, and named himself Gregory VII. His first act was a gesture of independence. Instead of waiting for Henry's agreement to his election, he merely sent him notification that it had taken place. Immediately afterwards, he excommunicated his nominal ally,

Robert Guiscard, for his continued attacks on church property in Apulia and Calabria, and at the same time took up the fight against simony, nicolaitism, and other irregularities in the lives of the clergy. This personal crusade led him directly to the most significant conflict of his career, that with Henry IV over investitures.

Henry was the greatest lay lord in Europe and there were a great many bishoprics in his lands. He was also, and as a consequence, the most persistent offender against the canons concerned with simony. When, in 1075, he claimed that he was feudal overlord of all the bishops in the empire, and ruled that none were to be permitted to take possession of their sees and incomes until they had taken an oath of fealty and paid the customary feudal fine to him, Gregory promulgated canons in France, Germany and Italy forbidding princes to invest with temporalities and clerics to accept investiture by them. At the same time he circulated twenty-seven propositions, which became known as the *Sentences* or *Dictatus Papae*, setting out dogmatic conclusions regarding canon law on the authority of popes. Most important among them for their practical application were numbers two, three, twelve, nineteen, twenty-two, twenty-six and twenty-seven:

> Only the Roman Pontiff has universal rights of judgment and rule.
> He alone can depose and reconcile bishops.
> To him alone is it given to depose emperors.
> He can be judged by no one.
> The Roman Church has never erred, nor, as the Scripture bears witness, will it err in future.
> Anyone who is not at peace with the Roman Church cannot reckon himself a Catholic Christian.
> The pope can free subjects from fealty towards iniquitous persons.

At first, Henry appeared to ignore both the canons and the propositions but in January 1076 he called all the German bishops to a synod at Worms and forced them to declare Gregory deposed as a rebel heretic uncanonically elected.

The news of his deposition reached Gregory just as he was about to meet the annual Lenten synod at Rome, and a man of his independent character could make only one reply to such a challenge. He put his *Sentences* into effect, declared Henry deposed and excommunicated, and freed all those who owed him loyalty from their oaths: 'To Henry the King, son of Henry the Emperor, who with unheard-of pride has rebelled against thy [that is, Peter's] church,

I deny government of the whole kingdom of Germany and Italy, and absolve all Christians from the bond of the oaths which they have made or shall make to him, and I forbid anyone to obey him as king . . .'

Henry replied by invading Italy and appealing to Robert Guiscard—himself still excommunicate—for help. Robert refused to give it openly, but attacked Gregory's chief ally in the south, the Prince of Salerno. For a time, indeed, Gregory's position looked precarious, but he was not without his admirers in Germany, where the emperor had recently put down a rebellion among the princes. As Henry marched into Italy, his bishops led a revolt against him which received lay support. In October 1076, a national Diet ratified his deposition by Gregory, and his supporters began to drift away. By the beginning of January, he had to acknowledge himself temporarily defeated. Meeting the pope—already on the road to Germany and a council to elect a new emperor—at the castle of Canossa, within the domains of the arch-papalist Matilda of Tuscany, he did penance standing in the snow until Gregory was ready to absolve him.

It was a humiliation which could only be the prelude to further trouble. The German rebels ignored the reconciliation at Canossa and, acting as though Henry were in fact permanently deposed, elected Rudolf of Swabia as their ruler. Gregory remained neutral throughout the war which inevitably followed, until the moment when Henry began once more to nominate bishops, when he re-excommunicated him and recognized Rudolf. But Henry was stronger now than he had been for some time, and the German bishops remained loyal to him. In June 1081, synods at Maintz and Brixen declared the pope deposed and elected the Archbishop of Ravenna to rule the church as 'Clement III'. In that same year, Rudolf was killed in battle and Henry marched on Rome, gaining supporters as he went. He laid siege to the city in 1082 and a year later had fought his way to St. Peter's, although Gregory still held the Tiber crossing. The pope was virtually a prisoner, immured in the Castel Sant' Angelo, until being forced in March 1084 to flee from the city altogether, when a traitor opened the gates of the fortress. 'Clement III' was installed at the Lateran, and the humiliation of Canossa had been extinguished.

Once again the Normans were the key to the situation. Both sides appealed for their support, Henry offering Guiscard more land,

Gregory promising both reconciliation with the church and support in the Norman's chief ambition, the conquest of Constantinople. Dazzled by a vision of himself on the imperial throne, Guiscard accepted the pope's offer and was confirmed as the ruler of southern Italy, and the Normans marched on Rome in support of their new ally. As they advanced, opposition melted away until, when the vanguard reached the gates of the city, the only Germans left in Rome were a few of Gregory's supporters who had never left in the first instance. True Normans, Guiscard's men sacked the city nonetheless and, when they abandoned its ruins, took Gregory with them, whether as their leader or their prisoner no one quite knew. Gregory was carried to Salerno, Clement III returned to Rome, and Guiscard left for Greece, to join his son Bohemund, who was fighting his way towards Constantinople. When Gregory died at Salerno in May 1085, the whole world knew that 'the man who could be judged by nobody' had been judged and condemned by enough of his own contemporaries to make it impossible for him to hold the throne which had given him juridical power.

Chapter III

THE POPES AND THE PRINCES

THE REIGN of the German pope Clement III marked the temporary triumph of caesaro-papism in the West. The Holy Roman Emperor, who was in a very real sense the creation of the papacy, had subdued the Holy See. Both the emergence of the emperor and the subjection of the papacy were the outcome of pressures not fully understood at the time. Other solutions to the problems left by the evaporation of the original Roman Empire in the West could be imagined—but not, it seems, by the popes, who twice co-operated in attempts to recreate the Western empire, first under the Franks, then under the Germans, and finally claimed universal sovereignty for themselves.

No pope in the Middle Ages was capable of thinking in terms of spiritual authority alone; in fact, it was not until the Italian Concordat of 1929 that the papacy surrendered all claims to temporal power in Italy. Even Gregory VII did not repudiate the machinery of power. He accepted feudal oaths and attempted to give protection like any other feudal lord, and in such declarations as the *Sentences* was struggling for authority within the existing system. He attempted not to separate the church from the state, but to subject the head of the empire to the head of the church. To both him and Henry IV, power and authority were personal endowments. He challenged the emperor on the level of personal authority, and lost. But in losing he gave later popes new grounds on which to face the world. Five and a half centuries after Gelasius had suggested that the authority of the popes might be greater than the power of kings, Gregory declared that it was so, distilling the essence of the feelings of earlier generations—feelings expressed in such forms as the False Decretals—into authoritative statements of law. After this, it did not matter if earlier claims were proved false, the only consideration was whether the pope's estimate of his authority was accepted by enough people to make it a fact. At the time of Gregory's death, it was not sufficiently widely acknowledged, but within a hundred and fifty years papal claims were to be admitted almost universally.

After Gregory's death, it took eight years for the supporters of the concept of the sovereign papacy to win back the Lateran. For two of those years, there was no free pope anywhere. When one was elected, in 1087, he lived only a matter of a few months, but the following year the cardinals elected a man who had been close to Hildebrand: Odo, a former prior of Cluny, who had served Gregory VII as his principal legate. He ruled as Urban II with the support of the Normans, Matilda of Tuscany and the French. Barred from Rome until 1093 by imperial opposition, he travelled widely in Italy and France, presiding at synods designed to push forward the reform and romanization of the church. It was at first a holding action, but gradually internal German division and a growing desire for reform among Christians gave him the upper hand. Even after it had become possible for him to return to Rome, he did not neglect the important local synods, and it was at one of them, held at Clermont in 1095, that he preached the First Crusade. It was typical of him that the idea was not his own, but had been one of those schemes of Gregory VII's frustrated by his death.

In Gregory's dream no less than in Urban's preaching, the crusade had three aims, religious, political and financial. The religious aim was to unite Western Christendom in a common purpose under the pope and his legates and to secure the reunion of the Eastern and Western churches, while freeing the Holy Places from the Turks. The need to liberate the Holy Places had arisen because, after seizing Jerusalem in 1077, the newly dominant Seljuk Turks had put such restrictions on the pilgrim traffic that trade to and from the ports of eastern Italy had dropped catastrophically. Thus the restrictions were a financial as well as a spiritual disaster.

Relations between the papacy and the Eastern churches and empire had improved slightly in 1095. Early in the year, the Emperor Alexius had sent ambassadors to a synod at Piacenza, where they reported that although Seljuk power appeared to be declining, to be certain of holding the Bosphorus he needed more troops from the West to reinforce his Anglo-Saxon and Scandinavian Varangian Guard. It was within a few months of receiving this appeal that Leo preached the Crusade.

He died shortly before the First Crusade reached the apogee of its success with the foundation of the Kingdom of Jerusalem in 1100.

Yet in a very real sense the crusaders' victories were his victories, and resounded in the Western world to the glory of the papacy. They did not bring about the downfall of Henry IV or end the investiture controversy, but they made ultimate acceptance of papal views more certain. Although after the death of Henry IV in 1106 his son was crowned as Henry V by his father's antipope and not by Urban's legitimate successor, the Germans were by then alone in the world in their continued support of the schism.

Compromise on investitures was finally reached at Worms in 1122 on the basis of proposals made by the legitimate pope, Calixtus II. Henry guaranteed to end simony and promote electoral freedom, while acknowledging the pope's right to invest all bishops and abbots with their spiritual authority, symbolized by the ring and the staff. For his part, the pope recognized the emperor's natural anxiety about the loyalty of powerful men in his realm, and conceded to royal power the right to invest with the temporalities of an appointment by the touch of the imperial sceptre.*

Within a few years it became obvious on the continent that the apparently equitable compromise embodied in the concordat signed at Worms was in fact very favourable to the popes. Under its operation, the power of the emperor declined rapidly even inside Germany (although the concordat was not the only factor in that decline) and the importance of the lesser princes rose with that of the independent bishops and abbots, to whom they were often related by ties of blood as well as anti-imperial interest.

A generation of peace between the papacy and the empire began with the first purely Western council to be called 'general', the Council of the Lateran of 1123. It introduced no unexpected new legislation, but attempted to standardize the mass of laws passed in the previous half century against simony, nicolaitism and lay investiture. In the years following the council there were often difficulties in applying these canons, but Calixtus and his successor Honorius II proved to be reasonable men who, although always firm on the principles of Gregory VII, saw the importance of keeping the peace between themselves and the secular rulers of Europe.

* The arrangement made at Worms was essentially similar to one reached in England sixteen years earlier between Henry I and Anselm of Canterbury, and may well have been based on it. Under the English agreement, bishops were elected by cathedral chapters, received the ring and crozier from the papal legate, and did homage to the king for their temporalities.

Firm application of Hildebrandine principles established the papacy in a position of great practical influence, and was to lead to a restatement of papal claims to secular authority over the whole world. Although, as Hildebrand himself had frequently pointed out, earlier popes had claimed universal jurisdiction and had both crowned emperors and occasionally succeeded in deposing kings, general acceptance of their right to perform such actions was something new. That so many in the twelfth century were willing to support the claims was in part due to the obvious value of the reforms accompanying them, and in part to the far-ranging intellectual and spiritual gifts of the chief non-papal advocates of the sovereign papacy.

There were as yet no universities, but there were many influential monasteries with active schools where the study of the law was intensively pursued. The fact that such schools were associated with monasteries which were themselves deeply committed to the reforming movement meant both that the studies they produced tended to support Hildebrandine teaching and that the greatest scholars were often also the most devout men of their time. An obvious example is Anselm, who before becoming Archbishop of Canterbury was abbot of the Benedictine monastery at Bec, and after his death was canonized for his sanctity as well as for his political skill. Another is Bernard of Clairvaux.

Like Urban II, Bernard was not an innovator. He was the disciple both of Gregory VII and more directly of the reforming founders of the Cistercian Order, especially Abbot Stephen Harding of Citeaux. He is probably most widely remembered in the Church for his devotion to the Virgin, vividly expressed in his commentary on the Song of Songs, and in the secular world as the man who, in 1146, preached the Second Crusade, or perhaps as the opponent of Peter Abelard. It should not be forgotten, however, that his commitment to Hildebrandine ideas was total. He accepted and taught not only the reformers' standards of personal piety, but also their evaluation of the rightful position of the church in the world. Like them, he insisted on the absolute sovereignty of the pope. 'The fullness of power over all the churches in the world has been conferred by a special privilege on the Holy See,' he wrote in 1135. 'Anyone who resists that power, resists the divine order.' And in his view the secular power of the papacy was scarcely less, although it had to be exercised through princes. To explain its operation he took the doctrine of the two swords—of spiritual and secular power—from

St. Augustine and argued that both swords belonged to the papacy, in an exposition which was soon to become the classical statement of papal authority. Bringing together two texts, one from St. Luke's Gospel in which the apostles expressed their readiness to fight for Jesus ('And they said, Lord, behold, here are two swords') and the other from St. Matthew in which Jesus forbade Peter to fight for him ('Then Jesus said, Put thy sword up into its sheath'), Bernard wrote:

> The two swords belonged to Peter. The one (the spiritual sword) is in his hand, the other (the temporal sword) is at his disposal whenever it shall be necessary to unsheathe it. It is, however, to be kept by Peter in that condition in which it is least useful: 'Put up thy sword into its sheath.' Thus is belongs to him, but he may not use it with his own hand.

In other words, the pope has actual spiritual power, but only potential temporal power. If the second sword has to be drawn in defence of the church, it must be wielded by the pope's champions, the secular authorities, emperors and kings. But both swords belong absolutely to Peter and his successors.

Bernard's was the extreme position. It was not accepted universally. Even among those who claimed for the church the highest imaginable authority there was no agreement about the distribution of power within the church. Did authority belong solely and absolutely to the pope personally, as the extremists claimed? Or was it shared in some way between the pope and the cardinals, those bishops and priests of the city of Rome whose importance had increased dramatically in recent years? Or again, did it belong in a manner as yet undefined to the whole church? What was the real power of the council and the synod, those institutions which popes had used so frequently during the reform? At the time of the death of Honorius II some of these questions had not yet been asked in their plainest form, but they were already in the back of men's thinking, and they were to become increasingly important as the years passed until the Great Schism brought them into the very forefront of the debate.

Bernard of Clairvaux's letter ascribing total power within the church to the pope was written to Milan in circumstances that in many ways foreshadowed those of the Great Schism two hundred and forty years later. At the death of Honorius II, the machinery of papal election had once again proved itself inadequate to deal with the harsh realities of Italian politics. In 1378, the Romans were to riot in support of their demand for a Roman pope. In 1130, the struggle for power was not between Romans and non-Romans, but between two warring Roman families, the Frangipane and the Pierleone, both of which had candidates they wanted to see elected to the papacy. As Honorius lay on his deathbed, the papal chancellor suggested that to forestall violent demonstrations in support of either candidate, the dying man should be moved to a fortified monastery on the Caelian Hill and guarded there while a committee of eight cardinals, drawn from both factions, decided who should succeed him. As soon as he was dead, five of the committee elected a member of their faction, the Frangipane, to rule as Pope Innocent II, and their choice was ratified later the same day by other cardinals supporting the family. Within hours, the rival Pierleone faction had also held an election. Their choice was Cardinal Pierleone, who took the name Anacletus II.

At the time of the Great Schism, the question was to be which pope had been canonically elected; in 1130, there was no real doubt that neither of them had been. Innocent II had been chosen only by a minority, before Honorius's death had been announced or the conference of all the cardinals required by the canons had been held. Anacletus's election had proceeded without a cardinals' conference and regardless of the outcome of the only united discussion which had taken place, that appointing the committee.

On the day after the election a Pierleone mob drove Innocent II out of Rome. If he had been merely an unsatisfactory feudal lord, that might have been the end of the matter, but as he claimed the papacy, his fate interested all Europe. Unsafe in Italy, he fled to France, where he was championed by Bernard of Clairvaux on the grounds that he had been elected by the 'sounder' part of the cardinalate—six out of the ten cardinal bishops having voted for him. The argument had some weight because Nicholas II's decree on papal elections ruled that the cardinal bishops were to play the greatest part in elections, conferring to choose a pope and presenting their choice to the cardinal priests and deacons for confirmation of his election.

On the advice of Bernard and other leading churchmen, Louis VI called a synod at Etampes which recommended acceptance of Innocent, and the king swore allegiance to him. A few months later, Lothair III of Germany also recognized him. The following January,

Henry I of England, after a visit from Bernard, made the journey to Chartres and did homage to Innocent there. Italy, however, was strong for Anacletus II, the Pierleone claimant. In 1135, Bernard succeeded in persuading the Milanese to accept Innocent—the letters on papal authority already quoted were part of his campaign—but in the south Roger of Sicily, despite Bernard's pleading, maintained the schism until Anacletus's death in 1138 when the candidate proposed by the Pierleone to succeed him went immediately to Innocent II and made his submission.

A little over a year later, Innocent demonstrated his complete control over the Western church by calling a second oecumenical council at the Lateran. It is variously estimated that between five hundred and a thousand bishops attended. They did not, as might have been expected in the circumstances, examine the procedure for the election and recognition of popes, although the ease with which the Roman factions had ridden over the canons at the elections of Innocent and Anacletus, and the facility with which Bernard had been able to find a law to prove that what he wanted to believe was in fact true, were clear indications that the mass of legislation passed by the Western church in the course of its history was in urgent need of codification. The earlier decretals were now in some cases centuries out of date and the new scholars needed authorized and generally-accepted texts from which to work. There was also a revival of interest in law of all kinds, for it had been recognized that only law kept mankind from the anarchy and chaos into which the Western world had collapsed after the decay of the old Roman Empire. Commentaries on Roman law were being used at the schools as one of the foundations for secular law, but there was no code governing the church.

Early in the twelfth century, two notable, although notably imperfect, collections of canon laws were utilized to support local regulations, those of Anselm de Lucca and Cardinal Deusdedit, but neither took full account of the new situation stemming from the Hildebrandine revolution. Cardinal Deusdedit's, indeed, had been partly designed to reduce the importance of the pope and elevate the cardinals whom, by a false etymology, he said were the 'hinges' on which the church turned—the exact position claimed for Peter and his successors by Leo IX in his letter to the emperor and patriarch of Constantinople in 1053, the year before the Eastern schism. The cardinals had certainly gained much in importance over the preceding century—but the pope had gained more. A new code was needed, accurately reflecting the new situation. It appeared, probably in 1140, under the title *Concordantia discordantium canonem*, but soon became known simply as *Decretum*: the Decretal. Little is known of its author, except that he was a monk named Gratian who taught law at the School of Bologna, but the influence of his work on the later Middle Ages was incalculably wide.

As the original title of his decretal reveals, Gratian's concern was to produce concordance between apparently contradictory canons. The method he adopted was that being developed in the schools for disputations, setting text against text, making distinctions, setting out objections and answering them with more texts until concordance was reached. In all, he brought together 3,458 canons demonstrating, partly by art in arrangement and argument, that Gregory VII's teaching had not been innovatory, but had expressed the true tradition of the Roman Church. They showed the pope dominating the church through his right of jurisdiction over local bishops and synods, and the church as totally independent of lay power and politics, with the rights of princes reduced merely to that of expressing *consensus* with decisions already reached by the pope or local bishops, and imperial claims to a role in papal elections totally extinguished.

Gratian did not solve all the problems, and it was his failure—and that of commentators and glossators on his work—which made possible the Great Schism as well as many other disputes of less permanent significance. But at least after the appearance of his concordance, scholars, bishops and kings knew what they were arguing about. The timeliness of the publication of the Decretal is underlined by the nature of the controversy with the German emperors Frederick I Barbarossa and his grandson Frederick II which loomed so large over the following decades.

Frederick Barbarossa seems really to have believed the legend that he was the true successor to the emperors of ancient Rome. Like Otto, the first German Emperor, he spoke and wrote of himself as the new Constantine and—having absorbed the significance of the Roman Law recently 'rediscovered' at the schools—also as the new Justinian. Justinian's sixth-century code had described the emperor as the source of all power and authority but, since Gregory VII, the canon law of the church had made precisely the same claim for the popes. The doctrine of St. Peter's two swords was incompatible with the exalted view of Frederick's office encouraged by his advisers. If the new 'bible' of the popes was Gregory's *Sentences* and Gratian's *Decretum*, showing that the papacy was 'founded by God alone' and subject to no one, Frederick's was the *Digest* of the law, proving that he ruled 'at a nod'. Believing that it was the divine will that he should rule, Frederick was the first actually to speak of his kingdom as the *Holy* Roman Empire. Tensions were inescapable. They appeared even before the imperial coronation in 1155. The ceremony itself was a struggle for dominance between two equal and opposing wills.

At the moment of the coronation, Pope Hadrian IV was in the ascendency, simply because Frederick was not yet wholly secure. He demonstrated his authority over the emperor by presenting Frederick to the world as his vassal, the feudal tenant of the papacy. Hadrian has sometimes been represented as a proud man, deliberately humiliating the emperor by compelling him to perform such feudal tasks as holding the stirrup of the papal horse and altering the order of the coronation to emphasize his own authority. It was not, however, his own power only that he was demonstrating, but that of the reformed papacy. There was nothing hypocritical in Hadrian's attitude: his actions merely expressed his reading of the existing situation. But it made a breach with Frederick inevitable. Less than two years after the coronation, Frederick publicly denounced the pope for daring to suggest in a letter to the imperial Diet of Besançon that the papacy had conferred the empire on him as a *beneficium*, a 'benefice', just as though he were merely a feudal tenant. Hadrian later tried to explain that he had used the word simply to mean 'benefit' or 'gift', but he was unconvincing. In 1158, Frederick showed his independence by creating the Kingdom of Bohemia by an act of his own will, although since the time of Pepin the Short it had generally been admitted that new kings received their lands from the emperor but their authority—a spiritual gift—from the clergy. When protests were made, the imperial chancellor told the Diet of Roncalia (held before the first glow of success after a victory over Milan had faded) that 'the law is whatever the emperor wills'. His contemporaries realized how revolutionary this statement and the action it followed were: a court chronicler reflected that Frederick had made himself 'the sole ruler of the world'.

The following year it became known that Hadrian was seeking a new alliance with the Normans of Sicily, and to counteract such a move the emperor invaded Italy. By the end of that summer's campaigning, he was indeed 'sole ruler', for the pope, whom he had made his prisoner, suddenly died at Agnani. The majority of the cardinals immediately elected to succeed him the canonist Roland Bandinelli, a pupil of Gratian, who announced that he would reign as Alexander III. The new pope was fully committed to the Hilde-brandine vision of the sovereign papacy and was well equipped to defend it. He had already produced valuable commentaries on the *Decretum* and was soon to issue decretals of his own important enough to be included in the full code of canon law promulgated in the following century under Gregory X. Immediately after his election, he began negotiations with the Lombard Guelphs and Roger of Sicily. Frederick Barbarossa's counter-blow was to secure the election of an antipope, a cardinal priest who became Victor IV. Both Alexander and Victor had grounds for claiming that they had been validly elected, but Victor had the immediate support of the imperial army. Alexander fled from Rome.

The schism which began in September 1159 lasted until 1180. In all, four antipopes opposed Alexander III. The third of them, Paschal III, both crowned Frederick a second time and canonized Charlemagne at his request. But Alexander's diplomatic and legal skills ensured that the schism did not spread into France, England and Spain. Indeed, as late as 1179 he was strong enough to hold a general council, the third at the Lateran. It passed a number of decrees, the most important of them being that, to prevent schism arising in the future as the result of inconclusive papal elections, a two-thirds majority of all the cardinals would be required for a valid election. In further measures against simony and nepotism, it also decreed that no one should be made a bishop unless he had been born in wedlock and had reached the age of thirty years.

Alexander died two years after this council ended, and there followed a period of seventeen years of confusion and disarray, during which five popes briefly occupied the throne. If Jerusalem had not fallen in 1187 to the forces of Saladin, Barbarossa might have conquered all Italy. As it was, the task fell on his son after he had met an ignominious death on his way to the Third Crusade, being drowned in the River Saleph near Antioch in June 1090. Within four years the new emperor, Henry VI, had almost achieved the great German ambition of an empire unbroken from the Baltic to Sicily. The aged Pope Celestine III, virtually without allies, was no match for him and when Henry died suddenly in 1197, his son, the three-year-old Frederick of Sicily, inherited the whole of Germany and all Italy except a small part of the Papal States.

Pope Celestine died the following year and was succeeded by his nephew, the thirty-seven-year-old canonist Lothario di Segni who, wiping out the past, took the name used by the last of the antipopes to Alexander III, calling himself Innocent III.

During the whole of Innocent's term of rule, Frederick was his ward and the empire was in disarray. The pope made the most of his opportunities. The four incidents for which his reign is chiefly remembered, the sacking of Constantinople by the knights of the Fourth Crusade, the 'crusade' against the Albigensians of Provence, the first moves towards the establishment of the Inquisition, and the interdict on England, all stemmed from his conviction that he was the divinely appointed ruler of the world. A canonist himself, pupil of the famous Hugaccio, taught from his schooldays that 'whatever God can do, the pope can do', he called himself the Vicar of Christ, seeing himself as the plenipotentiary regent of God on earth, given divine authority to rule the world. During his papacy, an English poet wrote: 'The Pope is the wonder of the world.' No canon lawyer was willing to deny it, least of all Innocent III himself. In the first year of his reign, in October 1198, he wrote in condemnation of Philip of Swabia, a younger son of Frederick Barbarossa:

> The creator of the universe established two great luminaries in the firmament of heaven, the greater to rule the day, the lesser the night. In the same way, he appointed two great dignities in the firmament of the universal church, which is spoken of as heaven . . . These dignities are the authority of the pontificate and that of royalty. Moreover, the moon derives her light from the sun, and is actually inferior to the sun in both size and quality, position and effect. In the same way, royal power derives its dignity from pontifical authority.

The movement begun by Hildebrand reached its apotheosis in Innocent III, ruler of 'the universal church which is spoken of as heaven', king-maker and king-breaker, strong enough to desert the Guelphs and proclaim Frederick of Sicily as emperor, but forbid him ever to unite the kingdom of Sicily and the empire, so throwing all alliances into confusion, and gaining for himself room to manoeuvre. The Fourth Crusade grew partly out of the failure of the Third and partly out of a flattering appeal from the boy-emperor Alexius of Constantinople, brother-in-law of Philip of Swabia, made in person to Innocent at the beginning of his reign. The story of its degeneration from a pious undertaking with political overtones, to a commercial enterprise born of an alliance between France and the Venetians, and finally to a piratical attack culminating in the establishment of a 'Western' Frankish emperor at Constantinople in 1204, is too familiar to recount in detail. What needs to be emphasized is Innocent's intention in calling for it. He made it a pilgrimage, remitting taxes and offering indulgences to all who would take the cross, and there can be little doubt that, horrible as the outcome was, Innocent's original aim was to fulfil his spiritual and temporal obligations at one and the same time, promising military support to the suppliant emperor and the opportunity to win grace to Christian knights. He was both wielding the spiritual sword and calling for the temporal sword to be unsheathed in defence of the universal church.

Innocent's success—and there can be no denying that he was very successful—depended on the degree to which his claim to be the universal ruler was accepted both by the clergy and by the mass of the people in the West. The extent of their obedience to him was clearly demonstrated by the success of the interdict he placed on England in 1208. The situation in England which led to the imposition of the interdict was a somewhat outmoded one, reminiscent of the investiture controversy a hundred years earlier. When Archbishop Hubert Walker died in 1205, the monks of Canterbury secretly elected their sub-prior to succeed him and sent him to Rome for Innocent's approval. The bishops of England protested on the grounds that they had been given no opportunity to participate in the election. King John forebade both the appointment and the appeal to Rome, and ordered the bishops and monks together to elect his own nominee, John de Grey of Norwich, and then asked Innocent for the *pallium*. Innocent rejected both elections on canonical grounds, and sent Cardinal Stephen Langton to fill the vacant see. The king refused him admission to the country, and confiscated the estates of the monks of Canterbury. In 1208, Innocent put the whole country under an interdict, forbidding the celebration of any sacrament except baptism and extreme unction, and closing the churches and their cemeteries. The measure of Innocent's authority—the measure, that is, of the acceptance of papal supremacy—was the universality of obedience to this edict. There was no schism in England, even when in 1212 Innocent formally declared John deposed and freed his subjects from their allegiance to him. Philip of France, allying himself with Frederick of

Sicily, assembled his army against John, and some Welsh chiefs rose. John made an ally of Innocent's old enemy in Germany, Otto IV, but pressure in England proved too much for him. There was no formal rising, but in 1213 he was compelled to receive both Langton and a papal legate, to whom he did homage for the kingdom, surrendering it and receiving it back as a papal fief.

Although ordered by Innocent to cease his preparations for war against John, Philip of France refused to abandon his campaign. In 1214, John sent an army under the Earl of Salisbury to Flanders to unite with the forces of Otto IV, now himself excommunicate and threatened by Frederick of Sicily. At the battle of Bouvines, John lost his last hopes in France and Otto his crown. The following year, John signed the Great Charter and Innocent, at the height of his power, summoned the fourth Lateran Council, which was to give the empire to Frederick.

In the Fourth Crusade, Innocent had intended that the temporal sword should be drawn against Islam. In 1212, by the act deposing John, he ordered it to be unsheathed against a rebellious king. Midway between these two dates, in the Albigensian Crusade, first preached by Innocent in 1208, it was actually drawn against heretics.

The threat represented to orthodoxy by the religious dualism of the Albigensians or Cathars had been recognized at the third Lateran Council of 1179, which issued a decree against the heretics 'in Gascony, Albi and around Toulouse' who 'publicly manifest their error and draw simple and unbalanced folk into their conspiracy', prohibiting anyone from having any dealings with them, and excommunicating 'them and those who receive them and abet them'. Albigensian teaching, forbidding as it did normal marriage and the taking of any oaths, threatened not only the clergy but the whole pattern of mediaeval life. At the beginning of his reign Innocent moved against these non-conformists with the traditional weapons, the canons of the Lateran Council and the arguments of skilful preachers, using first the Cistercians and then the Spaniards Bishop Diego de Osmar and Sub-prior Dominic Guzman; but the Albigenses did not yield. Ugly incidents multiplied until Innocent, losing patience, preached a crusade against Provence in the most fiery phrases: 'Arise, Christian Soldiers! The blood of the righteous cries to you to protect the church with the shield of faith against its enemies! Arise and gird on your swords!' The holy war began, in July 1209, with the siege of Beziers. It lasted twenty years—so good was the plunder of the unique civilization of Provence—and at first the only voice raised against it seems to have been that of Dominic Guzman. By 1215, however, it was clear that the war was no longer a crusade in any true sense of the word, and ways of ending it became one of the chief matters discussed at the Lateran Council secretly summoned that year to consider—although it was never said openly—how best the church could wield its undeniable power to make all Europe a single City of God.

This fourth Lateran Council was the high water mark of papal power in Europe. It was attended by bishops and abbots from all over the continent, and by the founders of two new monastic orders, Francis of Assisi, and Dominic Guzman, prior of the Order of Preachers, to which was soon to be entrusted most of the work of the Holy Office of Inquisition. Its pronouncements ranged wider than those of most former councils, from the war against heresy to the clothing of the clergy, and the necessity for papal supervision over monasteries—and kings. Innocent was a demanding master as far as the clergy were concerned. He had previously said that 'all corruption of the people comes mainly from the clergy' and had devoted much time to the correction of the lives of bishops and abbots. Now he ordered (for the canons of the council were the embodiment of his ideas) strict control of every aspect of the priest's life. Nor were only priests to be subject to examination; the laity too were to be made true inhabitants of the City of God. The Albigensian heresy and the excesses of the Waldenses—who had begun as popular preachers but were now teaching revolution—had badly frightened the episcopate and made it clear that close control was necessary if the papacy was to be truly sovereign. To meet these dangers, the council ordered that henceforward no one was to be allowed to preach or teach without episcopal permission, and that every parish was to be inspected twice a year by the bishop or his archdeacon. It further decreed that information about suspected heretics should be collected on oath, that secular authorities should be required to swear to expel the guilty from their dominions, and that the property of anyone condemned for heresy should be confiscated. More important still, however, it also laid it down that:

> Every faithful Christian of either sex, having reached the years of discretion, shall confess his own sins once in the year at least to his own priest and seek to fulfil the penance inflicted on him on account of them reverently receiving the sacrament of the Eucharist at least once at

Easter. . . . If for a reasonable cause anyone wishes to confess his sins to any other priest, let him first seek and obtain permission from his own priest, otherwise the other priest may not absolve nor bind him. . . .

Never before had Christians been bound to confess at specified intervals, although the practice of confession had been known for many centuries. The canon was carefully worded, both to exclude informers ('his own sins') and to safeguard the secrets of the penitent. Yet the conclusion is inescapable that its main purpose at the time of its composition was to enable parish priests to know the degree of their parishioners' loyalty—the general report of which was to be collected twice every year. As only those who had received absolution were permitted to receive the Eucharist at Easter, it also gave the informers for which the century was notorious valuable indications as to where fresh victims might be found.

In the course of the Lateran Council, Innocent III also told the assembled fathers of his 'burning desire to snatch the Holy Land from the hand of the infidel' and announced the Fifth Crusade, to be financed by generous gifts from the papacy and a tax on the clergy. He proclaimed a total armistice in Europe—but made no reference to the sack of Constantinople in 1204. In calling for a new crusade, he was echoing Frederick of Sicily. In July of that year, the latter had been crowned Frederick II of Germany by the Archbishop of Maintz, and immediately called on all true knights to follow him to the Holy Land. Now in November, Innocent was pressed to crown him as Holy Roman Emperor, although years earlier he had made the prince promise never to unite Sicily and the empire. The electors of Germany were strongly advocating his claims and, although Otto IV still had some supporters among the bishops, Innocent had been speaking of the young king as emperor-elect for some time past. However, he left it to the council fathers themselves to vote for the deposition of Otto and the election of Frederick—so betraying the Guelphs, who had for so long been generally faithful to the papacy. Frederick was duly proclaimed emperor of the West.

Innocent died in Perugia in April 1216, before Frederick II could show him how badly his trust had been misplaced. The election which followed his death was more like a modern conclave than any which had preceded it. The people of Perugia seized the nineteen cardinals then in their city and locked them up until they had elected a pope; and it was only by good fortune that their trap closed around one cardinal more than the two-thirds needed for valid election. The cardinals' choice fell on an aged Roman, during whose reign of over ten years as Honorius III papal power already began to show signs of decline from the high point marked by the rule of Innocent III. Indeed, in the opinion of many, all that saved it from disaster was the force of character of the pope's chief adviser, Ugolini, the Cardinal Bishop of Ostia, who was destined to be the next pope, Gregory IX. Honorius proved powerless to stop the war against the Albigensians or to persuade his former ward, Frederick II, to launch the crusade against the infidel in the Holy Land.

The situation changed for the better, however, with the election of Ugolini in 1228. The new pope was a relation and a protégé of Innocent III, sharing something of his character as well as his attitude to the papacy and the world. Annually for eleven years, Frederick had said that he would sail for Jerusalem: Gregory IX, disturbed by his continuing hostile activity in northern Italy, gave him one final chance to prove that he meant to carry out his promise and, on being denounced for his importunity, excommunicated Frederick on the grounds that he had broken his solemn oath. In a grand gesture of defiance, Frederick immediately set out for Jerusalem—and took it, insofar as he made a temporary alliance with the sultan, was admitted to the Holy Sepulchre, and there crowned himself King of Jerusalem.

In his absence, Gregory conquered Sicily, thus starting a war which was to last until 1230, when a peace treaty was finally signed at San Germano. By that time, Frederick had retaken Sicily, subdued most of the Papal States and, by the violence of his revenge, made his name feared wherever he went. Surprisingly, the peace lasted for nine years before Gregory, able to endure the insults of 'the Wonder of the World' no longer, suddenly renewed the excommunication of 'the beast, the so-called emperor, Frederick II'. There was ample provocation. Not only had Frederick finally separated the Lombard League from the papacy, he was also trying to persuade the cardinals that Peter's primacy was only a matter of honour, and not of authority, and that they should summon a general council on their own authority to rid the church of the 'unworthiness' of Gregory's rule and elect a true pope. The bull of excommunication listed charges against him ranging from 'sedition against the Holy See' through failure to nominate bishops to vacant sees and the collection of the revenues from them, to extortion and 'manifold injury of nobles, poor persons, widows and orphans'.

Frederick II's initial reaction was to march on Rome, but he was forced to withdraw in the face of stiff popular opposition. Then, a few months later, he snatched from the Genoese fleet two cardinals and more than a hundred archbishops and bishops on their way to Rome for a council which, he correctly feared, had been called to depose him. A further six months later, Gregory IX died, aged a hundred, mourning the fate of the imprisoned prelates and fearful for the future of the city with a new imperial army almost under its walls. On receiving the news of his death, Frederick II again withdrew his forces, but the threat of violence still hung over the cardinals as they assembled for the new election. They would not elect an imperialist and dared not elect anyone else.

After a delay of two months the senator commanding the city guard arrested them all and kept them under restraint so severe that three of them died before they could agree on a compromise candidate. They finally elected the Archbishop of Milan, who himself died within a fortnight, leaving chaos behind him. The Romans rioted for a Roman pope. Some of the surviving cardinals fled to Anagni. Frederick II, while maintaining his threats, tried to buy a majority for an imperial candidate by freeing the two cardinals he had arrested and bribing the rest. On June 23, 1243, the cardinals elected a Ghibelline, Sinisbaldo Fieschi, a noted jurist and former lecturer at Bologna, who announced that he would reign as Innocent IV. Expecting sympathetic understanding from him as an imperialist, Frederick continued the armistice signified by the release of the cardinals, and sent legates to Rome to convey his congratulations to the new pope. Innocent refused to receive them.

Later in his career, in his *Commentaries* on the decretals, he was to declare that the excommunication of an emperor could be ordered only for 'notorious excesses' (*pro notoriis excessibus*), but that any bishop could decree it. By refusing to admit Frederick's legates into his presence at the very beginning of his reign, he let it be known that he had already judged the reigning emperor in his own mind and found the sentences passed on him by Gregory IX fully justified. His judgment cost him the city of Rome. Hunted by Frederick's troops, he fled first to Genoa, then to Lyons, from where he could continue the diplomatic struggle under the protection of Louis IX.

Frederick called the whole affair 'a game of chess' but he played it in deadly earnest. Innocent IV's aim now was to destroy him. In

June 1245, Frederick sent an ambassador to a small council called by Innocent at Lyons, to make promises of reform in his name. His promises were unacceptable. On July 17, after a formal disputation had examined all the legal questions involved, he was condemned on four counts: perjury, breaking the peace with the church 'frivolously', sacrilege in arresting the prelates, and heresy. He was sentenced to be 'deprived of and deposed from all his dignities and honours'. The bishops added the solemn injunction: 'We command strictly and definitely that in future no one shall obey him ever again as king or emperor. . . . In Germany, the princes entitled to do so may now proceed to the election of a new king. . . .' The bull of deposition was read at a scene of the greatest solemnity, all the bishops standing to hear it with lighted candles in their hands, and extinguishing the flames against the stone floor at its end. In theory, Frederick's reign ended at that moment: in fact, he continued to war and scheme against Innocent until he died in 1250. The struggle was then continued by his son Manfred until 1266, when he was killed by Charles of Anjou, to whom the papacy had offered the crown of Sicily.

Making the deposition of Frederick II effective was not the only important business to occupy the bishops in the years following the Council of Lyons. The war against heresy still continued, although actual fighting had stopped in Provence in 1229. Innocent III's plan for commissions of enquiry to seek out not only Albigenses but all aberrant thinkers and teachers had borne fruit in the reign of Gregory IX with the establishment of the Holy Office and courts of inquisition in 1233. It was a field in which the church and the empire could and did co-operate. Already in March 1232 Frederick had extended to the whole empire a law previously operative only in Sicily decreeing that heretics should be 'put to death by fire in the sight of the people' as guilty of a crime against the common good of the state. Similar laws were passed in France by Louis XI in 1233. They were based on earlier Roman law, which was held to support Gregory IX's view that European heretics, regarded as traitors, were no better than foreign enemies, the Saracens and Turks. Thomas Aquinas likened them to coiners, but held that counterfeit ideas were worse for the state than counterfeit money.

Heretics were executed under the old Roman law, as dangerous to the state. The first trials had been held about the year 385, under the Emperor Maximus, and the accused on that occasion were a bishop

of Abila named Priscillian and his following who, like the Albigensians, taught a gnostic dualism. Their trial and execution were a
valuable precedent to the lawyers of the Middle Ages. Papal attitudes
hardened on this subject as they did on so many others during this
century of lawyers. The third Lateran Council in 1179 merely
pointed to the fact that the church expected help in dealing with
heresy: 'Albeit the discipline of the church does not carry out bloody
retributions, being content with priestly judgment, it is nevertheless
aided by the regulations of Catholic princes'; but the fourth Lateran
Council in 1215 demanded that help: 'Convicted heretics shall be
handed over for punishment to their secular superiors or the latter's
agents ... Clerics shall first be degraded ... Catholics who take the
cross and devote themselves to the extermination of heretics shall
enjoy the same indulgence and privilege as those who go to the Holy
Land.' The reaction of Catholic princes to this instruction was the
passing of laws such as that which in Sicily required the public
burning of heretics. In 1233, branches of the Inquisition were set up,
under Dominican control, in every Western country, and in 1252
Innocent IV circulated a directive setting out strict rules for the
procedure of the courts of inquisition, laying it down, for example,
that inquisitors themselves were not to enter the torture chamber,
but that 'it shall be obligatory for the ruler to force all the heretics
whom he has arrested—but without cutting off a limb or bringing
them nearer to death—overtly to confess their sins as robbers and
murderers of souls and thieves of the sacraments of God and the
Christian faith, and to give the names of other heretics known to
them'. It was this last clause, more than any other, which made the
courts of the mediaeval inquisition the vile places they were, for who
could judge when the suffering prisoner had no more information to
give ?

Innocent IV died in 1254, and was succeeded by a close relative of
Gregory IX's, a vacillating man who ruled as Alexander IV and lived
in growing fear of Frederick's son Manfred. Manfred was never
accepted by the German Electors, but neither were the papal candidates for the thrones of Sicily and the empire, Edmund, the son of
Henry III of England, and Richard, Earl of Cornwall, Henry's
brother. Richard was actually crowned as King of the Romans, and
consequently emperor-elect, at Aachen, but civil war in England
made him ineffectual as a papal ally on the continent. The truth was
—although no one saw it at the time—that imperialism was a dying

force, and the new nation-states were claiming the allegiance that men had previously given to the concept of universal empire. In the circumstances it was ironical that neither of Alexander's immediate successors was able to set foot in his capital, Rome, after his election: both were French and neither was acceptable to either the people of Rome or the Germans. When the second died, in 1268, it was almost three years before the cardinals could be persuaded to elect his successor. Fears of the Germans, of the French, of Charles of Anjou (whom the papacy itself had enfeoffed with the Kingdoms of Naples and Sicily in order to be free of the Germans), and of the Romans held them back, until the citizens of Viterbo imprisoned them in the archbishop's palace there, and when they still hesitated, took the roof off to leave them without protection from the weather. On September 1, 1271, they elected an Italian, formerly Archdeacon of Liège, who announced that he would reign as Gregory X. It appeared to him that, in this century of lawyers, what was supremely lacking was a set of firm rules for the election of popes, one which would leave the electors really free to make the best choice. At a general council held at Lyons in 1274 in an abortive attempt to reunite the Eastern and Western churches, he issued a decree in which he co-ordinated all the earlier canons relating to elections and added new rules based on his own experience of electoral failure. His rules were substantially those still applied in papal elections today to make over-hasty election impossible and long delays very difficult. Adopting Alexander III's dictate that only cardinals should take part in the election, Gregory laid it down that on the tenth day after the death of a pope, the ceremonies of his funeral then being complete, the electors should be locked up together, with only one servant-adviser each, and no contact with the outside world except for a single window through which food could be passed. The regulations required a guard to be put on the door, and the reduction of rations if an election were not made within three days, with a further reduction —to bread and watered wine—after eight. They further demanded a secret ballot—which proved all but impossible to achieve for many years—and a two-thirds majority for election.

Valuable as they were, these rules marked the final transformation of the Bishop of Rome into the sovereign pope. In early centuries, Bishops of Rome had always been elected at Rome by the clergy and people: now only the college of cardinals, often largely composed of non-Romans, was to play any part in the election, and theoretically no one was to know what any individual cardinal had said or done during the conclave. In the following century it was to become clear that it was no longer necessary for the nominal Bishops of Rome even to want to live in Rome, and at the election of Urban VI, which triggered off the Great Schism, the people of Rome were to show how conscious they were of the loss of their bishop to the world.

At the time of their formulation, the first aspect of Gregory X's new rules to become apparent was that they were not going to be permitted to work. The 'game of chess' formerly played between the emperor and the papacy now had new contestants but the stakes remained the same: the Papal States and influence in world affairs. The States themselves were too big a prize to be left merely in the gift of cardinals—or so it seemed to the most powerful ruler in Europe now that Germany was in chaos, the King of France, the successor to St. Louis, Philip IV 'the Fair'.

In the eighteen years between the death of Gregory X in 1276 and the election of Boniface VIII in 1294, no less than eight popes briefly appeared and as rapidly vanished again. The state of the game may be judged from the fact that two were French, two came from Rome, three from other parts of Italy and one from Portugal, while for more than three years out of the eighteen the see was vacant.

After the death of Nicholas IV in 1292, it looked as though this vacancy would never be filled. The cardinals were split between the Colonna and the Orsini factions, and faced with urgent problems, over which there could be no compromise, concerning the future of the Kingdom of Sicily which had slipped from papal control after the massacre of its French garrison in the Sicilian Vespers of March 21, 1282 and its seizure by Peter III of Aragon. Two years passed in argument before such of them as had survived two summers of deadly heat and fever compromised in electing—partly from cynicism, partly from superstition—an aged but saintly peasant from the Abruzzi, the founder of an order of hermits named Peter of Murrone, who had been prophesying that if no election was made soon, all the cardinals would die. They sent Benedetto Gaetani, a jurist and cardinal legate, to persuade the old man to come to Perugia for the formalities of election, but he refused to move from his mountain hermitage. The situation soon proved to be not as simple as the old man's thinking. Some of the new pope-elect's closest advisers were indebted to Charles II of Naples, who was intriguing to regain the Kingdom of Sicily, and it was to him, however unwillingly, that Gaetani had to turn for help. Even then it took two kings, Charles II of Naples and his son Charles of Hungary, to persuade Peter to leave the mountains. When they had at last succeeded in this, they took him south, away from the Papal States into the French and formerly Norman city of Anagni, Cardinal Gaetani's own birthplace. The other cardinals followed, and Peter of Murrone was crowned as Pope Celestine V outside the gates of Aquila in August 1294.

Immediately after the ceremony, Charles II removed him to Naples, where again the cardinals had to follow if they were not to lose all their influence over events. As it was, under Charles's guidance, Celestine appointed enough French and Neapolitan cardinals to outvote the surviving Italians, assigned the whole of the church's tithes in France to Philip the Fair—the pope himself practised and encouraged apostolic poverty—and made Charles's son Louis Archbishop of Lyons at the uncanonical age of twenty-one. But he was altogether too unworldly for Gaetani and his allies. He did not want to be pope, and said so, but there was only one doubtful precedent for a pope abdicating, that of Gregory VI in 1046, and Charles II was joined by a multitude of devout people, grateful for a holy pope, in appealing to Celestine to continue in office. His own order, the Spiritual Franciscans, thus found themselves allied with the most worldly of monarchs in trying to persuade him to carry on in office. Many, including the poet Jacopone da Todi, saw him as 'the Angel Pope', 'the good pope to come' predicted at the beginning of the century by Abbot Joachim of Fiore, who though condemned for heresy by the fourth Lateran Council, was still regarded widely as a prophet. It was later said that Gaetani pressed Celestine to resign—his enemies went so far as to suggest that he made heavenly voices speak in the pope's bedchamber by means of a secret speaking-tube—but it is probable that he did no more than tell the pope that there was nothing in the canons to prevent his resignation if he felt that it was necessary; this judgment was subsequently upheld by the majority of canonists. What made it seem to smack of self-interest at the time was the fact that Celestine resigned on December 13 and on Christmas Eve Cardinal Gaetani became pope, being crowned as Boniface VIII, with the support of some French and Neapolitan cardinals. But if he made promises to his supporters, they were not kept.

His first move after election was to leave Naples and the sphere of

French influence. Celestine tried to return to his hermitage, but Boniface insisted that he should travel to Rome with the cardinals, for the rumour was already spreading that the new pope would die— or even already had died—and the Angel Pope return to the throne. The hermit tried to escape to Greece, but a storm drove his boat back to port in Italy and he was handed over to Boniface, who kept him as it were on permanent exhibition at Fumone Castle in the Campagna until he died in 1296.

Meanwhile Boniface busied himself with foreign affairs. He arranged a truce between the French and the Aragonese in Italy and, after many difficulties, between Edward I of England and Philip the Fair in Gascony. But in his own Papal states he was not so successful. It was the era of interminable small, inter-city wars, and many men as skilful as Boniface and more popular had failed to bring peace. Moreover, he had enemies even closer to him, chief among them the Colonna cardinals, uncle and nephew, Jacopo and Pietro, appointed by the Colonna pope, Nicholas IV. They, and the Spiritual Franciscans, refused to admit the validity of his election, and the whole Colonna family began to put ever-mounting pressure on him. On May 3, 1297, Stephen Colonna seized a convoy carrying taxes and other treasure to the pope, excusing his banditry by arguing that Boniface was no true pope and could not therefore have any use for papal income. On the 12th the Colonna cardinals issued a manifesto, denouncing Boniface as a simoniac, usurper and heretic, and demanding a general council to try him. The manifesto—and two more which rapidly followed it—listed thirteen arguments against the acceptance of Celestine's resignation, the main point being that no one, not even the pope himself, could demote a pope, because the papal power came from God himself, who alone could take it away by death. Yet they also argued that a general council could depose an heretical pope: an old canonist view, recently supported by the commentator Hostensius in his *Summa* and *Lectura* on the decretals.

Boniface summoned the two cardinals to Rome to defend their views, and when they refused to make the journey, held a consistory at which he deprived them of their office, with the angry comment: 'I will root out this accursed family and its diseased blood.' On May 23, faced with what looked like the beginnings of a full-scale revolt, involving the Franciscans and the Spirituals as well as the Colonna, he issued a bull denouncing the whole family as schismatics. The Colonna literally took to the hills, preparing for war in their castles outside Rome. They had repaid the stolen treasure, but Boniface was implacable. His intractability alienated more of the cardinals, but the supporters of the Colonna were strong enough neither to summon a viable general council nor to elect an antipope who would be widely recognized; and in the end, despite their strong foreign connections especially with Naples and Sicily, the Colonna found themselves facing a papal 'crusade'. Powerful as the family was, it had made too many enemies in the Papal States to hold out for long. Castle after castle surrendered to the papal armies, until all that remained loyal to them was the city of Palestrina, defended by Sciarra Colonna 'the Savage': when it fell, Boniface ordered the site to be levelled and sown with salt, and its inhabitants resettled nearby at a place to be called Civitas Papalis, the Pope's City. The Colonna were forced to do penance, dressed in black with ropes around their necks. They never forgave Boniface either the crusade or their humiliation. Soon they began to complain that the pope was violating the peace terms, alienating their fiefs and giving them to others. He renewed the excommunication and they fled. Stephen soon reached France by way of Sicily and England; Sciarra followed him not much later but by a more romantic route, taking service first with the corsairs of the Barbary Coast and then with Philip the Fair, after being captured, put in irons at Marseilles, and ransomed by the king at his nephew's request. Boniface had not heard the last of them.

By the year 1300, the pope seemed once again to be master of the world. He celebrated his victories in the glittering Holy Year of Jubilee which so fascinated Dante. The plenary indulgence which had hitherto been offered only to those who took part in crusades to free the now totally inaccessible Holy Places was transferred to the churches of Peter and Paul at Rome. It was estimated that two million people from all over Europe made the pilgrimage to this Christian version of the old Saecular Games. 'The Church heaped up treasure and the citizens became rich through the sale of their wares,' one chronicler wrote, adding that Boniface appeared several times in imperial dress, surrounded by the cardinals in the new scarlet cloaks he had designed for them, declaring 'I am Caesar: I am the emperor'.

It was a superficial triumph. In France, Philip the Fair had learned years before from Aegidius Romanus, the Archbishop of Bourges, that 'Jesus Christ gave the church no temporal sovereignty, and the king derives his authority from God alone'. As early as 1296,

Boniface had found it necessary to publish a bull, *Clericis laicos*, directed primarily against England and France, excommunicating any cleric who paid taxes to anyone except the Holy See contrary to ancient immunities. The bull was remarkable both for the completeness of its claims to these immunities and for the arrogant terms in which it was phrased from its very beginning: 'Boniface, bishop, servant of the servants of God, for the perpetual record of the matter. . . . That laymen have been very hostile to the clergy, history relates—and it is clearly proved by the experiences of this present time. . . .'

Philip's reaction to this bull was to forbid the export of gold and silver and the activities of foreign clerics on French soil: Edward I's to outlaw the clergy altogether, and on the pope's claiming Scotland as a papal fief—the *filia specialis* of the Roman Church as it had been called since at least 1189—against which no king could legally make war, to obtain an act from his parliament at Lincoln prohibiting him from being answerable to the pope for his temporal authority, so renouncing his predecessor John's submission and oath of fealty.

Boniface slowly withdrew from the extreme position he had taken up in *Clericis laicos*, admitting that kings could tax the clergy in times of national necessity. The peace lasted until 1301, when Boniface appointed a new Bishop of Palmiers without the consent of Philip IV, and the king arrested the bishop on charges of preaching against royal authority. This was the moment for the clash between the two views of sovereignty then current, papal and national. Boniface's reply to the arrest was a bull entitled *Ausculata fili*, summoning all the bishops of France and doctors of law of the University of Paris to Rome for discussion of ways and means to protect religion in France and addressing Philip the Fair in terms that could more fittingly have been used by Innocent III: 'Let no one persuade you that you have no superior and are not subject to the supreme authority of the ecclesiastical hierarchy.' This was in fact exactly what Philip did believe. In a letter to Boniface beginning 'Before there were clergy . . . *Antequam essent clerici*,' he had already asserted that the French king had been sovereign in France before the conversion of the country, and hinted that French kings would be sovereign there again. The king's reply to *Ausculata fili* was twofold. He summoned an assembly of his own to discuss the rights of the pope in France and wrote to Boniface in a style recalling Frederick II's defiance in 1239, but reflecting the new nationalist spirit: 'The church is not

made up only of clerics, but also of laymen. . . . With the consent of the temporal power the popes have hitherto given the clergy special liberty, but this must not operate to the detriment of the state. . . .'
It was a severe blow to papal prestige when most of France's bishops and lawyers obeyed their king—partly because the version of Boniface's bull circulated in France was a forgery, possibly prepared by Pierre Flotte, the royal chancellor, crudely denying that Philip had any rights except those granted by the Holy See, but principally because the canonists of Paris were not convinced that Boniface's reading of the law could be justified. Writing to Boniface, Philip, fully aware of the presence of the Colonna in his kingdom, was sarcastically abusive: 'Philip, by the Grace of God King of the French, to Boniface who pretends to be pope, little or no greeting. Your High Foolishness must know that we are subject to no one in the affairs of this world . . .'

Philip's defeat that summer in the battle of Courtrai took the edge off the quarrel for some months, but before the council summoned by *Ausculata fili* could assemble at Rome, Philip had passed new laws forbidding the clergy to leave the country. When the Lateran Council of 1302 opened in late October it was found, however, that four French archbishops and thirty-five bishops, together with a smaller number of abbots and doctors of theology, had defied the ban. On November 18, pope and council together promulgated the most famous of all statements of papal claims, the bull *Unam Sanctam*, setting out the doctrine of the two swords in the strongest terms and claiming that all secular authorities were necessarily subject to the pope:

> We are obliged by faith to believe and hold to one holy catholic church —the apostolic church—(and for ourselves we do firmly believe in and sincerely confess it)—outside which there is no salvation, nor yet remission of sins: the spouse foretold in the Canticle: 'One is my dove, my perfect one . . . the only one of her mother, the chosen of her that bore her', representing the one mystical body whose head is Christ. . . . Therefore there is only one church, and of this unique church one body and one head—not two heads, as though it were a monster—namely, Christ, and Christ's vicar, Peter and Peter's successor, the Lord having said to this same Peter: Feed my sheep. . . .
> And we are taught by the words of the Gospel that in this [Church] and in its power there are two swords, namely, the spiritual and the temporal. For when the apostles said, 'Behold, here are two swords' (that

is, in the church, since it was the apostles who spoke), the Lord did not reply, 'It is too much,' but, 'It is enough.' Truly, he who denies that the temporal sword is in Peter's power, misunderstands the Lord's words, 'Put up thy sword into its sheath.' Both are in the power of the church, the spiritual sword and the material. But the later is to be employed for the church, the former by her . . .'

. . . It is absolutely necessary for every human creature to be subject to the Roman Pontiff . . .

Nothing could have been better calculated to antagonize French nationalism. On March 12, 1303, Guillaume de Nogaret, the new chancellor of France, indicted Boniface before the Council of State demanding—as the Colonna had demanded years earlier—that he should be brought before a general council to answer charges of heresy and usurpation of the papal throne. The pope's response was to recognize Albert I of Austria as ruler of Germany and appeal for his help. The next step would logically be the excommunication of Philip the Fair and war with Naples and France, a war which, as Philip was surrounded with enemies, the papacy might well win. To prevent it, Philip gave his consent to a scheme proposed by de Nogaret and Sciarra Colonna to seize Boniface and bring him to Lyons for trial.

The conspirators found support in Tuscany, mustering men at a castle belonging to a Florentine banker named Musciatto, whose trade was suffering as a result of the international situation and for which he blamed the pope. To exacerbate the French attitude towards Boniface still further, charges were laid against him at the Council of State ranging from the murder of Celestine V, through heresy and simony, to publicly declaring that he would rather be an ass or a dog than a Frenchman. Those French prelates remaining in France voted with the rest of the council for action to free the world from 'the monster with the double crown'.

At daybreak on September 7, 1303, three hundred knights led by de Nogaret and Sciarra Colonna surrounded the palace of the Gaetani at Anagni and broke in to find the pope, it is said, deserted by the cardinals, sitting alone and unarmed in an empty hall. For three days, they tormented him with words and rough handling, until he was rescued by some of the townspeople. It is not known why de Nogaret and Colonna stayed so long at Anagni, but the delay cost them complete success. They withdrew their soldiers, leaving the pope apparently victorious. Boniface returned to Rome in something like a triumphal progress across Italy, but within a month he was dead. No one realized it then, but in a very real sense the papal monarchy died with him. Later popes were to claim plentitude of power in the secular as well as the spiritual sphere but none of them was to come close to its universal exercise.

Chapter IV

ON BAPTISING ARISTOTLE

THE TWELFTH century was crucial for the development of
the intellectual life of the Middle Ages. When it opened,
Western culture was illumined only by the Scriptures, the
writings of the Fathers, the laws of church and state, and the *logica
vetus*, comprising Aristotle's *Categories* and *Peri Hermeneias* and
Porphyry's *Isagoge*. By the year 1205, however, thanks to the work of
scholars like Anselm of Canterbury, Peter Abelard, William of
Saint-Thierry and Aelred of Rievaulx, the texts available for study
at the first University, formed that year by uniting the schools of
Paris, included Latin translations of most of the Greek authors
whose names are familiar to students today, together with commentaries on them produced by the greatest of the Arab scholars of
Spain.

Although the Arab invasions had destroyed the last Roman
schools in Carthage and cut Spain's links with Rome, they had not
led to a dark age in those provinces comparable with, for instance,
that which fell upon the old province of Gaul after the coming of the
Franks. On the contrary, in many respects they led to a raising of
cultural and intellectual standards above the highest achieved by the
Vandals and Visigoths, although, of course, in a different tradition,
one alien to the struggling Christian civilization of Europe.

At every period throughout the early Middle Ages there were
occasional contacts between the Arab and Christian worlds, but it
would be as wrong to over-estimate their cultural importance as to
overlook them altogether. The majority of Western travellers to the
lands ruled by the caliphs were pilgrims and those hoping for some
profit from the pilgrim traffic. They were more interested in curiosi-
ties of Eastern manufacture and in relics of early Christianity than in
the learning of the East. It was not until after the virtual closure by
the Seljuk Turks of the trade and pilgrim routes had brought the
first crusaders to the Holy Land in the last years of the eleventh

century and led to the foundation there of semi-permanent Christian kingdoms and principalities—and perhaps even more significantly bishoprics and monasteries—that Christian scholars were made aware of the learning of the Saracens, or indeed of the educational achievements of the surviving Byzantine empire.

Even more important for the development of Western intellectual life, however, was the more or less contemporaneous crusade in the West against the Moors of Spain. Attempts to win back the Iberian peninsula for Europe had actually begun as early as 722 and were not to be successfully completed until 1212, but the turning point was Rodrigo Diaz's victory at Valencia in 1094, which made Aragon and Castile safe from anything but a major assault—a victory used by the agents of Urban II to spur the ambitions of those being asked to volunteer for service in the East. The Spanish Moors of the recovered areas were neither driven out nor reduced to slavery by their Christian masters, but efforts were made to convert both Arabs and Jews to Christianity, and for the purpose primarily of this mission Archbishop Raymond I of Toledo established a school in his city for the instruction of the clergy in the arts of logic. At first the school relied on the texts of the *logica vetus*, but contacts with the Moors soon revealed that their leading scholars knew more about Greek learning than did the Christians set to argue with them. The archbishop therefore turned his scholars to the work of translating all the classical texts available in Arabic into Latin. At about the same time, attention was drawn to the fact that in the seventh century a Christian named Boethius had made translations of hitherto neglected texts from Aristotle; and as a result of the resurrection of his work, and studies at Toledo, twelfth-century schools were inundated with 'new' ideas, not only in logic but also in philosophy, metaphysics and the natural sciences. The texts transmitted by both Boethius and the Toledo school were of uneven quality and many of the commentaries made available under the umbrella of Aristotle's suddenly semi-divine name were Neoplatonist rather than truly Aristotelean. But their effect was revolutionary. For centuries, mystics had maintained that learning was unnecessary: the Scriptures and the Fathers taught all that Christians needed to know. Generally, the Church had agreed. But the 'new' texts seemed to make all the warnings of the mystics out of date. At Chartres, students with a curiosity as lively as that which had driven earlier generations to 'stand on their heads to learn grammar' went so far as to study the

Koran and debate its value in comparison with the New Testament.

The first volume of the *logica nova* had already appeared when, in 1140, Gratian published his logical study of the inconsistencies of canon law, the *Decretum*. Soon afterwards, German studies of Roman law, made at the court of Barbarossa, also became available to students, and from then on, law and logic, philosophy and theology —although nominally kept separate by the authorities at the schools —were forged together in the minds of both scholars and students, each subject influencing the aims and methods of the others, and altogether giving a distinctive flavour to all mediaeval intellectual work. The results of this conflation were uneven. Undeniable advances were made in those disciplines, such as philosophy and law, which depend on logic, but true and sustained progress in the natural sciences was delayed, as it had been in Hellenistic times, by the emphasis put on argument at the expense of observation, and by the shortcomings of Aristotle's own physics.

In about the year 1150 at Paris, Peter the Lombard published the first of four books of theology—the *Sentences*—in which he set out to examine Christianity logically, as a philosophical system, dealing with such subjects as the Trinity, the creation, the angels and the revelation made in the Gospels, in the same way as Aristotle and his followers had speculated about the world they knew, and following the pattern of propositions and distinctions used by the logicians and the lawyers such as Gratian. Just as Gratian's *Decretum* became the basic textbook used by all mediaeval canonists, and writing commentaries on parts of Gratian was soon the standard way in which students of law showed their ability and learning, so Peter Lombard's *Sentences* became the classical manual for Christian philosophers and speculation on some point taken from the synthesis of 'the Master of the *Sentences*' the principal exercise of schools of theology. Within a generation or so of the death of Peter Lombard, then Bishop of Paris, in 1160, the first attempts were being made to produce complete syntheses of Christian philosophy, theology and cosmology, the forerunners of the *Summae* of philosophy and theology left incomplete by Thomas Aquinas at his death in 1274. One of the most influential of these early *summae*, that produced by Alain de Lille, who died in 1202, was remarkable for its deliberate attempt to reconcile the world-despising theology of the ascetics and mystics, and the current philosophical 'humanist' view of creation. He argued that the world was naturally good and pleaded that all nature—

including human nature—should be set free, so that by natural development of a respect for law, learning and civilization, the race could produce a new kind of man, whom Alain called 'the Youth', who would live naturally at harmony with himself and the whole creation.

Freedom to speculate of the order needed to produce such works as Alain's *summae* was not without its dangers. It is impossible now to determine how far, if at all, the successors of the Albigenses and Waldenses, the 'Poor Men' of Lyons and Flanders, were attributable either to the freedom of the new scholars or the narrow legalism and logic of the higher clergy, but traditionally-minded Christians were in no doubt that heresy and scholarship went hand-in-glove together. Francis of Assisi's injunction to his Friars Minor, 'Lesser Brethren', to own no books, although forming a section of his general rule calling on them to separate themselves wholly from the world, was not made solely as part of the warning against valuable possessions. Books and book-learning were suspect. Sermons preached at Paris during the early years of the university are full of warnings to students against damaging the health of their souls either by riotous living or by overlong study, both of which would keep them from their prayers. The original Poor Men were enthusiasts for mystical religion, and forbade book-learning, claiming that true preachers needed no scholarship. A man called to preach by the Spirit does not need a bishop's licence—or so they taught. It was not long before they denied that the church needed bishops or sacraments: direct inspiration serves all needs. When they began to deny the Eucharist and denounce marriage, they were equated in the official mind with those other heretics, the Albigenses, against whom Innocent III turned his crusaders in 1208.

In fact, however, the origins and aims of the Waldenses and Albigenses were very different. The 'Poor Men' were Christians who shared the enthusiasm so characteristic of their times, the enthusiasm that founded the Orders of Friars, precipitated the tragedy of the Children's Crusade in 1212 and lit the fires that burned heretics. But the Albigenses were, beyond all reasonable doubt, not so much Christian heretics as 'pagans', the spiritual descendants of the dualist gnostics and Manichees whose teachings had so troubled the early church. Their challenge was offered from concealment within the regular life of the church, and it threw the authorities into something close to panic. It was the fact that they produced and made use of vernacular versions of the Scriptures which led first local synods, such as that of the clergy of Flanders in 1230, and then the church as a whole to forbid the circulation of the Bible in the Romance languages. The Holy Courts of Inquisition were allowed to assume the infamous forms they took in France and Germany under Inquisitors Robert le Bougre and Conrad of Marburg during the reign of Clement IV because both the pope and orthodox Christians generally felt surrounded by invisible enemies. As early as 1157 a synod at Rheims legislated against the Manichee weavers as 'men of the lowest class who frequently move from place to place, changing their names as they go'—and so remaining nameless and unknown. Weaver—*textor*—became the common name for the Albigenses in the north, but they were not the only travellers who carried heresy about with them. So too did pilgrims and mercenaries, jongleurs and goliards, usurers—or so it was believed—and wandering scholars, and the great centres of heresy were strung along the chief pilgrimage and commerce routes. The dualism of the Albigensian Cathars (the 'clean ones') is said to have entered Italy from Bulgaria, and Provence from Italy, along the main trade route. (Hence, probably, the name 'bougre' given to Cathars: Robert le Bougre himself had been a member of the sect at Milan before his re-conversion to Christianity and employment as an inquisitor.) The suspicion of the inquisitors fell on all those who travelled from place to place; and not without reason, for there was plenty of evidence to show that they carried not only orthodox books and the ideas of orthodox scholars, but also the teachings of the 'heretics' and the epics and lyrics of the first flowering of Romance and Teutonic literature, including cycles such as the Romances of the Grail and the Rose which, if not originally inspired by heresy, were certainly capable of heretical interpretation. The life of the Provençal courts of love was far removed from that of the weaver's shed in Flanders—or the baker's shop at Rheims whose proprietor, one Echard, was condemned as a 'Poor Man' in 1230—but the students, who could go anywhere, linked the two together. It would appear an even longer step from them to Aristotle, but again, to the official, suspicious mind, the students provided the link. In the prevailing atmosphere of warfare against hidden enemies, it is not surprising that the speculations of the scholars soon came under suspicion. The Aristoteleanism of the scholars of Paris did not, it is true, of itself tend to either Catharism or Waldenseanism, but it did lead

Photo : Mansell Collection

THE PALACE OF THE POPES AT AVIGNON

THE TOMB OF BALTHAZAR COSSA, JOHN XXIII, BY DONATELL
AND MICHELOZZO, IN THE BAPTISTERY, FLORENCE

THE TOMB OF URBAN VI IN THE VATICAN

away from pure theology, and so, it seemed, undermine the authority of the church. Innocent III preached the crusade against Provence in 1208: only two years later, he forbade the use of any part of Aristotle except the texts relating solely to logic. In 1215, Aristotle's philosophy was banned at the University of Paris, under regulations approved by Innocent's legate, Robert of Courson: 'Neither Aristotle's books on metaphysics, nor *summae* treating of them, nor the teaching of Master David of Dinant, nor Amaury the heretic, nor Maurice of Spain, are to be read.' This attempt to ban Aristotle failed, as did many others in later years. It would have needed a crusade against Paris and the scholars as violent as that waged against the Albigenses to have crushed scholasticism.

In 1228, Gregory IX, already preparing to give inquisitorial powers to seek out heretics to the learned Dominican Friars, felt obliged to write to the theologians of Paris, solemnly warning them against the dangers of heresy to which they exposed themselves by the study of 'profane' natural philosophy, and so 'adulterating the Word of God with the figments of philosophers'. Yet within a short time, he found it necessary to order the Franciscans to take up advanced studies, so that they would be equipped to meet the objections of the philosophers, and in 1231 was reduced to the despairing suggestion that a papal commission should be appointed to purge Aristotle's works of their errors. Nothing, it seemed, could halt the triumphant advance through the schools of Aristotle, and his Arab and Jewish commentators, Avicenna and Averroes, Ibn Gabirol and Moses Maimonides of Cordoba.

Paris was the first and chief centre of the new learning: 'the Italians have the papacy, the Germans the empire, and the French learning' as the saying went. But once both the Dominicans and the Franciscans were free to study, they carried it wherever their preaching took them—which was wherever there seemed to be a danger of heresy. Soon after 1231, Aristotle was being taught by Franciscans at Oxford under the chancellorship of Robert Grosseteste, who himself made translations directly from the Greek and wrote a commentary on Aristotle's *Posterior Analytics*. It was this 'baptism' of Aristotle by the two orders of mendicant friars, whose basic orientation was towards traditionalism and mysticism, which finally solved the problem of philosophy for the authorities of the church. Amid a galaxy of great names from the universities of the thirteenth century, most widely remembered are perhaps those of the

Franciscans Roger Bacon and St. Bonaventure, and the Dominicans Albertus Magnus and his pupil Thomas Aquinas: Bacon for his universal interest in alchemy and the physical sciences as well as philosophy and theology; Bonaventure, Albert and Thomas for the intellectual brilliance with which they bent Aristotle's methods to Christian purposes, so that, for many generations of Catholic students after them, 'philosophy' meant the Christian Aristotle-leanism of Aquinas's *Summae* of philosophy and theology, a form so individual that it became known universally as Thomism.

The victory of Thomism was not by any means immediate. In fact, for much of his working life Aquinas seemed to have more enemies than allies in the church, and at the end his own mystic conscious-ness betrayed him. He left the *Summa theologica* incomplete because, as he said, the visions he had seen reduced all that he had written to nothingness. His most active opponents were, however, the tradi-tionally-minded, old-fashioned teachers of religion, who thought that he neglected the true learning of the church as recorded by the Fathers: in fact, the only 'father' he quoted as often as Aristotle was Augustine. In March 1277, three years after Aquinas's death, Robert Kilwardy, the Dominican Archbishop of Canterbury, condemned thirty propositions which had found support in disputations at Oxford. Most of them were taken from Thomism. Seven years later, his Franciscan successor, John Peckham, renewed this condemnation and in January of the following year wrote to Rome denouncing the whole Thomist approach to theology, pointing out that 'the teaching of the Two Orders'—Dominicans and Franciscans—was by then 'almost totally opposed on all disputable questions: the teaching of one of the orders [the Dominican] has abandoned and to some degree now scorns the opinions of the Fathers, being founded almost exclusively on the positions adopted by the philosophers'. Later in that same year of 1285, Peckham explained that his real objection was not to philosophical studies 'serving the mysteries of theology' but to the 'profane novelties' of Thomism 'introduced into the profundity of theology about twenty years ago'.

In the same month as Kilwardy made his original attack on Thomism at Oxford, the Bishop of Paris condemned 219 theses mainly drawn from Averroes and his principal Christian commen-tators Siger of Brabant and Boethius of Dacia, but including some taken from Thomism. The problem as the authorities saw it was that in their enthusiasm for Aristotle Christian teachers such as Siger were being led into denial of the truths of revelation: one of the theses condemned at Paris denied that to humble oneself was a virtuous act—a total repudiation of New Testament ethics in favour of Hellenistic ideals. The succeeding half-century was rent by the conflicts between Averroism and Thomism, the Franciscans and the Dominicans, and the victory of Thomism was not completely won until many years after Aquinas's death, although Aristoteleanism was firmly entrenched in the thinking of Western scholars. Indeed all the controversies of the fourteenth century—including that concerning authority, marked by the Great Schism—were fought out in the language and style of Hellenistic debate, employing logic and philosophical concepts taken as frequently from Aristotle and the Arabs as from the New Testament and Fathers of the Church. Even those who, like the Franciscan John Duns Scotus and the nominalist William of Ockham, were most strongly opposed to the Thomist synthesis could not escape the influence of Aristotelean logic and ideas.

The degree to which this style of thought and debate had captivated the minds of the learned by the end of the thirteenth century is vividly illustrated in its use by Guillaume de Nogaret, the chancellor of France, to win over doubtful theologians and unconvinced noblemen to Philip the Fair's view of the pontificate of Boniface VIII, when he decided to hold a formal disputation at the University of Paris to prove by law and logic that Boniface was not worthy to be pope and to justify in advance the military action planned against him. Remote though some of the more arcane speculations of the philosophers and logicians were from everyday life and from the decisions on policy taken by princes and popes, the philosophers themselves frequently played very active parts in the affairs of their times.

PART THREE

THE CHURCH DIVIDED

Chapter I

THE BABYLONIAN CAPTIVITY
OF THE CHURCH

THE FOURTEENTH century began amid the tinsel glitter of the Year of Jubilee staged by Boniface VIII but the brilliance lasted only until the pilgrims had all gone home. In the succeeding months Boniface came under renewed attack from France, replied with a claim to universal sovereignty in the Bull *Unam Sanctam* and was shortly afterwards frightened to death by de Nogaret and Colonna the Savage.

His successor, Benedict XI, ruled only from October 1303 to July 1304, stubbornly resisting to the last the demands of Philip the Fair that he should lift the sentence of excommunication placed on the French chancellor and renewed on the Colonnas for the outrage at Anagni. After his death, despite the rules calling for the immediate election of a successor, the papal throne was kept vacant for a year by the inability of the cardinals to agree upon a candidate. At last, however, the conclave elected Bertrand de Got, the Gascon Archbishop of Bordeaux, who chose to reign as Clement V.

At the time of his election, Clement was in France. When he received the news he first visited his see of Bordeaux, then turned towards Italy, intending to go to Rome for his coronation, but a combination of evil circumstances prevented him from travelling further than Vienne. Weakened by a cancer, he lost his courage when he learned that a revolt in the Papal States would make the journey to Rome dangerous, and surrendered to Philip's insistent demands that he should be crowned at Lyons. Only six cardinals attended his coronation, but Philip himself was there. The meeting between the king and the pope showed that Clement could not match Boniface VIII in determination. He allowed himself to be persuaded to stay in France, reinstate the Colonnas, and appoint nine French cardinals, enough to give the French party an overall majority in the sacred college.

Philip, who had been so well satisfied by the election of Celestine V, was still not content. He would have liked to have seen all record of the reign of Boniface VIII swept into oblivion, but as that was impossible, he demanded that Clement should personally preside at a new session of the trial of Boniface for heresy and murder. Clement refused, but in February 1306 he went as far in appeasing the king as to withdraw the Bulls *Clericis laicos* and *Unam Sanctam* 'in so far as they injured him'. It was still not enough. The pope struggled for freedom of action, but physical weakness drained his resolve. He refused to live at the French court, but could not summon the energy to break away into Italy. In 1306, he was too ill to leave Gascony, but the spring of 1307 found him at Poitiers, where he met Philip again. They reached no agreement on any of the issues between them, and that autumn Philip struck a terrible blow at the power of the church in France by arresting every member of the Order of Templars within his realm, on charges ranging from plotting treason, through sexual perversion, to insulting and defiling the cross and denying Christ and the sacraments. How far these accusations were justified remains uncertain as they were the stock ones brought against mediaeval heretics and secret societies. The real complaint against the Templars seems to have been that they held the purse-strings of the kingdom and were loyal to the papacy.

Although individual Knights of the Order were bound by the usual monastic vow of poverty, the Order itself was one of the richest proprietors of land and property in Europe, and its treasurers were noted for their skill in handling money. For a hundred years before 1295, they had been official bankers to the French court, maintaining links between the royal treasury and Lombard and Jewish bankers throughout Europe. In that year, Philip IV, in pursuit of his policy of national self-sufficiency, had taken the management of affairs out of their hands, only to be forced to restore it to them in 1305, when the expulsion of the Jews from France, the debasing of the coinage and a ban on the export of money had all failed to bring him solvency. The new national awareness of the French found this dependence on the Order intolerable. Vague, general accusations against the Templars which had been circulating for some time crystallized into definite charges and were brought to the notice of both the church and the king. Philip welcomed them, but it was two years before his chancellor could collect enough evidence for their master, Jacques de Moulai, to feel it necessary to appeal to Clement for a proper enquiry. The request was made while Clement was at Poitiers in 1307, and the papal investigation had scarcely begun before the knights were imprisoned and their rents sequestered to the royal treasury.

It is impossible to judge whether Philip himself really believed the charges against the knights, but he certainly made cynical use of them in his attempts to force the concessions he wanted from the pope. When Clement complained that he had already ordered the Inquisition to investigate the Templars, his officers were permitted to question a hundred and twenty of them, but they had already been tortured and all but four were ready to admit to any crime rather than face torture again. In November 1307, Clement was compelled by the overwhelming 'evidence' to issue bulls enjoining all Christian princes to arrest the Templars and sequester their property in the name of the papacy. Only in Provence, Naples and the Papal States was any evidence found to support the French charges although royal and inquisitorial courts in every country sifted the Temple's affairs. In Cyprus, the Templars were massacred before the enquiry could be completed. In France and Italy, the more closely the confessions were examined, the less likely they seemed, and in 1308 the pope suspended the inquisition of the Order.

Immediately, de Nogaret released a stream of vituperative pamphlets against both Boniface VIII and Clement himself, accusing the one of murder, the other of nepotism and extortion, and calling on the king to see justice done in spite of the pope's refusal. An assembly at Tours in May judged the Templars worthy of death, but Clement refused to condemn them and protested so vigorously that the king permitted the transfer of the lesser prisoners to papal gaols. But he kept Jacques de Moulai under his own jurisdiction and sent a string of witnesses to the papal court at Poitiers with tales vivid enough to reawaken Clement's doubts. That summer, Clement reopened his own enquiry and summoned a general council to meet at Vienne in the autumn of 1310 and examine the evidence he collected: then to escape the influence of the French court he removed his household to a Dominican Priory at Avignon. The priory stood on papal property, and Avignon itself was within the domains of King Robert of Naples, a loyal vassal of the pope and papal *vicarius* in Italy. At the time, the choice seemed a good one, but events soon showed that Avignon was not far enough away from the King of France. After the murder of the German emperor in

1308, Clement did stand firm in support of the electors' choice of Henry VII of Luxemburg to succeed him, despite Philip's championship of his own brother's claims, but he was forced to agree to the re-opening of the case against Boniface VIII. That affair dragged on, used as a weapon against the pope whenever he was not sufficiently subservient to the royal will, but the case of the Templars was not allowed to do so. In May 1310, the Archbishop of Sens, a royalist and brother of one of the king's ministers, convened a synod in his archdiocese which condemned fifty-four Templars as 'relapsed heretics' one day and burned them the next. The surviving Templars took the point: only twelve of the more than two hundred heard by the papal court at Avignon before it rose the following month attempted to withdraw the confessions they had made in the royal prisons. When the Council of Vienne met, a year late, in October 1311, the only solid evidence against the Templars was that contained in the confessions collected in France.

By then, Clement and Philip were allegedly allies. In February, Philip had agreed to forget the case against Boniface if Clement would lift all the papal bans against France made since 1300: *Unam Sanctam* disappeared with the rest. At the Council the pope proposed Philip's policy of condemning the Templars unheard, and when the delegates would not agree, closed the discussion, turning the council's attention to the questions of a new tax to pay for a crusade and the need for reform. Philip, seeing his advantage slip away, revived the question of Boniface's trial and when public opinion in France was aroused against the pope, went to Vienne in person to discuss the question of the Templars. In March 1312, a secret consistory of the Commission on the Templars voted for their condemnation and on April 3 a plenary session of the council heard Clement read his personal sentence on the Order: it was to be disbanded, and its property throughout the world transferred to the Knights of St. John and the Knights of Spain. The ruling was not popular either with the council or with the princes who had hoped to enrich themselves from the spoils of the Temple. Clement silenced the complaints of the council by forbidding the delegates to discuss his judgment on pain of excommunication but it was in some instances several years before the Hospitallers gained control of what had fallen to them.

The final grim act in the Templars' tragedy was played out at Paris on March 18, 1314, when the leaders of the Order, Jacques de

Moulai and Geoffroi de Charnay, were condemned to life imprisonment on the evidence of the confessions they had made many years
earlier. Shocked by the savage sentence, they cried out that they
were not guilty, and were immediately re-arrested as relapsed
heretics. Before darkness fell that day, they had been condemned by
a royal tribunal, taken out and burned.

The affair of the Templars demonstrated to the Christian world
how hollow was the pope's claim of universal sovereignty. A determined king had shaped papal policy to his own ends. But Clement's
subservience was not his only fault in the eyes of Europe. Both papal
taxation and papal nepotism reached scandalous levels during his
reign. At his first consistory in 1305, he raised to the cardinalate five
men closely related to himself, and when he died in 1314 his kinsmen
occupied important posts throughout France and Italy. He himself
lived frugally—perhaps because his illness imposed frugality on
him—but his retinue was so rapacious that his progresses through
France left bishops and abbots forced to entertain him close to ruin.
He died worth more than a million gold florins, but three-quarters
of his fortune went to relatives and a fifth to charities under his will.
Only 70,000 florins were found in the treasury by his successor
John XXII. Although neither the suppression of the Templars nor
the nepotism of the pope led to any immediate revolt against the
papacy, they both helped to create a climate of opinion dangerous
for the future.

Already by 1310, the Italians living in the Papal States, deserted
by their ruler the pope, and at the mercy of rapacious officials, more
of whom seemed to be Frenchmen as every year passed, had appealed
to Henry VII of Germany for the protection that an emperor could
give. There was a revival in Rome of the old imperialist spirit, and
talk of a new World Empire, independent of the papacy. The rediscovery of Greek and Latin literature had reawakened dreams of the
Rome of Aeneas, Augustus and the Caesars. Dante echoed a common sentiment when he wrote to Henry VII in 1310, 'Come—look
on thy Rome ever-tearful! Widowed, lonely, wailing night and
day: Why, O Caesar, art thou not by my side?'

Henry VII joined the Widow Rome as soon as he could. He would
have arrived earlier, but she was in law only a grass widow, and the
legates of her legitimate husband, Clement, caught and delayed him
at Lausanne, threatening him with intervention by Philip the Fair
and Robert of Naples until he took an oath that he would not harm

the rights of the church in Rome and the Papal States. At Milan, he was crowned with papal permission as King of Lombardy, and cardinal-legates prepared to conduct him to Rome. By the time his party reached the Lateran Palace, however, Neapolitans had occupied the Vatican, Castel Sant' Angelo and Trastevere, in an effort to delay the coronation until the ambassadors of Florence and the Guelph towns could persuade the pope at Avignon to forbid it. Henry appealed to 'his' Romans, and the cardinal-legates, threatened with assassination if they waited for the pope's ruling, crowned him at the Lateran in June 1310. But he could not hold the city and, as soon as he had withdrawn, the Romans elected a People's Captain to rule them. At Tivoli, he received a letter from the pope ordering him to leave the Papal States and make a truce with the papal vicar, Robert of Naples. Realizing that unless he made a show of strength, he would lose all influence in Italy, he chose instead to make an alliance with Robert's enemy, Frederick III of Sicily, and in 1313 felt strong enough, with the support of the Ghibelline towns, to march on Rome again. Two miles from Siena, he suddenly sickened and died; rumour said that he had been poisoned by a Dominican monk. With neither pope nor emperor to rule her, Rome sank into disorderly obscurity.

During this unsettled period, when papal, imperial and republican government had all failed in northern Italy, the city-states turned to a semi-autocratic and aristocratic system of government by councils of leading citizens, the *Signoria*. Conflicts between these petty governments were watched with regret by the most able political thinkers of the time. Emotional though Dante's appeal to Henry VII was, it reflected a longing for stability shared by many. Boniface VIII and Clement V had both recognized that the new consciousness of national self-sufficiency abroad in western Europe, and the failure of the Germans to find a competent emperor, had made the empire irrelevant to the situation except as an item of propaganda. Boniface's claim in *Unam Sanctam* to universal sovereignty was an attempt to fill the gap that the empire had left. On the other hand, Clement's admission that the provisions of that bull could not be enforced in France showed that Innocent III had been right a century earlier to admit that the Kings of France had no superiors there in secular matters. But papal clear-sightedness on this point was not universally shared. Many were unwilling to grant that if there was ever to be a universal ruler again, he could only be the pope. Some, like

Dante, still yearned for an emperor who would be, in Frederick of Sicily's words, 'the Lord of the world and Head of Nations in temporal things', to whom all kings and princes would be legally subject. Dante's *On Monarchy* shows that to him even the failure of Henry VII's successor, Lewis of Bavaria, to re-establish a stable empire, did not indicate the end of the imperial ideal. There should be, he argued, a universal society of civilized men, ruled by a single man—the emperor—whose primary tasks it should be to ensure peace, correct local constitutions and guarantee justice, so reconciling and modifying for the common good 'the policies of kings, aristocrats, those called optimates, and those zealous for popular liberties'. Not all the kings, aristocrats, optimates and popularist republicans would have agreed to accept an emperor on these terms. Civil conflict was as common in fourteenth-century Italy as short-tempered debate.

Another place where debate was often short-tempered after the death of Clement V was Carpentras, where a conclave of ten Gascon, six French and seven Italian cardinals was trying to agree on a new pope. The Carpentras conclave finally broke up in disorder, and the papal interregnum outlived both Philip the Fair, who died in November 1314, and his elder son Louis X. It was not until the summer of 1316 that, just before his death, Louis X succeeded in persuading the cardinals to come to Lyons for an election: they were assembling there when they heard of the accession of his brother as Philip V. Before the conclave could disintegrate again, the Dominican convent where they were staying was surrounded by troops and effectively shut off from the world. Even so the cardinals remained deadlocked from June 28 to August 5, when Napoleone Orsini, becoming suspicious in a typically Roman manner of the intrigues of his fellow-Roman Pietro Colonna, persuaded a faction of the Italians to support the Gascon candidate, Jacques Duese, a seventy-two year-old canonist, Bishop of Avignon and Cardinal-Bishop of Porto. He was duly elected on August 7 and announced that he would reign as John XXII.

His reign opened dramatically, with an attempt to end his life by witchcraft supplemented with arsenic. Its instigator was Hugues Gérard, Bishop of Cahors, who then stood charged at Avignon with simony and peculation. The conspiracy was originally kept small: only two papal stewards inside the palace, a wizard named Bonmacip, the bishop's treasurer and a messenger knew what was afoot.

Bonmacip first practised against the pope's nephew, Jacques de Via —John XXII was already proving as avid a nepotist as his predecessor had been—and whether the spells worked or not, de Via died. Certain then of success, Bishop Gérard brought the Bishop of Ganos and other credulous persons into the plot. Three wax figures were baptised at Toulouse by the Bishop of Ganos in the names of the pope, Cardinal de Jean and Cardinal de Poujet, and packed into a hollowed loaf to be smuggled into the palace at Avignon. But the suspicions of the papal guards were aroused and the wax figures came to light. The messengers revealed nothing, even under severe questioning, but Bishop Gérard himself boasted of the plot among his friends. He was arrested in May 1317, tried on various charges, including attempted murder by witchcraft, stripped of his episcopal rank, and handed over to the Marshal of Justice for judgment. The sentence was death and he was burned at the stake.

This domestic crisis was by no means the only trouble the pope had to endure. In Germany, two princes were fighting for the crown: Lewis of Bavaria and Frederick of Austria. John XXII named them both 'King of the Romans' and, leaving them to fight it out, confirmed a decree of Clement V's, to the effect that the pope 'to whom God hath assigned power on earth and in heaven alike' is the lawful administrator of the empire, and that during an interregnum 'the power of the emperor devolves upon the church'. He also made Robert of Naples vice-regent of the empire in Italy and, in a neat legal reversal of the usual mediaeval situation, in which kings drew the incomes from bishoprics and abbacies during vacancies, decreed that all the imperial officers in Italy who had been appointed by Henry VII should be regarded as disenfeoffed until they had sworn allegiance to him as the administrator, and that all taxes should be paid to him until an emperor was crowned.

He needed not only the recognition but also the money. Clement's relatives and two years' interregnum at Avignon had left the papal treasury empty. To bring in the essential funds, he remodelled the administration of the church, so that it became the most fully centralized and effective instrument of government in the Western world. Soon there was plenty of money but the pope's efficiency in collecting it had made him unpopular. Not only were there understandable objections from tax-payers, but there were also those who believed that the church had no right to levy taxes on the clergy or anyone else. The great debate on Apostolic Poverty which ended with the condemnation of the Franciscans and the detention of their General Michael of Cesena in 1323 thus had practical as well as theoretical significance.*

Moreover, the Franciscans and tax-payers were not John XXII's only enemies. In Italy, Matteo Visconti talked of setting up his own Italian pope, with a papal state to support him. The pope replied by preaching a crusade against Milan. Visconti appealed to Lewis of Bavaria for help, and when the emperor promised it, the pope first ordered him to abdicate, then declared him deposed. Lewis protested that the pope lived in France and could have no temporal jurisdiction in the empire and, in March 1324, published his *Declaration of Sachshausen*, questioning the legality of the pope's election and accusing him of teaching error, breaking the peace and ignoring the law. The pope replied by excommunicating 'the brazen serpent of Germany'.

Outwardly the situation was thus far relatively normal, with the pope and the emperor-elect at loggerheads over Italian politics. But in this instance it was made extremely dangerous by the fact that several of the best philosophers of the age found it impossible to justify the pope's stand against either the Franciscans or Lewis of Bavaria. The result was that Lewis found himself with some unexpected but welcome allies: Michael of Cesena, kept at Avignon, whether as prisoner or hostage nobody knew, William of Ockham, an English Franciscan genius, called to Avignon to answer charges of heresy, and Marsilius of Padua, the rector of the University of Paris who, with another professor named Jean of Jandun, had just produced a seminal treatise on authority entitled *Defensor Pacis*, the Defender of the Peace, in which papal claims to universal sovereignty were swept aside as irrelevant to the actual state of the world.

Although Marsilius was teaching in Paris, his book reflected conditions in his native Italy, and drew its conclusions from them. A few years earlier, his own city of Padua had brought popular republican government to an end by electing Jacopo de Carrera as *Signore* for life. He had in fact ruled for no more than a year before being overthrown but in that short time the old freedoms had vanished and in 1324 his family was able to regain control of the city. Marsilius recognized the inevitability of this change in the existing circumstances, but set himself the task in *Defender of the Peace* of outlining the ideal constitution for Italy, and so for the world.

* See pp. 125-9.

Granting that there had to be rulers for the sake of peace, he concluded that monarchy was 'perhaps preferable' to all other forms of government, but that it could exist 'in one city as well as in several'. In other words, the Lord of Padua or of Milan could be as true a king in his single city as the Kings of England or Sicily in their countries. But, he added, all 'monarchs' should be elected by their subjects, as the council at Padua had elected Carrera. Hereditary monarchy could only lead to civil unrest. No monarch should rule 'without the laws or contrary to them' but all should allow their actions to be 'regulated by the laws'. The role of the emperor was to mediate between monarchs and moderate their rule when it became harsh. The authority to make new laws 'belongs to the whole body of citizens, or the weightier part thereof' because the common good and justice require it. In short, the true Defender of the Peace is the law made by the people.

Marsilius rejected Thomas Aquinas's judgment that a king or senate of wise men could know better than the people what was best for the state; he also denied the doctrine of papal sovereignty in temporal affairs, as later thinkers at the time of the Great Schism were to deny it in spiritual matters, using his argument that the authority to make laws lies with the 'human legislator', the people itself or the monarch to whom a people voluntarily delegates its powers. The general trend of *Defender of the Peace* was popularist and favourable to small states. In the final chapter, Marsilius summed up his reasons for writing it: to show the masses of the people 'the extent to which it is possible to ensure that the ruler does not assume arbitrary power for his own advantage, to pass judgments or perform other acts of government contrary to or apart from the laws'.

Marsilius's views earned him the enmity of the court at Avignon, where the pope was still accepted as the Sovereign Pontiff, endowed with the plenitude of divine authority. Excommunicated and forbidden to lecture, he went to Germany for safety's sake, and became a fiery supporter of Lewis of Bavaria, identifying the pope as the real enemy of peace in Italy and the emperor as its true defender.

In 1327, Lewis, encouraged by the antipapal movement among the philosophers, announced that he was going to Rome for his coronation, and that the pope has no right to forbid him because he was himself 'a savage and tyrant, exploiter of the Christian religion, suppressor of the poor and of the life of Christ, enemy of the apostles, who by his cunning and deceit utterly destroys perfect poverty'. He set out so determinedly for Rome that John XXII was soon receiving appeals from all over Italy begging him to come at once and save his people from the Germans. The pope, now over eighty, wrote that he could not come. The cardinal-legates in Italy combined their forces to try and bar Lewis from Rome, but they could not hold the Vatican and were forced to flee, leaving the city under an interdict. Lewis was crowned first as King of the Lombards, then as Emperor of the World in January 1328.

In April of that year, hearing that the pope had called for a crusade against him, he replied by trying the pope publicly in the square in front of St. Peter's, and condemning him as antichrist. A second session of the court in May declared the pope deposed, and Lewis presented to the people a Franciscan named Pietro Tainalducci as their new pontiff, Nicholas V. At Avignon it was discovered one morning a fortnight later that Michael of Cesena and William of Ockham had evaded the papal guards and fled. When next heard of, they were both at Lewis's court. The schism between the pope and his Imperial and Franciscan subjects appeared to be complete.

However, it was one thing to make a schism and another to maintain it. The people of Rome and the Papal States had never ceased to hope that the pope would one day be persuaded to return to Rome, and the interdict on the Romans hurt them no less than Innocent III's interdict had hurt England a century earlier. Within two years, in fact, Nicholas V was to travel to Avignon and make his submission. Resistance to Lewis had by then forced him out of Rome, first to Pisa, then to Trento. He was reported to be ready to submit, when John made two mistakes fatal to the quick success of his cause. First he insisted that Lewis should abdicate and proposed to set up a anti-emperor: then he slipped into undeniable heresy himself.

In three sermons in the winter of 1331–2 he taught, contrary to received opinion, that 'before the resurrection of the body, the souls of the dead possess neither eternal life, nor true beatitude, nor the beatific vision'. The acceptance of such views would have required the re-writing of a large part of mediaeval theology, including the popular doctrine of the communion of saints, and the theory behind canonization. Guiral Ot, the newly-appointed papalist General of the Friars, supported the pope, but among the Franciscans in Lewis's camp there was something very like rejoicing, for they had always said that John was a heretic.

At Avignon, Cardinal Napoleone Orsini condemned the pope, but Cardinals Fornier and Ulrich defended his right privately to hold any views that seemed probable to him. John himself, now a very old man, seemed puzzled by the trouble he had caused. He consulted bishops and theologians in search of the truth. But Ot, preaching the pope's doctrine in Paris, shocked prelates and king alike. Preparations were made for a formal disputation—which might well have ended with the condemnation of the pope—but before it could be held, John fell ill in December 1334, recanted, allowing departed souls the beatific vision 'so far as the state and condition of a separated soul permits', and died.

The next election was made precisely in accordance with the canons. Nine days after the death of John XXII, the cardinals were locked up under guard in the palace at Avignon, and seven days later they emerged to announce that they had elected a pope, the Cistercian Jacques Fornier, formerly Bishop of Palmiers and Cardinal-Priest of St. Prisca's, now Benedict XII.

The new pope was a cold, remote man, an expert inquisitor whose victims called him 'the devil' and 'the spirit of evil'. He loved justice, and despised inefficiency and muddle because they led to injustice. Almost his first act as pope was to start a general reform of the administration of the church. There were, he said, 'abuses without number' to be corrected. After a study of corruption in church courts and taxation, he fixed a scale of charges and salaries in all departments and established a system of examinations for candidates for important curial posts. To prevent bribery to secure the early presentation of petitions, he opened a registry for all documents reaching Avignon. He imposed reforms on all the major religious orders, except the Dominicans, who he said needed nothing but an improvement in discipline. As a reformer, he achieved most of what he set out to do, yet his short reign of eight years is usually called unsuccessful, since he failed to control Lewis of Bavaria, who continued to receive encouragement from Marsilius, the German Franciscans, the Ghibelline cities of Italy, and the German Diet itself.

In 1338, the Diet meeting at Frankfurt passed an ordinance— *Licet iuris*—denying the pope any rights in German elections, although insisting that emperors-elect should continue to be known as Kings of the Romans. *Licet iuris* was an attempt to secularize the empire fully in keeping with the spirit of the age. It might have been avoided if the pope had lived in Italy, but so might much else besides. As it was, the Italians themselves were coming to despise the papacy. Petrarch, who visited Avignon and found nothing sympathetic in the cold correctness of Benedict XII, nevertheless continually urged the return of the curia to Rome, for its own sake and Italy's. He ridiculed the Frenchified Avignon curia on the one hand, yet on the other caricatured its residence in France as an exile imposed on the papacy by an alien king, so opening the way to the dubbing of this period in papal history as 'the Babylonian Captivity of the Church'. However, neither he nor the advocates of apostolic poverty ever forgot that there were two Babylons in the Bible: Mesopotamian Babylon, where the Jews were carried as captives, and Apocalyptic Babylon, 'the Great Whore', whose orgies shamed the saints. To Italian nationalists, and to the Fraticelli, the 'little brothers' of the Franciscan Order, who refused to own property and preached apostolic poverty in spite of the relaxation of the primitive Rule of St. Francis, Avignon-Babylon was a combination of them both. Austere though the private lives of some of the Avignon popes were, the papal court was generally splendid and extravagant. It was universally said that the cardinals and their favourites were living in luxury while neglect destroyed what little stability the Papal States had once enjoyed. *Signori* like the Visconti of Milan were swallowing Italian freedom and Benedict's policy was one of appeasement to whoever seized power. All he asked of the *Signori* was peace for the church and the prompt payment of taxes to keep the machinery at Avignon well greased. At the time, the Visconti were paying regularly, so Benedict overlooked their aggressive expansionism. He sold Parma, Verona and Vicenza to the della Scala brothers for an annual tribute of 5,000 florins and the promise of five hundred soldiers when he needed them. The Gonzaga were confirmed as Lords of Mantua and the Estense were granted Modena, Comacchio and Ferrara on similar terms. But in the Papal States there was continual unrest because the rectors and vicars appointed to rule were so often Frenchmen. Only Florence remained constantly loyal to the popes until just before the end, when she too rebelled.

The result of Benedict XII's failure to control either Italy or Germany was that his successor inherited a markedly uncomfortable throne. To all appearances, though, he was well fitted to make the best of it. Pierre Roger, a former Benedictine abbot, Bishop of Arras and Archbishop of Rouen, was a man admired by theologians for his learning and by politicians for his urbanity. The conclave chose him unanimously. He ruled as Clement VI.

His first task was to try and end the war between Philip VI of France and Edward III of England before it became more than an affair of skirmishes at sea. He failed, perhaps because Edward was determined that there should be a war, and was certainly not willing to allow a Frenchman to rob him of it. After fighting began in earnest on land, with an invasion of Normandy in 1346, Clement intervened several times and arranged truces, but none of them proved lasting.

The German problem was temporarily solved, however, by the death of Lewis of Bavaria in 1347 after his attempts to enrich his own family had led to a revolution, the wounds of which had scarcely begun to heal before the Black Death of 1348–50 swept across the continent.

The plague distorted the whole of the rest of Clement's reign, and indeed the history of the rest of the century. At Avignon itself, in its first season in 1348, it had destroyed half the population by April: in March alone, 11,000 corpses were buried in a new cemetery provided by the pope. The chroniclers of the time praise Clement for his generosity while the plague raged. Providing medical help and what would now be called welfare services, he spent his income without thought for the future; but as Dante and Petrarch both remarked, that was his habit throughout life, whatever the object in view.

The plague brought the pope not only financial distress but also pastoral problems which money could not have solved even if it had been available without restriction. In Germany first, then throughout Europe, fear of the disease induced a hysteria the symptoms of which included the rejection of orthodox thinking on many matters, especially religion. The first victims of this mental disturbance were the Jews of Germany. Accused of poisoning the wells and so infecting their neighbours with the plague, they were subjected to such terrible persecution that in July 1348 Clement took them under his special protection in an attempt to save them. The following year, mass hysteria took even more frightening forms. Germany was overrun by flagellants who, having convinced themselves that the sickness was a punishment for sins, concluded that expiation by suffering was being demanded of them by God. As a penance, they whipped themselves with leather thongs made more wounding with barbs of bone. It was said that thirty-three and a half days of self-inflicted torment would save either the body or the soul. The flagellants went from village to village, spreading both plague and delirium wherever they went. Other hysterical symptoms manifested themselves: there was an outbreak of biting in nunneries, and barking or mewing replaced human speech there. In many places, as Boccaccio recorded, hysterical penances alternated with equally hysterical feasting and sensuality. The problems presented to Clement VI by this psychological catastrophe can easily be imagined. The flagellants rejected all human institutions, including the church. In October 1349, when they reached the Avignon district and the pope saw for himself how great a peril they represented, he condemned their movement, and ordered bishops and priests everywhere to try and stop it. No one accused him of overharshness: the movement was too dangerous to be allowed to continue.

The damage the plague did outlasted both the epidemic and its accompanying hysteria. The terror itself and the loss of life, the incompetence of established authorities to do anything effective towards controlling either, and the ensuing economic chaos, were all factors in the complex revolutionary situation in which Europe found itself in the third quarter of the fourteenth century. The total effects of the plague are as difficult to assess as the total effects—economic, social and psychological—of the First World War. But although imponderable, they were by no means negligible. Those at school and university during the plague years were just beginning to take control of affairs in the decade which saw such outbreaks of rebellion as the Peasants' Revolt, the Lollard movement in England and Bohemia, the War of the Eight Saints in Florence (itself touched off by a new outbreak of plague), and the Great Schism.

The first results of the economic troubles of Europe after the plague were noticed as early as 1349. In England that year an attempt was made to stabilize society on a reasonably equitable basis by the enactment of a Statute of Labourers, the intention of which was to reimpose on the peasant the wages and duties he had accepted before the plague appeared. A second Statute of Labourers followed in 1351 complaining that 'servants, having no regard to the said Statute [of 1349] . . . do refuse to serve . . . unless they have livery and wages to the double or treble of what they were accustomed to take'.

In the same year, Parliament enacted the first Statute of Provisors, reflecting both the shortage of money and growing English antipathy towards the centralization of the church at 'French' Avignon.

The Statute made it illegal for the pope to 'provide' benefices in England for his own nominees, and for money to be sent abroad to pay absentee bishops, abbots and rectors. The act came as the culmination of almost ten years of dispute about the rights of the pope in England. Measures taken by Edward III's parliament of 1344 had denied the papacy all but purely spiritual powers in the kingdom. A counterblast from Clement VI had claimed 'full authority to dispose of all churches and ecclesiastical dignities, offices and benefices', and in 1346 Edward had ordered the confiscation of all benefices held by absentee foreigners. The measure passed in 1351 was not actually implemented, except as a threat. In fact, England had sent no money to Avignon since 1332, so this Act of Provisors did little more than legalize the existing situation. A year after Clement's death, a new statute, *Praemunire*, was to make illegal the arraigment of any of 'the king's subjects' before a foreign court and all appeals to foreign courts. No one hid the fact that the courts so repudiated were those of the pope, and the appeals forbidden, ecclesiastical appeals. The punishments envisaged by *Praemunire* were draconian. Anyone who did appeal to Avignon was to be given two months to make his excuses—or his escape—'at the expiry of which time his procurators, advocates, executors and notaries, and he himself and his abettors, shall be out of the king's peace; his lands, merchandise and chattels shall be forfeit to the king; and if he is seized, he shall be imprisoned until the payment of a ransom fixed by the king'. Again, the statute was not used; but it was there, on the rolls, a clear expression of English nationalism, and English rejection of the old-fashioned concept of the universal jurisdiction of the popes.

The antipathy of England was only one of the problems facing the new pope, Innocent VI, a canonist, who had been Bishop Etienne Aubert of Nyon and Clermont and Cardinal-Bishop of Ostia. There were signs that even the cardinals were beginning to be anxious about the growing personal authority of the popes. Before confirming his election, in December 1352, they imposed conditions on him intended to safeguard the freedom of the cardinalate. They laid it down that there should never be more than twenty cardinals, so that Innocent could not create enough to outvote them, that no cardinal was to be stripped of his authority unless two-thirds of the sacred college voted for his degradation, and that no one was to be appointed to or dismissed from high office in the church without the agreement of the college. They banned all relatives of the pope absolutely from any significant appointment, and required the agreement of the cardinals to any proposal to levy subsidies from kings or taxes from the clergy, adding that all sums so collected should be shared equally between the treasuries of the pope and of the cardinals. Finally, they said, cardinals were to be free to discuss whatever interested them, and to express their opinions on it.

The new rules were observed from December 1352 to June 1354. In July of that year, the pope repudiated them, as contrary to the canons. His reputation before his election had been that of a weak man. His reforming zeal and determination after it gave the lie to all the earlier reports concerning him. He was especially harsh towards the clergy—if it was harshness, as they protested, to expect them to reside at their benefices and perform the tasks for which they were paid. He turned the full force of the inquisition on to the Fraticelli and Beghards, and later began to make his own enquiries into the affairs of the more orthodox members of both the Franciscan and Dominican Orders.

His biggest problems were, however, in Italy, where control of the Papal States had by now slipped almost entirely out of papal hands. In 1347, his predecessor Clement VI had accepted the claim of a brilliant but mad layman, a protégé of Petrarch's, named Cola di Rienzo, to be his tribune in Rome, and granted the city a Year of Jubilee in 1350 to help Rienzo restore its fortunes. Petrarch's description of the city in those years draws a frightening picture of conditions there: 'Houses are falling down, walls collapsing, temples being overthrown, laws trodden underfoot. The Lateran Palace is razed, and its basilica, the mother of all churches, stands roofless, open to the wind and rain. The sacred dwellings of Peter and Paul are tottering; the temple of the apostles is a shapeless heap of ruins, a heap of stones to move one to pity.'

Cola di Rienzo was not the man to do much to right this situation. Instead he devoted himself to making his dreams of grandeur come true, giving it out that he was the illegitimate son of the Emperor Henry VII, having himself knighted and crowned, and soon identifying himself with the universal emperor of Dante's early dreams, calling all the kings and princes of the world to come and justify themselves to him, in a proclamation beginning 'I, Nicholas, the stern and gracious, Liberator of the City, Zealot for Italy, Friend of the World, Tribune, Augustus . . .' It is surprising that he lasted as long as he did, from May to December 1347. At this point Clement excommunicated him, and the nobility restored the senate.

Senatorial government, however, proved no more successful. The Jubilee was a failure, and there were revolutions in 1351 and 1352. The second of these brought to power a popular hero, who was proclaimed 'second tribune and august consul'. Innocent VI, who still had the first tribune, Cola di Rienzo, under restraint at Avignon, released him and sent him to the new cardinal-legate, Albornoz of Toledo, to see what use he could make of him. By this time, however, the 'second tribune' had been murdered, and Albornoz allowed Rienzo to approach no closer to Rome than Perugia, although granting him the courtesy title of Senator. In 1354, however, he escaped the cardinal's vigilance long enough to hire a band of mercenaries and reach Rome, entering the city to a liberator's welcome on August 1. For many months the Spirituals had been saying that he was the ruler who was to inaugurate the kingdom of the Holy Spirit foretold by the Abbot Joachim, but he behaved like a newly-liberated devil. On October 8, alarmed by his arbitrary arrests and murders, the mob set fire to his palace on the Capitol and he was killed as he tried to escape.

Rienzo was mad, but his behaviour was only a little more extreme than that of many of those whom Cardinal Albornoz was trying to control in the pope's name. He had few regular troops under his command, and was forced to rely on mercenaries hired from one or other of the Great Companies terrorizing Italy at that time. Even so, he was remarkably successful in fulfilling his orders once he had realized that he could rely on no one but himself and nothing but the weight of the pope's purse. The pacification of the Papal States was to take thirteen years, but already by 1354 he had won substantial successes in the southern areas, where the Visconti found subversion difficult owing to distance.

His task was made somewhat easier than it would otherwise have been by the fact that it was no longer practical for the Ghibelline towns to appeal for help from the emperor. The secularization begun under *Licet iuris* in the reign of Lewis of Bavaria was carried further by his successor Charles IV of Luxemburg without objection from the pope because its immediate effect was to separate Germany from Italy and reduce the effective size of the empire to the area north of the Alps.

Charles IV had been elected in 1346, as a rival and anti-emperor to

Lewis of Bavaria, at the instigation of Pope Clement VI. He was called at first 'the priests' emperor' by German isolationists, but he showed few signs of subservience to the pope even in ecclesiastical affairs. Fearing his ambition, Clement VI did all he could to keep him out of Italy, even though that meant refusing him coronation at Rome. Within two years of Cardinal Albornoz's arrival in Italy, however, the situation there had so improved that Innocent VI did not object when Charles announced his intention to march to Rome, but even sent a cardinal-legate to meet him there and crown him in 1355.

That same year, after the Diet had met at Metz, Charles published his 'Golden Bull' on future German elections, a document which, by ignoring the question of papal rights in imperial elections, effectively denied them. In the past, imperial elections had been theoretically subject to papal veto and in practice, as Charles's own career illustrated, papal rejection of a ruling emperor gave strong support to any would-be usurper. After the final promulgation of the Golden Bull in 1356 the electoral system was seen to have been as it were nationalized and the theory of universal papal sovereignty exploded. Henceforward the electors were to be four named princes and three named archbishops, all German. The secular power would always be able to outvote the ecclesiastical, and 'foreigners'—as the popes now became, silently but nonetheless really—would not be able to intervene.

Innocent VI accepted the Golden Bull calmly, realising that it had immediate advantages for Albornoz's campaigns in Italy, where the emperor now became a foreigner. It was only a threat for the future —and there was nothing he could effectively do about it. But shortly afterwards a threat did arise which he could not ignore. In the spring of 1357 and again in 1358, Avignon itself was besieged by a mercenary company, one of many then ranging the country, consisting of soldiers discharged from the armies of both France and England after the Treaty of Bordeaux had brought another temporary halt to the Hundred Years' War. It cost Innocent a thousand gold florins to persuade them to go and besiege someone else. But new companies were formed after the Treaty of Bretigny in 1360 had resulted in the release of thousands more men, and Avignon was again cut off by a band which settled at Pont St. Esprit, at the crossing of the Rhône. The second blockade lasted until March 1361, when Innocent again bought off the besiegers, paying them 14,500 gold florins to go to

Italy and fight for his ally, the Duke of Montferrat. This unexpected charge on the treasury left him in desperate straits. Opposition to papal taxation had never been fiercer. The collectors were often met with outright refusals to pay. In some places, plague, famine and war had swept away the tax-payers without trace. To the common people and clergy of Europe no less than to princes and prelates, the papacy seemed insatiable. Dante called the Avignon popes 'wolves in shepherds' clothing' and many were ready to echo his opinion. But seen from Avignon, the need for money was very real. When Innocent died, in 1362, the treasury was empty, although the papacy was hated for its avarice. The Franciscans are said to have sung *Gaudeamus* 'Let us rejoice', instead of the customary *Requiescat in pace* 'May he rest in peace', on receiving the news of his death, and Briget of Sweden, the pious foundress of the Order of Brigetine Nuns, a widow who had devoted her last years to helping the papacy in its troubles, wrote: 'Pope Innocent has been more abominable than the Jewish usurers, more treacherous than Judas, more cruel than Pilate. He has devoured the sheep and slain the shepherds: and now at last for all his crimes, [God] has thrown him into the pit.'

The first man elected to succeed the unhappy Innocent was Hugues Roger, brother of Clement VI. Each of the fifteen cardinals voting for him is said to have done so because he believed that no one else would. But Roger refused to reign, and there were days of argument before a second compromise candidate could be found. He was Guillaume de Grimoard, a former Benedictine abbot and teacher of canon law who over the previous ten years had come to know the situation in Italy well while acting as the head of several papal delegations to the peninsula. At the time of his election in 1362 he was in Naples as papal nuncio to the court of Queen Joanna, daughter of the former vicar in Italy, Robert of Anjou. A delegation was sent to Naples to bring him to Avignon for his coronation. On October 27, he assumed the tiara as Urban V.

The ascetics and mystics of the church saw his accession as a blessing from God, for although a learned scholar and man of affairs, he was by nature one of them. In one respect at least, the idealists were not disappointed in him. Neither as nuncio nor as pope did he ever forget that his primary vocation was to be a monk. He made his day revolve around the monastic timetable as he had kept it in his youth. His contemporaries had nothing but praise for his generosity especially, although not solely, to monasteries and schools and for his determination to rid his court of its multitude of useless and costly dependents. His Constitution *Horribilis* laid down the severest penalties then recorded for those who absented themselves from their benefices even to attend him, and he succeeded in reducing taxes by cutting curial expenditure.

His years as a nuncio had, however, not taught him the dangers of political appeasement. He failed to understand developments even in Italy, the country he knew best, and came close to wrecking what Albornoz had built.

At the beginning of his reign he took the grave step of condemning Bernabo Visconti of Milan for heresy and preached a crusade against him as an enemy of the church, but in 1363, when Albornoz was poised with an army gathered from all over eastern Europe to destroy him, the pope accepted his promise that he would restore church property, and suddenly withdrew his legate's authority in the north, transferring him to Naples. The result was that when the pope was seized with the idea of gathering all the mercenary companies into a single army and sending it to crusade against the Turks, he had first to make peace in Italy with a Visconti swollen with fresh victories. It cost him half a million gold florins to buy back cities in Romagna and around Bologna which could have been his at little expense beyond continued trust in Albornoz.

The idea of a crusading army made up of the Great Companies came to nothing, but another of Urban's grand schemes, that of returning the papacy to Rome, almost succeeded. Innocent VI had often talked of return. Petrarch, Briget of Sweden and the Romans themselves had often urged it. When Urban V decided in 1365 that the time was right, practical men said that it could not be done, but the pope gave orders for the Lateran Palace to be rebuilt ready to receive him. The cardinals, the emperor, Bernabo Visconti, the King of France and the Guelph towns of Italy were all warned of the coming move. They reacted as might have been expected, the strongest opponent of the plan being the French king, and its warmest supporters the Florentines and poets of Italy. 'Rome calls to her spouse, who will also be her saviour,' the Florentine ambassador told Urban. 'The Golden Age will come again.'

'Holy Father, Israel has left Egypt at last,' Petrarch wrote with equal fervour, 'The House of Jacob is no longer in the midst of a strange people.' But Charles V of France prophesied a disastrous end to the expedition. The final French embassy to the pope at Avignon in April 1367 recalled the famous story from the apocryphal *Acts of Peter* of the apostle's flight from Rome and his encounter with Christ on the Appian Way, but altered the dialogue to make the King of France ask his 'father' the pope, 'Lord, where goest thou?'—'To Rome'—'Then wilt thou be crucified.'

Urban V left Avignon on April 30, 1367. Northern Italy was unsafe so he sailed to Corneto and entered Viterbo on June 8, staying there until the autumn. He was not crucified, either at Viterbo or when he entered Rome on October 16, but there were riots in September, marked by the ominous cries 'Death to the Church!' and 'Long live the People!'

He spent the winters of 1367-8 and 1368-9 in Rome and the summers in the Italian countryside. The first year was a brilliant success. He achieved more in months by his mere presence than legates had previously been able to do by years of hard work. But his appointments showed that he was still a Frenchman at heart and the Romans turned against him. When Perugia rose against its legate and hired mercenaries under Sir John Hawkwood to help win its freedom, the Romans made common cause with the Perugians, and in the spring of 1370 Urban withdrew to Viterbo, to write to the Romans, 'If the Holy Spirit brought me to Rome, the Holy Spirit is now taking me away again, for the glory of the church.' In the autumn, he sailed back to France, and within weeks of reaching Avignon was dead. Petrarch noted, 'Urban would have been counted among the greatest of men, if when he came to die he had had his bed put before the altar of St. Peter's, and passed to another world from there. . . .'

The conclave which began on December 29, 1370 elected Roger de Beaufort, a forty-two-year-old cardinal deacon, to the papacy on January 5, 1371. A nephew of Clement VI's, Beaufort had risen rapidly through the church by a combination of nepotism and ability. He announced that he would rule as Gregory XI.

From the beginning of his reign it was clear that if the papacy was to survive as an effective force in Europe, and especially in Italy, he would have to lead the cardinals back to Rome. He told Edward III of England that to do so was his 'dearest wish'. Cardinal Albornoz was dead, and the system of government he had devised for the Papal States, with papal vicars in the chief towns co-operating—or, perhaps equally often, quarrelling—with elected councils, required the presence of a strong ruler to play the part ascribed to the monarch-moderator in Marsilius's *Defender of the Peace*. Bernabo

Visconti was still working to extend his power southwards and there was fighting in Piedmont. The free Tuscan republics, Pisa, Florence and Siena, caught between the Milanese and the Papal States, were uneasy. The reoccupation of Perugia by papal forces in 1371, following the surrender of the Bolognese forts to the pope some years earlier, was an added cause of anxiety. Florence refused to join the league formed by Gregory to fight the Visconti, but the significance of her refusal was masked by the readiness of Joanna of Naples and the King of Hungary, together with the Lords of Montferrat, Savoy and Carrera, to help him. The forces of the pope's league quickly won apparently important victories, taking a number of towns, and with the tide running for the papacy, Gregory announced to the sovereigns of Europe that he intended to return to Rome. But it was more than four years before he actually left Avignon.

The delay caused bitter disappointment in Italy. Catherine of Siena, on whom had fallen Briget of Sweden's mantle as female adviser to the popes, expressed fears that the pope had lost his nerve. 'I should like to see a manlier spirit in you,' she told him, 'free from fears and self-seeking, and free from earthly love of kindred.'

Gregory's detractors had always said that he was weak and vacillating, but he was not idle during those four years, and his work was decisive enough to give the lie to the charges levelled against him. The life of the church did not stop merely because Italy was in turmoil. Every pope in the fourteenth century had similar problems to face: heresy, the nationalism which threatened his international position, and the need for reform, especially among the friars. Gregory XI faced them all and dealt with them firmly. The Franciscans and Dominicans both felt the weight of his authority. So too did the Cathars and Jews of Spain, who were suspected of witchcraft, the Jews and Fraticelli of Sicily, and the remaining flagellants and Beghards* of Germany.

In the diplomatic field, too, there was important work to be done before Gregory could leave France. His representatives were deeply involved in negotiations at Bruges intended to repatch the peace made by his predecessors between England and France. A truce was

---

* The Beghards, and their female counterparts the Beguines, many of whom had by this time adopted the extremist opinions on apostolic poverty favoured by the Fraticelli, were members of an originally wholly orthodox lay Order, founded in Flanders in about 1180.

achieved in 1375, but by then relations between England and the papacy were severely strained. The cost of the French wars and the intensification of national feeling partly attributable to those wars had led Edward III to threaten to put into operation the antipapal statutes of *Praemunire* and *Provisors*. Three years earlier, the pope had been forced to ask the rulers of Europe for a subsidy to help pay for his own wars in Italy. Edward had refused to pay England's share and had sent the Bishop of Bangor to Avignon to protest against the operations of the papal courts involving Englishmen and the provision of English benefices to non-resident foreigners. Protracted wrangling followed this visit, during which Gregory was forced to concede many of the king's points, granting him the right to provide benefices, cancelling unpaid taxes and quashing legal proceedings against Englishmen. All these negotiations with England naturally took a good deal of time—much of it wasted, because they were followed by no improvement in English sentiments towards the papacy. When Gregory was forced again to ask for money from England, it was put about there that the concessions he had made earlier regarding unpaid taxes constituted a treaty excusing England permanently from payment of annates and tithes, and that in renewing his appeals for money, the French pope was trying to tear up his treaties, so as to have English gold to ransom French prisoners or pay bandits to go and fight his Italian wars.

The most pressing problem of these years was in fact these Italian wars and their aftermath. Florence was growing more uneasy with every change in the situation. The truce made in Piedmont after the victories of Gregory's league left the Tuscan towns isolated, an apparently easy prey to unscrupulous enemies. Moreover, the Papal States had actually helped their most obvious potential enemy to remain in being, by engaging Sir John Hawkwood's mercenaries to fight the pope's battles. That in itself seemed to Florence an unfriendly and undiplomatic act. More unfriendly still was the refusal of the Papal States to sell grain to her during a famine following a new outbreak of plague in 1354. That there was a general shortage of foodstuffs and that the Papal States had binding contracts with other cities and states weighed little with men threatened by starvation. Wherever Florentines went, they began to talk against the French popes and against the French rectors who administered Italian cities in his name. Once the fires of nationalism were lit, there was no power in Italy to extinguish them. Scandals involving Frenchmen added fuel to the flames. In July 1375 the Council of Eight—the 'Eight Saints' of Florence—led her into war against her oldest ally, the papacy, adding the word *Libertas* in letters of silver to the red banner of Florence, and doing nothing to restrain the people when they tore a monk to pieces in revenge for the abduction of a noble-woman by the Abbot of Montmajeur. In the city of Florence itself, church property was confiscated, the offices of the inquisition were pillaged, priests were charged with civil crimes and outlawed. Abroad, in Tuscany and the Papal States, her envoys carried on a war of propaganda against the papacy. The message, in whatever words it was framed, was always the same: 'Now is the time to revive ancient liberties. . . . Let all nations unite with Florence, and tyranny will melt away.'

The Florentines' campaign won quick successes. In October 1375, Orte and Narni joined the Florentine League. In November, Citta di Castello, Montefiascone and Viterbo rebelled against their rectors. In December, Perugia joined the rebellion, and in March 1376, Bologna expelled her papal vicar.

Catherine of Siena wrote to Gregory: 'Unfurl the banner of the Holy Cross, and we shall be freed from our discord, war and many vilenesses: you may even reform the shepherds of Holy Church. Vampires have sucked so much blood from the church that she looks deathly pale.'

The crusade Catherine wanted was one of love and reconciliation. But it was already too late for diplomacy. Attempts at negotiation achieved nothing. Towns from coast to coast joined the revolt, until only Rome remained loyal to its prefect. On March 31, 1376, Gregory put Florence and all Florentines throughout the world under a ban of interdiction, excommunication and outlawry. Florentine trade came to a standstill. Breton mercenaries were marched into Italy in May. Florence tried to subborn both the Bretons and Hawkwood's Englishmen. Cardinal Robert of Geneva, commander of the Bretons, believing that Bologna was wavering in her allegiance to the Florentine League, gave orders for the country-side around the city to be laid flat, to demonstrate to the citizens where their best interests lay. The Bolognese, expecting reinforce-ments, stood firm until the success of the mercenaries' pillage reduced the besiegers themselves to starvation rations and, in 1377, the cardinal was forced to withdraw them to the coastal area around Cesena and Rimini. This retreat heartened the Florentines, who marched on Ascoli and captured it. Hawkwood's mercenaries, loyal to the pope but unwilling to mix with the Bretons, made life miserable in the heart of the country—and so intensified the rebels' hatred of the pope—as they continued to live off the land.

The position was one of stalemate. It continued to be so until Gregory XI, having borrowed enough money to put on a brave show, landed at Corneto on December 6, 1376 and entered Rome in splendour on January 17, 1377.

'Do not come with armed force,' Catherine of Siena had told him. 'The magic wand of justice must be wielded by the hand of love.' But the War of the Eight Saints was not yet over, and he and his fifteen cardinals were guarded on the road and in the city by a mercenary army of two thousand men. The only 'hand of love' that the pope could offer Tuscany and the rebel States was that of Cardinal Robert of Geneva.

War flared up again at Cesena, late in January, when a brawl between some of the cardinal's mercenaries and certain local butchers brought the townspeople out into the streets with cries of 'Death to the Bretons and the Pastors of the Church!' Besieged in the citadel, the cardinal sent urgent appeals to Hawkwood for his help. On February 3, Hawkwood reached the city, and by nightfall four thousand of its citizens lay dead in the streets.

The shock of this massacre, following so closely on Gregory's triumphal arrival in Rome, was a blow from which the Florentine League could not recover. One by one throughout the summer of 1377 the towns in revolt either returned to their allegiance or were smashed into submission by the mercenaries. By winter, the Florence of the Eight Saints once again stood alone in the world. The interdict weighed heavily, with trade as well as religion halted. When Barnabo Visconti offered to mediate, Florence reluctantly accepted.

Early in 1378 a congress met at Sarzena to settle the affairs of Italy once and for all time; Papal and Florentine envoys, Visconti's mediators, and the ambassadors of the Emperor Charles IV, the Kings of France, Hungary and Spain and of Queen Joanna of Naples met together to bring peace to the Church and to the World more or less on the terms dictated by the pope.

In that victorious moment, Gregory XI died at the new papal palace of the Vatican.

Six months ahead lay the Great Schism.

JOHN WYCLIFF

THE EMPEROR SIGISMUND
From the portrait attributed to Konrad Laib in the Kunsthistorisches Museum, Vienna

Chapter II

THE FIRST PROTESTS

THE INTENSIFICATION of national and regional conscious-
ness in the fourteenth century, the decay of serfdom and the
growth of towns, the first stirrings of the Renaissance in
Italy, and the strengthening of local dialects until they became
capable of supporting national literatures, uneven cultural development and educational opportunities in different areas despite the
spread of universities to every part of Europe, and the 'Avignon
Captivity' of the papacy—all these factors were instrumental in the
crumbling of the monolithic structure of the universal society, the
unitary City of God, envisaged in the papal and imperial claims of
the earlier Middle Ages.

It was the early possession of a well developed language—the
Langue d'Oc—which made possible the brilliant regional civilization
in thirteenth-century Provence destroyed by the Albigensian Crusade.
French in its two forms was the first of the Romance languages to
achieve a literature, and it was in France that nationalism first
became a problem to the popes and partisans of a united Christendom. By the end of the century the Italian dialects had developed to
a point at which they could support a literature, and Tuscany
produced Dante Alighieri, a nationalist, who dreamed of the return
of *romanitas* and the empire which had supported it, matching
Christian heroes against those of antiquity, and judging them
all by the standards of his own humanism. Dante had little time
for sovereign popes, and none for the Avignon *curia*. Despite
his appeals to the Emperor Henry VII to save Italy, however,
his visionary empire would not have suited a German ruler of
those times. German regionalism, fed on German self-awareness,
left the German princes less conscious than their forefathers had
been of the affairs of the rest of Europe. The emperors still
claimed to rule the whole empire with 'the fullness of imperial
power' (*plenitudo potestatis imperialis*), but in fact their authority—

and generally their interest—was limited to northern and eastern Europe.

In England, as in Italy and France, nationalism grew with the perfecting of the vernacular, and it would be difficult to decide which fed upon the other. The reign of Edward III was marked both by the French Wars and the coming-of-age of the English language. In 1362, Edward ordered that English should be spoken in all the law courts of England, as French was by then 'much unknown in the said realm', and it was probably in the same year that Langland published the first edition of his *Vision of Piers Plowman*. The next generation saw Wyclif's revolt against papal autocracy and the Peasants' Revolt against feudal aristocracy, as well as the appearance of Chaucer's *Canterbury Tales*.

Important as these and parallel national developments were, however, they did not mark the end of that international scholarship and interest in antiquity which had been so characteristic of the previous century. The work of rediscovery and reinterpretation went on, although Greek remained virtually an unknown tongue (even Wyclif's Bible was a translation not from the original Greek and Hebrew, but from the church's Latin Vulgate). The century actually saw a great revival of Latin, especially in Italy, where Dante's dreams of empire and Petrarch's of a restored Rome were both stimulated by and in turn stimulated the rediscovery of the great Latin poets of classical times, especially Virgil and Ovid. The study of Virgil— whose hero Aeneas founded Rome as 'the New Troy'—aroused a new interest for Homer in Petrarch and his younger contemporary Boccaccio. At Avignon, they met a possible teacher in one Barlaam of Calabria, whose knowledge of Greek history, grammar and philosophy was reputedly unparalleled. But although profoundly learned himself, he was a poor teacher, and after he had left France for Constantinople, Petrarch complained that he had learned only enough to realize how little he understood. When a Byzantine ambassador presented him with a copy of Homer, he mourned, 'Alas, Homer is dumb, or I am deaf . . .'. He remained deaf to Greek, although not to the influence of the Greeks in Latin dress, until he died.

Boccaccio was more fortunate. In 1360, he encountered at Avignon a pupil of Barlaam, and succeeded in persuading the city of Florence to engage him as a teacher. From him, Boccaccio learned enough to produce a prose version of the Iliad and the Odyssey, and a treatise

On the Pagan Gods which had a great influence on the direction taken by the Florentine Renaissance. But the Greek school at Florence closed after only three years, when its teacher decided to leave the city.

It was not until the end of the century that the study of Greek was firmly re-established in western Europe, by Manuel Chrysoloras, a Byzantine nobleman related to the reigning emperor, Manuel Paleologus. He first visited Venice in 1394–5, on an embassy from the emperor, to seek military help against the Turks. During that first stay, he had to refuse a Florentine invitation to teach his native language there, but the invitation was renewed when he returned to Italy, and he began to teach Greek at Florence on February 2, 1397. The rest of his life he divided between diplomacy and teaching. In 1400, he went to Pavia with his emperor, who was touring Europe begging for help against the Turks, and held classes there until 1403, when imperial politics took him back to Constantinople. He visited Florence again in 1404 and 1406, and later lectured in Bologna and Rome. His books included a study comparing the teachings of Rome and Constantinople, intended to further the cause of reunion, and the first 'modern' Greek grammar for foreign students, as well as a Latin translation of Plato's *Republic*. When he died, in September 1415, he was attending the Council of Constance as his emperor's ambassador.

Although intellectual curiosity may account for a large measure of the Italian humanists' interest in the classical Greeks and their gods, the direction in which their curiosity led them—away from orthodox religion—was also in some measure due to their disillusion with the church during the period of the Avignon papacy. It was one of many signs of revolt during the century, and although later experience has shown that it was one of the most potent for the future, at the time it seemed one of the least threatening. To the popes at Avignon, apostacy of the kind alleged against the Knights Templar and open rebellion like that of the Franciscan Order seemed much more immediately menacing.

The charges brought against the knights were designed to suggest that they had rejected Christianity altogether in favour of a dualism similar to that taught by the Cathars of the previous century. Whether they were in fact guilty is an unanswerable question, because the only available evidence is that preserved by their accusers, obtained either from the Order's renegades, who were naturally anxious to denigrate it, or from serving knights through torture. At their trials the Templars were accused of having shown their apostacy at secret initiation ceremonies by spitting at the cross and calling Christ 'a false prophet, and not God'. The chaplains of the Order were alleged to have omitted the words of consecration from the Mass, and to have permitted laymen to give absolution after confession of sins. They were said to have practised sodomy and onanism as quasi-religious rites. Some were even denounced for having worshipped an image called Behemoth (although few witnesses would admit to having seen such an image themselves) and to have worn the little cord *cordula* and the thread *filum* that had been the badges of the Cathar weavers, and before them of the Bogomils, Bulgarian weavers who had preserved the teachings of pre-Christian dualism in the remote valleys of their land.

According to the Cathars (again, as their teaching was preserved by their orthodox opponents and inquisitors), the godhead is the ultimate source of both good and evil, light and darkness, and men may serve either the right hand or the left hand of god. The creation itself is evil, the work of a devil, and the Perfect, the Clean, the *Catharoi*, must despise every aspect of the physical world, including organized religion, which unknowingly worships the creator-devil and in its sacraments makes use of material things. But those who are merely initiates, and not perfect, may use the world as they like, because all material things are equally evil. The only 'evil' to be avoided if possible is begetting or bearing children, because to do so is to increase and perpetuate the misery of the world.

It is certainly possible that, at the beginning of the fourteenth century, the Templar Order had become tainted with this dualism, or with the closely related craft of the witches. These were usually accused of worshipping the black god, the god of darkness and the lie, Satan, 'the Lord of the World'. Their trials make confusing reading, however, because—except for a few eccentrics among them, like the Bishop of Cahors who tried to bring the reign of Pope John XXII to a premature end—they did not accept their accusers' terminology. Anne-Marie de Gourgel, tried for witchcraft in the Archdiocese of Toulouse in June 1335, a very articulate witch, confusingly spoke of her deity as the king of heaven, and called both the Lord of the World and the God of the Christians 'Satan'. The two gods were, she said, co-equal, co-eternal and continually in conflict—although the final victory of her Lord was assured.

Confused though her theology was, it was obviously related to that of the Cathars and Bogomils (and of the Templars, if the accusations against them were true). But the Bogomils, Cathars, Templars and witches were certainly not branches of a single underground conspiracy against Christ, existing over a period of several hundred years, although that is how the more fanatical of the inquisitors saw them. The Templars were probably arraigned for a hotch-potch of dualist doctrines because such accusations were likely to be accepted as authentic by those who genuinely feared secret societies and dreaded that they might one day actually witness the open triumph of the devil. It is only surprising that, given the credulity of the times, so few were ready to believe them guilty.

However, if the Templars were not dualists, the Cathars certainly were, and after the crusade in Provence had destroyed their centre and scattered them through Europe, their teachings gradually lost their individuality, and became confused with those of other revolutionary groups, such as the Beghards, who taught similar doctrines of perfection. The inquisitor's chief problem was to know where orthodoxy ended and heresy began. The problem posed by the Spiritual Franciscans was a case in point. There had always been two views on the questions of poverty and spiritual perfection. The majority believed that it was possible to be both a good Christian and a property-owner at one and the same time and had always preferred to think of the Holy Spirit as working through the organization of the visible Church. Mystics, however, had always quoted against them those texts from the Gospels suggesting that poverty and spirituality go hand-in-hand. But these were also the teachings of the early gnostics and later dualists. Francis of Assisi's emotional attachment to 'My Lady Poverty' looked to many in the church like an indictment of the church herself, and he was saved from the heresy-hunters only by the personal protection of the Sovereign Pontiff. The majority of Christians felt less uncomfortable with the more intellectual Dominicans than with the early Franciscans, and the decision of the Franciscans of the second generation to relax the stringency of Francis's original rule and allow their communities to possess houses and books was greeted with some relief. But not all Franciscans were satisfied with the new rules, and the mystery of poverty continued to attract some in every generation. Unfortunately, those who were drawn by the vision of reaching perfection through self-denial were also magnetized towards the most fanatical preachers of the age, and especially to the romantic apocalyptic speculations of the Cistercian Abbot Joachim of Flora.

The abbot himself belonged to the twelfth century, and died in 1202. But his speculations lived on after him. He taught that the history of the world fell into three ages, each lasting forty generations of thirty years. The first age was that of the Father, from Abraham to the birth of Christ, and was dominated by the flesh. The second age was that of the Son and the visible church, when flesh and spirit ruled together: it would end in the year 1260. The third age would be that of the Holy Spirit, and the Visible Antichrist, who, the Abbot thought, would be revealed in the person of an evil pope.

The appeal of this teaching to romantic mystics is easy to understand. Those Franciscans disappointed by the growing worldliness of their Order had no difficulty in identifying themselves with the 'Spiritual Men' foretold by the abbot, especially after the plague of 1348–50 had seemed to presage the coming of the end of the world ruled by the Son. The abbot's three books of prophecy were reissued under Franciscan patronage in 1254 with an introduction which identified them with the first volumes of the 'Eternal Gospel' foretold in the Apocalypse (Revelation XVI. 6) and made much of by the abbot himself. This introduction, but not the abbot's works, was almost immediately condemned. When 1260 came and went without a visible end of the world, new calculations were made to show that although the reign of the Spirit had begun, there must first be a time of trial, during which it would be an invisible kingdom, subject to persecution. While Bonaventure ruled the Franciscans, he managed to keep the Spirituals under control, but after his death in 1274 the question of poverty was raised again, the Spirituals arguing that as Christ and the apostles had been poor, true Christians should own nothing. Five years after Bonaventure's death, Pope Nicholas III tried to resolve the problem in a bull (*Exiit qui seminat*) pointing out that although the rule seemed to have been relaxed, the Franciscans in fact possessed nothing, because everything they used belonged absolutely to the Roman Church.

This argument satisfied many, but not all, of those who had been troubled. Among those unconvinced was Peter of Murone—the later Pope Celestine V—who founded an Order of Spiritual Hermits later to be suppressed by his alleged murderer Boniface VIII. The mystics immediately identified Celestine with the Angel Pope of Joachim's prophecies, and Boniface with the Visible Antichrist, and the debate about poverty and perfection went on, both inside the Franciscan Order and among the doubtfully orthodox on its fringes. In 1305, a book appeared purporting to record conversations with St. Francis himself in which the Founder of the Order foretold and condemned the relaxation of the rule. It also taught that the Second Age of the World was divided into seven missionary eras, the last of which was marked by the coming of St. Francis and St. Dominic, who were really none other than Enoch and Elijah, the two Old Testament figures whose return at the End was confidently forecast in Jewish apocalyptic writings. Their task, and that of their followers, was to combat the Visible Antichrist—the ruling pope, Clement V, who lived in France and refused to condemn the murderer of Celestine V.

These fresh speculations revived the discussion of the Spirituals and poverty. The Dominicans, who were already at daggers drawn with the Franciscans over the role of Thomist philosophy in the church, did not welcome the place assigned to their founder in this version of the trials of the End. Partly at their insistence, the teachings of the Abbot Joachim were condemned at the Council of Vienne, together with those of the Beghards, who also preached perfection.

It had taken a long time to decide that Joachim actually had been a heretic. The effect of the judgment was to drive the Spirituals into open rebellion. The Franciscan Order split. Some, loyal to the papacy and the hierarchical church, accepted the ruling; others could not. The question of poverty still continued to worry them and the apparent avarice and undeniable nepotism of the papal court at Avignon convinced them that the church had become 'Babylon, the great whore, who has maimed and poisoned mankind'. Their reaction was to begin a lawsuit against the orthodox 'conventual' Franciscans with the aim of having primitive poverty restored throughout the order. In two bulls, dated December 1317 and January 1318, Pope John XXII condemned them by all the names under which they were known: Fraticelli, Beghards, Beguines, and Brethren of Poverty, writing in the terms of the three-fold monastic vow, 'Voluntary poverty is a great thing, and greater still is chastity, but obedience is a virtue to be esteemed more highly than either,' and drawing the attention of the Inquisition to them—a move that caused relations between Franciscans and Dominicans to deteriorate even further.

This attack on the Spirituals might have succeeded quickly if there had not been so much support in Scripture for their views, and if the politicians of Italy and Germany had not become involved in the dispute. In the early 1320s, however, first the conventual Franciscans and then the Dominicans took up the debate about poverty, and it became one of the most important points at issue between them at the universities. John XXII allowed himself to be drawn into it, and set up an enquiry, but before regular methods could produce an answer, Michael of Cesena, the General of the Friars Minor, led the General Chapter of his Order at Perugia in 1322 to the decision that Christ and his Apostles had lived in absolute poverty, and that Christians ought to follow their example. John XXII's reply to this challenge was a bull entitled *Ad conditorem canonem* reminding the Franciscans of what Nicholas III had told them: that everything they had belonged to the papacy, which granted them the use of it. Instead of ending the discussion, the bull only exacerbated it, and the debate grew continually more acrimonious until November 1323, when the pope condemned the teachings of the Chapter at Perugia as heretical in an Apostolic Constitution entitled *Cum inter nonnullos.* The effect was shattering, for the condemnation of the General Chapter implied that the whole order was in rebellion and any Franciscan remaining loyal to it was a heretic. Michael of Cesena was ordered to Avignon, and held there in semi-imprisonment until he rebelled in earnest in 1328 and fled to Germany.

Meanwhile, the Spiritual Franciscans, the Brethren of Poverty, fell into open heresy after their condemnation in 1318, and rejected the hierarchy altogether, denying that the sacraments administered by an organized priesthood were necessary to salvation—as the Poor Men of Lyons had done before them and Wyclif's Lollards, the Poor Preachers, were to do subsequently. They were persecuted for the rest of the century, but managed to survive in Germany and Southern Italy.

There was no actual continuity between the Poor Men of Lyons, the Brethren of Poverty and the Poor Preachers of England. What linked them was the appeal of certain ideas to certain temperaments. Angel popes and nationalist poets, rebel peasants and devout nuns, visionaries and professors all inveighed at different times against the wealth of the church and the luxury and immorality of her princes. The actions into which their protests led them varied as widely as their origins. At least one group of peasants in France began to pray to Satan 'the Chief of the Serfs' to save and enrich them. At least one pope, Urban VI, came close to madness in his zeal to reform the church. Dante and William of Ockham turned to the Emperor of Germany for relief. Briget of Sweden gave up comfortable widow-hood to found a religious order. Catherine of Siena took to writing admonitory notes to the popes. There was no uniformity about these protests except that they all came from the same general direction, that of mysticism and visionary perfection. Catherine of Siena wanted her popes to be heroes. The Italian humanists looked back to a golden age of hero-emperors and hero-gods. There was not a single revolt, but rather a series of disconnected, disorderly shudder-ings of revulsion against various manifestations of the church's claim to universal sovereignty and the luxury in which the court of the universal sovereign lived.

Reasoned attacks on papal sovereignty came first from the French, then from teachers of law and logic such as Marsilius of Padua and William of Ockham. Many of these teachers were Franciscans, and already in revolt against the favour shown by the popes towards Thomism and its Dominican advocates. Marsilius and William of Ockham both attacked papal theory at its most vulnerable point, the imperfectly defined principle of the plenitude of papal power (*plenitudo potestatis*). Originally the phrase had been used to signify the plenary authority given to a legate or ambassador, empowered to bind his prince or his country with his word. In papalist theory it was first made to signify the fullness of authority given to Peter with the words 'Whatsoever thou shalt bind on earth shall be bound in heaven', but later canonists used it to describe the power of the popes, whom nobody could judge. Innocent III spoke of his own power as *plenitudo potestatis*. By the fourteenth century, he who wielded that authority, the pope alone, had become for the canonists, in the words of one of the ablest, Joannes Andreae, 'the *Apostolicus*, Lord of the Whole World', and 'the Wonder of the World, neither God nor man, but as it were a mean (*neuter*) between them', subject to no one, indictable for no crime except perhaps open and persistent heresy.

Against such extreme theories, Marsilius taught that the claim to papal plenitude of power was damaging to peace and disruptive of good order. Secular power belongs to the 'human legislator', the sovereign people, who might delegate their legislative powers to emperor, king or prince, but would never do so to the pope.

William of Ockham was an even more fervent opponent of papal sovereignty. He set against it the Pauline and Augustinian concept of the gospel as a new law of liberty: the easy yoke promised by Christ.

> It is plain that the Christian law does not allow for a servitude as complete as that of the Law of Moses. If Christ had so ordained and disposed matters that the pope possessed a fullness of power of such an order as to extend, properly and under all circumstances, over everything not opposed to either divine or natural law, the Law of Christ would be a law of terrible slavery—a servitude incomparably greater than that of the old law.

Therefore, he concluded, his own Franciscan Order and the empire had the right—given to them by Christian freedom—to oppose pontifical pronouncements and to defend the rights and individual freedoms of Christians against the pope. He pointed out that Christ had himself refused supreme temporal power, and asked how. His *vicarius*, the pope, could then claim to wield it in His name. He denied the infallibility of either popes or general councils: by the end of his life, he had reached the conclusion that both the pope and the clergy could fall into error, and that when they did so, it was for the supreme layman, the emperor, to correct them—as the emperors of Constantinople had corrected popes, by presiding over disciplinary general councils.

Rejection of the theory of the plenitude of papal power was one of the principles of the most extreme of the protest movements, that inspired by John Wyclif of Oxford and carried on by John Hus of Bohemia.

Wyclif (1320–84), a leading scholar at Oxford, absentee rector of Lutterworth in Leicestershire and many other English benefices, protégé of John of Gaunt, and adviser to Richard II, invented a religion which seems to have been an amalgam of all the forms of protest, both learned and popular, current in his time. With the Waldenses, the Spirituals and the disgruntled poor of England, he shared the idea that churchmen should live in 'apostolic poverty'. Like the Waldenses, he taught that anyone could preach, without license. With the rebel Franciscans of Germany, he shared the idea that the only source of inspired teaching was the Bible, and the only source of authority, God himself; thus denying, by asserting what he himself called the 'domination by grace', papal authority to teach and correct sinners. He rejected Thomism as non-scriptural, and the accepted theory of the operation of the sacraments as contrary to his own doctrine of domination by grace: if the power and authority to perform any religious act comes directly from God alone, and not through the hierarchy, he argued, God will withold the power to baptize, ordain and consecrate from those in mortal sin.

In other hands this mixture of all the heresies would probably have remained no more than an inarticulate cry of hate, but Wyclif, although a master of invective when he felt the need, was a highly-skilled and intelligent teacher and manipulator of men. When John of Gaunt, acting as chancellor to Edward III, began an attack on the properties of the magnates of both church and state, Wyclif supported him with texts and arguments to prove that churchmen should be poor, and that statesmen had a right to dispossess them if they were sinners—which, by the standards of Wyclif's teaching on poverty, they all were. In 1377 when, following a papal condemnation of ten propositions attributed to Wyclif, he was summoned to appear before Bishop Courtenay of London at St. Paul's, John of Gaunt answered the summons with him, and was so insolent towards the bishop, a man widely respected and even loved, that the London mob broke into the courtroom and brought the hearing to an abrupt end. That same year, Gregory XI, about whose pontificate and return of the curia to Rome Wyclif had been moderately polite, sent bulls to Oxford, Canterbury and London, and an Apostolic Letter to Edward III, forbidding the dissemination of Wyclif's teaching and ordering that he should be held in prison until his confession had been obtained and sent for examination to Rome. No action was taken on the bulls until six months after Edward's death, when it was clear that John of Gaunt had peacefully if unwillingly accepted a fall from favour. When Wyclif learned of their existence, in December 1377, and was summoned by Archbishop Sudbury to appear before him at St. Paul's and answer the charges contained in them, he cursed Gregory for 'a horrible fiend' and 'an abiding heretic'. Nevertheless, after a short delay, he did appear at St. Paul's. This second examination was no more conclusive than the first. The mother of the boy-king Richard II, the widow of the Black Prince, forbade the bishops to find against Wyclif, and before the arguments resulting from her intervention could be resolved, the mob had decided to play its part again, this time on Wyclif's side.

When Wyclif learned, in the summer of 1378, that the 'horrible fiend' Gregory XI was dead, and a new pope, Urban VI, with a reputation for asceticism, had been crowned, he wrote to Rome, apologizing for not having answered the bulls against him, addressing Urban as 'Christ's foremost vicar upon earth', and submitting in support of his own teaching that 'at the time of his earthly life, Christ was the poorest of men and declined all earthly rulership. . . . From this I deduce that none of the faithful should imitate the pope himself, or any of the saints, unless by doing so he also imitates the Lord Jesus Christ'. He welcomed Urban's reforms intended to reduce the wealth of the cardinals, but seemed doubtful whether the new pope's reforming zeal could long withstand the pressures of his office: 'Since God has given us a pope with true evangelical instincts, we are bound now to pray that these instincts may not be exterminated by deceitful counsel and that the pope and cardinals may not be moved to act against the law of the Lord. . . .'

At this stage in his career, Wyclif was still willing to grant that the pope had a certain spiritual authority, operative so long as he did not offend. But his ideas on this and many other points were still fluid. It was only a year or so later that he began to send out his Poor Preachers—the Lollards—arming them with parts of the Bible in the vernacular (the weapon the Cathars had used against orthodoxy, two hundred years earlier) and a set of doctrines denying the basic tenets of contemporary theology, transubstantiation, the sacrifice of the Mass and the real presence of Christ in the eucharistic species.

Until then, he had both respected and been respected by the friars, the orthodox 'poor preachers', but the open heresy taught by Wyclif's unlicensed followers made it impossible for them to continue in his support, and they were his most vociferous opponents during the four years of life that remained to him. He was willing to do battle with them: among his tenets condemned at London in 1382 was the proposition 'that he who gives alms to friars is by that very fact excommunicate' and another declaring 'that friars are bound to gain their living by the labour of their hands, and not by mendicancy'. Opposition to the friars brought Wyclif's preachers much closer to the popular view of them as expressed, for example, in the *Vision of Piers Plowman*, where they are stigmatized as those who 'preach to the people, glosing the gospel for their own profit', typified by the Franciscan Sir Enter-Houses, the physician of the soul, whose only prescription to strengthen contrition was 'a plaster made of private payment'.

How great a part Wyclif's preachers played in the Peasants' Revolt in 1381 it is difficult to determine. He was never charged with personal complicity in the plot, although his protest against tithes paid to unworthy bishops was used by Parson John Ball in his sermons of revolt. The rebellion was sparked off by commissions of enquiry sent into the shires to collect a shilling poll-tax from the thousands who had successfully evaded it. Its leaders, John Ball and the ex-mercenary Wat Tyler, were not Lollards, but probably made use of them to carry seditious letters. The peasants' victims in London were the natural enemies of the poor: the lawyers and their records, the Flemish weavers and Lombard bankers, John of Gaunt's palace and dependents (Gaunt himself was in Scotland), Archbishop Sudbury and Treasurer Hales.

The revolt collapsed on the intervention of the king, but the Lollard movement did not die, perhaps because the king protected it. In 1382, after the condemnation of Wyclif's propositions at London, steps were taken to expel all heretics from Oxford and Lollards were tried in several parts of the country, but Wyclif himself was permitted to retire to his Lutterworth rectory and live there unmolested until his death two years later. By then, Lollardy had already spread to the mainland of Europe, through the members of the Queen's household. Richard had married Anne of Bohemia, and it was in her native country, under the leadership of John Hus, that Wyclif's movement led to open revolt. In England, Lollards were afforded some protection by the court while the king lived, but after the accession of Henry IV in 1399, their position became continually more precarious, until Parliament proscribed them unconditionally in the Statute De Haeretico Comburendo of 1401, the first Act of an English parliament to make heresy punishable by the royal courts. The Act forbade anyone to preach without an episcopal licence, or to make or write any book contrary to the Catholic faith, or to form a conventicle or hold a school where heresy was taught, on pain of fines and imprisonment for a first offence, and public burning for a second. Not even the Templars had been so harshly treated in England. But the situation seemed to demand harshness. For more than twenty years, the Great Schism in the church had been undermining all authority in Europe, and no king now dared to permit a challenge to his power on any front. The government of Henry IV was fiercely loyal to the concept of a spiritually sovereign papacy, not only because the king believed the teachings of the church on papal authority, but also because some Lollards had begun to preach that just as the world needed no popes, it needed no kings either.

Chapter III

THE GREAT SCHISM

WHOEVER HAD been elected to succeed Gregory XI would have found himself in difficulties within a matter of weeks. The times demanded an impossible combination of qualities: firm convictions, a generous mind, an international outlook, a steady nerve, greatness of soul, saintliness, diplomacy, skill in war and love of peace.

The conclave of April 1378 produced Urban VI, Bartholomeo Prignano, formerly Archbishop of Bari, a man despised by the very cardinals who had elected him for the meanness of his birth and the commonness of his appearance. His intelligence, knowledge and devotion to his work were never questioned, but he proved neither strong enough nor sensitive enough to fill the role required of him, and within six months his inadequacy had destroyed his own mental balance and disrupted the delicate equilibrium of inner tensions which had hitherto given stability to the rock of Peter.

The most probable sequence of events leading to his election has already been outlined, but even that account may be inaccurate simply because all the surviving descriptions were written by men anxious either to clear their own names or blacken other people's reputations. Everyone realized that the schism resulting from the counter-election of Cardinal Robert of Geneva as Pope Clement VII in the September of that same year was a tragedy for the church, and might equally prove to be a personal disaster. All documents relating the events preceding the Great Schism must therefore be regarded with suspicion, except perhaps the diplomatic despatches recording the barest statements of the facts, such as Christofero of Piacenza's letters to the Duke of Mantua: 'The Lord Pope Gregory left this world on the twenty-seventh day of March . . . and on the eighth day of April the Lord Cardinals . . . elected to the papacy the Lord Bartholomeo, Archbishop of Bari.' So much was true. But later the cardinals were to deny even that.

When Gregory died, the Cardinal of Amiens was at Sarzena, representing the Holy See at a conference called by Bernabo Visconti of Milan to end the war between the Florentine League and the papacy and settle the future of Tuscany and the Papal States. Five other French cardinals were at Avignon, awaiting the day, confidently expected, when the papal curia would return to France. The conclave that chose Prignano, then, consisted of eleven Frenchmen, the Spaniard Peter de Luna and four Italians. Obviously, if the French had been united, they could have defied the Roman mob and elected one of themselves to the papacy. They were, however, divided into two factions, the Limousins led by Jean de Cros, 'the Cardinal of Limoges', and the Gallicans led by Robert of Geneva, 'the Cardinal of Geneva' and cousin of the French king Charles V of Valois.

The riots in Rome during the conclave in support of demands for a Roman pope probably had little influence on the cardinals' choice of the Archbishop of Bari to rule the church. The division between the two French parties was so deep that a compromise was inevitable, and Prignano was an obvious choice. He was well known to all the cardinals, for he had served the late pope as vice-chancellor to the curia both at Avignon and at Rome and they no doubt believed that they could control him. Robert of Geneva supported his candidature, and the first to vote for him was the leader of the Limousin faction, Cardinal de Cros. When Geneva's Gallicans, seconded by the Italian Pietro Corsini, 'the Cardinal of Florence', rebelled against him, they maintained that his nomination and election had been forced upon them, first by fear of the Roman mob, then by fear of Urban himself and his mercenaries. If they had been genuinely afraid for their lives at the moment of the election itself, their votes would have been invalid: canon law was quite explicit on that point. Their state of mind after the election was immaterial. There is, however, no proof that they were so terrified when they voted and the letters they wrote announcing Urban's election contain no references to such a state of mind. When they were asked about this omission after they had rebelled, they said that Urban had dictated to them what they should write. The Cardinal of Florence actually claimed that Urban had forged the letters signed with his name. But Corsini's letter to his old teacher John of Pistoris had just that courteous yet personal note one would expect, and was moreover proved to be in the Cardinal's own handwriting. 'On Thursday,' he reported six days after the election, 'we unanimously elected the Archbishop of Bari . . . We firmly believe and hope—counting on his knowledge, his blameless life, his numerous great virtues, his wide experience, and the help given to him by Him Whose Vicar he is—that he will rule the universal church profitably, according to the will and justice of God, and the whole Christian People will be comforted and consoled'. If the cardinals' fear was not significant enough to be mentioned in so personal a letter, the *Declaration* signed by the rebels at Anagni on August 9 must be regarded with suspicion, for in it they make their terror the justification for their rebellion:

> The cardinals were advised by some of the guards . . . immediately to elect a Roman or an Italian, if they wanted to protect their own lives. It was for this reason that the ultramontane cardinals condescended to the election of an Italian: merely in order to escape the danger of death . . . Being all anxious to escape danger, they hastily nominated the Archbishop of Bari . . . [and after the enthronement] treated him as pope. . . . Yet all this was in the city of Rome, where the cardinals, especially the ultramontanes, never felt themselves secure. They believed that if they had cast any doubt on the election, they would all have been killed. . . .

There was indeed a commotion in the city during the conclave, but the *Declaration* protests too much. Bari was certainly nominated hastily. The cardinals, however, voted for him not once, but twice, with an interval of some hours between the counts. There can be little doubt that they intended to elect Bari, and that the election took place in accordance with the canons.

When the revolt was underway, Urban VI had a statement drawn up, recording the details of his election. This document, known as the *Factum Urbani*, goes into the actions of each of the cardinals at some length. In the main it agrees with the account of the conclave written by the chaplain-servant of Cardinal Peter de Luna, but naturally it emphasizes the points telling in favour of the validity of Urban's election. Analysis of it reveals eight major arguments in support of Urban:

1. *The fact that the cardinals knew that the church needed an Italian pope.* It points out that as early as March 29, the day after the burial of Gregory XI, the Senator of Rome, Guido de Primis, asked the cardinals to elect a 'Romanus Pontifex' . . . 'for the good of Italy' because, as a result of the Avignon papacy and continual warfare, 'the church was notoriously exhausted and held in great contempt

everywhere'. He said that it was generally believed that a Roman pope would not fall into nepotism or favouritism, but would promote worthy men and not only 'those favoured by [particular] princes and from nations subject to them'.

2. *The fact that the cardinals recognized the need for an Italian*, and at the beginning of the conclave swore that they would favour no particular nation, but would elect a pope 'advantageous to the church of God and to the world, as God and their consciences bade them'.

3. *The fact* (disputed by the French) *that the cardinals themselves had insisted on making the election, despite the commotion in Rome.* Jacomo Orsini, the favourite of the Roman mob, and Corsini, Cardinal of Florence, did try to persuade the other cardinals that the mob should be pacified before any election, but they saw no cause for delay. The Limousins—who had most to fear, if anyone needed to fear—rejected as improper a suggestion by Orsini that they should dress up a Roman Friar Minor as pope, and present him to the people, then elect a genuine pontiff when all was quiet. Nor would they agree to Corsini's proposal that they should elect the ageing and dying Roman Cardinal Tebaldeschi as a temporary sop to the people.

4. *The fact that the Archbishop of Bari was proposed by the Gallicans on the night of April 7, and first voted for by the Limousins.* The cardinals were all willing to vote, despite Orsini's doubts about the temper of the mob. In voting first, the Cardinal of Limoges emphasized the genuineness and freedom of his choice by the use of a long and unusually explicit formula: 'I genuinely and freely elect and accept the Lord Archbishop of Bari as pope, [doing so] knowingly and willingly, that he may be the true pope.' Following his lead, all the French cardinals, both Limousin and Gallican, voted for Bari before the mob broke into the palace.

5. *The fact that when the Cardinal of St. Peter, Tebaldeschi, was presented to the mob that broke into the palace as the new pope, he himself told the people: 'I am not pope, nor do I want to be antipope. A better pope has been elected, the Archbishop of Bari.'* It was the ultramontanes who persuaded Tebaldeschi to pretend that he had been elected when the mob broke in. At that moment, they probably did need a few moments in which to escape, but by then the election had already been made. 'They implored the aged cardinal to pose as pope. . . . He was placed on the papal throne and arrayed with a cope

and mitre' and held the attention of the crowd while some of the
cardinals—Limoges, Aigrefeuille, Poitiers, Brittany, Viviers and de
Vergne—were fleeing to the Castel Sant' Angelo, and Robert of
Geneva, Peter Flandrin and William Noellet were finding other
places of concealment. The other cardinals merely retired to their
quarters, and were not seriously molested.

6. *The fact that each of the cardinals confirmed the election of Bari
on April 9.* The Archbishop refused to be called pope until he had
asked each of the cardinals at the Vatican that morning 'if he had
been elected sincerely, freely, genuinely and canonically'. They all
agreed that he had. Moreover, the Limousins confirmed the election
in a letter signed by them all and sent from the Castel Sant' Angelo
to the Vatican.

7. *The fact that Urban was proclaimed by a Limousin, and accepted
by all Rome as the true pope.* The formal announcement was made by
Cardinal Peter de Vergne on April 9 in the traditional form: 'I have
to announce joyful tidings. We have a pope named Urban VI', and
the same day the pope was visited by three of the other four Limousins, Jean de Cros, Aigrefeuille and Malesset, Cardinal of Poitiers.
They petitioned him for favours, asking him to grant a cardinal's hat
to the late pope's nephew and to bring pressure to bear on the English
for the release of the late pope's brother, a prisoner of war, just as
they would have petitioned a true pope. On Palm Sunday, all the
cardinals and dignitaries of Rome accepted palms from him, as they
would have done from any pope. On April 15, Holy Thursday, every
cardinal joined in the ceremonies surrounding the promulgation of a
papal bull against Florence, by which Urban made Gregory's XI
quarrel his own. On Easter Sunday, April 18, all the cardinals were
present at the Vatican to see Jacamo Orsini crown and enthrone
Urban, and played their parts in the elaborate ceremony. Later that
day, they all went to the church of St. John Lateran, Rome's cathedral, to see Guido de Primis offer the fealty of Rome to her new
bishop and, most significantly, on Easter Monday, all sixteen of
them signed the Letter of Election sent to the cardinals remaining at
Avignon.

8. *The fact that for three months, all the cardinals treated Urban as
pope.*

For the next three months the cardinals were constantly in the presence
of the pope; they treated him as pope, assisted him, publicly as well as
privately in his papal function, gave him gifts, addressed him as

'dominus noster' and prayed at their Masses for him as pope. Moreover, they treated him as pope even during their stay at Anagni, where—as they themselves asserted—they were safe.

If the *Factum Urbani* were the only surviving account of Urban's election, it would seem beyond doubt that the defection led by Robert of Geneva was pointless, seditious and probably malicious. In fact, however, the cardinals did not desert Urban without cause, although their election of an antipope could not be legally justified. It is difficult to believe that Robert of Geneva, who had commanded mercenary soldiers and ordered the massacre at Cesena, was ever afraid of Urban. The pope did not frighten the cardinals, but he made them first hate and then despise him.

On that Easter Monday, the day after his coronation, when the cardinals wrote to France announcing his election, Urban made his first attack on the members of his court, denouncing those prelates who lived and worked in Rome while drawing their incomes from neglected benefices. The attack was justified but ill-timed, for most of those who fell under his condemnation were well-disposed towards him—even if it was, as he said, only in the hope of their own advancement.

Two weeks later, preaching on the text 'I am the Good Shepherd' he attacked the same group again, and denounced the cardinals present in the church as simoniacs, living in luxury on the payment they had received for benefices while good Christians starved. He singled out for an especially violent denunciation the Cardinal of Amiens, who had arrived in Rome the previous week from the conference at Sarzena to offer his oath of allegiance to the new pope and report on the negotiations. Urban had been told that the cardinal had run short of money while at Sarzena, and had begged subsidies from the ambassadors of both England and France. In future, he said, cardinals would accept no gifts from outsiders in any circumstances and, to enable them to live within their means, they would eat only one dish at any meal. In the course of his sermon, he spoke of Cardinal Orsini as the *sotus*, the half-witted one, and after it the Cardinal of Amiens told him bluntly, 'Now that you are the pope, I cannot give you the lie, but if you were still the Archbishopkin of Bari, as you were only a few days ago, I should say that the Archbishopkin was lying in his throat.'

The first time Urban attempted physically to attack a cardinal, his victim was Jean de Cros, the Cardinal of Limoges. Growing furious with him in an argument about the new rules for cardinalate austerity, Urban would have struck him if Robert of Geneva had not stepped between them, asking, 'Holy Father—what are you doing?'

The next victim of one of the pope's rages was again the Cardinal of Amiens: purple in the face, witnesses said, the pope accused him of 'every evil deed in the world' and listed his crimes before announcing that he had degraded him from the cardinalate. Again, Robert of Geneva intervened, not this time with a shocked question, but with a blunt warning: 'Really, Holy Father, you are not treating the Lord Cardinals with the respect you owe them—as your predecessor used to do. You are diminishing our honour. I tell you for a fact (*dico vobis in veritate*), that the Lord Cardinals will find ways to diminish your honour.'

A stormy month later, pope and cardinals together were listening to a friar preach on the subject of simony when suddenly the pope leapt up shouting, 'You may add that excommunication may be used against simoniacs, of whatever rank or standing—even cardinals.' Fearing another of Urban's instant sentences, the Cardinal of Milan, Simon of Bursano, called out, 'Holy Father, there can be no lawful excommunication, unless you have warned the guilty three times.' Spluttering with rage, Urban shouted back, 'I can do anything—if it be my will and judgment.'

When it began to appear that Urban was determined to restore the universal sovereignty of the popes in the form of personal authority, the cardinals tried to persuade him that Italy was no longer the centre of the world, and that the church would operate much more effectively from Avignon. The problems of the Papal States should be left to the soldiers, who understood them. But Urban would not hear of it. 'It is neither possible nor permissible for us to go there, because Urban V and Gregory XI returned to Rome with the purpose of restoring this city, and its ecclesiastical and spiritual life, which were close to collapse, and this intention is not yet fulfilled.' It was soon after this that the cardinals began to slip away from the city, on the excuse that the climate was too hot in summer for Frenchmen, and to congregate at Anagni, to prepare their *Declaration* against Urban.

Even before that document appeared, however, someone had aroused the interest of the canon lawyer Baldus of Ubaldis of the University of Bologna, the teacher of Pope Gregory XI, in the question of whether a pope could be deposed. In 1378, Baldus was living at Padua, outside the Papal States, and so beyond the immediate reach of both the pope and the cardinals. His first judgment, given in July, was that there were no grounds on which the cardinals could repudiate a pope once they had elected him, and none on which the church as a whole could depose him, except persistent and open heresy. In 1380, he re-examined the question and reached the same conclusion, rejecting all but contemptuously the cardinals' claim that they had acted from fear. If any one of them had been afraid, he said, he could have protested. All that was needed at any time before the coronation was a notary and two witnesses. Cardinals were not, in his experience, 'of a fragile and faint-hearted nature'. The true intention of the electors had been shown by the words they had used—words such as 'that he may be the true pope'. The cardinals must have known what they were doing and must have known the meaning of the words they used. Moreover, the claim that the mob frightened them into electing an Italian when they had no intention of doing so, could not be accepted because, in the first place, they could not have gone into the election refusing to elect an Italian for 'there is in the sight of God no distinction between nations' and the Holy Spirit was the true elector; and secondly, they could not have hoped to pacify the Romans by electing a Neapolitan who had lived most of his life in France. They had elected Prignano, he concluded, for the soundest of reasons, because they thought him 'a good, experienced and well-known man'.

Nevertheless, the cardinals continued to maintain that it was from fear that they had elected Urban and treated him as pope until they could escape from him. Later, some of them came close to admitting that he had been validly elected. Bertrand de Lagery, the Gallican Cardinal of Glandève, once said, 'Certainly—if he had been prudent, and had known how to behave, he could have been pope', and Peter de Luna, the Spanish Cardinal, 'If he had not behaved as he did, we should still have been with him. But by his violence he turned everything upside down.'

The pope's bad temper, however, was no justification for supplanting him. Violence—even madness—could not strip him of his power. In more than three centuries of debate on canon law, nobody had seriously posed the question: what would happen if a pope went mad? And if anyone had, it is certain that zeal for reform, or even fanaticism for reform, would not have been acceptable as proof of mental instability and incapacity.

The cardinals' rebellion might not have been permitted to endure if Urban had not also alienated the princes. They were able to go to Anagni and issue their *Declaration* and to Fondi to elect Robert of Geneva as Clement VII, because Urban had made enemies of both the Queen of Naples and the Duke of Fondi. In both quarrels, Urban had maliciously bruised the sensitive honour of his antagonists. The Duke of Fondi had lent Gregory XI twenty thousand gold ducats, and when he asked Urban to repay them, was rebuffed on the grounds that there was no proof that they had been used for church purposes. The Duke had protested, and Urban had declared him deposed and outlawed, as a proven *comes companiae*, mercenary leader or bandit chief. In the months that followed, Fondi time and again proved himself Urban's bitterest enemy.

An even slighter incident touched off the dispute between Queen Joanna and the pope. In the wars of Piedmont and Tuscany, and at the conference of Sarzena, first Joanna's soldiers then her envoys had supported the aims of the papacy most loyally. But such help was expensive, and in 1378, Joanna was forced to ask the pope to remit her kingdom's taxes for one year. The request rankled with Urban. In May, only a month after his election, he suddenly ordered the queen's seneschal to leave his place of honour at the papal table, and go down lower, among the servants. The seneschal protested that, as the envoy of an honoured ally, he had occupied the same place through the reigns of Urban V and Gregory XI at both Avignon and Rome, as Urban himself must have known. Urban lost his temper, angrily repeating his order, and the seneschal walked out, taking with him the friendship of Joanna and her husband Otto of Brunswick, and all those in France, from the king down, who remembered that her father had been a prince of the House of Anjou. Urban added to the insult by publicly declaring that the Kingdom of Naples was being badly run, because it was ruled by a woman, and that he would depose the queen, putting a son of Charles V of France in her place. So it came about that, when the rebel cardinals sent a delegation to Naples under Cardinal Orsini, Joanna was willing to listen to its arguments against the validity of Urban's rule. She would not, however, countenance those in favour of the Roman cardinal's own candidature. She let it be known that her own choice would be the Cardinal of Florence, and so showed that she would be willing to revive the now defunct Florentine League with the purpose of expelling Urban. When the candinals elected Clement VII, she pledged her kingdom's allegiance to him.

Neither Urban VI or Clement VII could hope to last long without allies. The Italian reaction to the election and counter-election was especially important, because renewed warfare in Italy (the 'way of action' as it came to be called) could easily have been decisive before outsiders could intervene. Immediately the counter-election had been made, both popes began to reckon up their allies. Urban bound the families and friends of twenty-nine leading churchmen from several countries to himself by making them cardinals a week after he had deposed all those who had voted for Robert of Geneva. To counter the threat from Naples, he announced that he had deposed Joanna and intended to crown Charles of Durazzo as king in her place.

Clement VII re-established contact with his mercenaries, sending some to protect Joanna and keeping the rest in the Papal States as an ever-active threat to Urban. But now he reaped the bitter harvest of his nationality and his years as a ruthless soldier. Apart from Naples, whose queen was of French descent, no important territory in Italy declared itself willing to support him against an Italian pope. Peace had already been restored between Florence and the Italian pope by July 1378. That autumn and winter, not only Venice, Genoa and Naples, but also twenty mercenary companies, the 'Italian' companies led by Alberico of Barbanio, swore allegiance to Urban. Clement hung on in Italy as long as possible, but by the spring of 1379 it was obvious that he was going to find no more allies there. He laid siege to Rome, and from Sperlonga on April 17 issued a bull proclaiming the foundation of a new kingdom, carved out of the northern and eastern Papal States, to be known as the Kingdom of Adria and ruled—if he could win and hold it—by his cousin, Louis of Anjou. Following his lead, Queen Joanna named Louis as heir to her own Kingdom of Naples. But Louis was in France, and unable to leave for Italy. On April 30, Clement's forces received decisive set-backs at Castel Sant' Angelo and by Barbanio's crossing of the Tiber, and he was forced to lift his siege of Rome. He withdrew first to Fondi, then to Naples. On June 2, Urban crowned Charles of Durazzo as King of Naples at St. Peter's and sent him out to win his kingdom. He made such rapid progress that, by the middle of the month, help from France still not having reached Clement, the people of Naples were rioting in his favour, and Clement's position there became untenable. He left Italy, and arrived at the papal palace at Avignon on June 20. In Naples, Charles went from victory to victory. By the end of the summer, Queen Joanna had been driven out of her last safe retreat, the Castel d'Uovo in the city itself, and if Urban had not contrived to quarrel with his ally Charles, the war would probably have soon been over. But Urban did find grounds for a quarrel in the new King of Naples' refusal to set up a duchy for the pope's nephew, Francis Prignano. Soon Charles was fighting Joanna, the mercenaries of the Kingdom of Adria and Urban VI. The landing of an expeditionary force from France under Louis of Anjou in the year 1382 only further complicated a situation already too tangled to be easily unravelled. One incontrovertible fact is that central Italy in those years was a hell to the peasant farmers, since all the contending armies lived off the land.

However, if Urban had military problems, his cause was flourishing in other spheres. In 1380, when Baldus of Ubaldis published the second edition of his *Consilium* on Urban's election and the cardinal's *Declaration*, it was found to list twenty grounds at law for rejecting the *Declaration*. In the same year, another influential Italian jurist, John of Lignano, published a treatise challenging the supporters of Clement VII to show legal justification for his election. They said they had feared Urban but, he asked, 'Can we believe them?' and answered the question with a firm 'No'. Both Baldus and John concluded that the rebel cardinals should be brought to trial—in fact, they said, the whole question should be made the subject of a legal enquiry. But the problem was to decide how a court could be constituted to examine it. The only body with enough authority to do so would be a General Council, to be summoned by the only man who was legally entitled to call such a Council into being, the legitimate pope, Urban VI.

The idea that only a General Council could solve the problems of the divided papacy found other advocates in these first years of the schism. As early as November 1378 some jurists of the University of Paris had told the king that he should summon a council rather than recognize Clement VII, and German scholars working there had set themselves the task of elucidating the nature of the relationship between the papacy and councils. The year after the schism began. Henry of Langenstein made a first attempt to suggest a solution in the course of his *Epistola Pacis*, a moving appeal for peace in the church: 'What heart, however hard, can remain unmoved by the

agonies of its holy mother the church?... See if there be any
sorrow like unto my sorrow ...' Appeals failing, he and his fellow
teachers set out to convince the church that a General Council must
be called which could legally solve the problems raised by the
Schism. In 1380 Conrad of Gelnhausen produced a reasoned
argument for a council, entitled the *Epistola Concordiae*. Against the
usual view that only a pope could validly summon a general council
and preside at it, he argued that the common good must prevail, even
over established law. If the citizens of Paris were attacked by an
enemy, they could take up arms and defend themselves, without
waiting for the king to repeal the decrees against the use of weapons
in the city. It was admitted by the canonists that a general council
could be summoned to deal with an incorrigibly heretical pope:
should it not then be permissible to call one to deal with a pope
incorrigibly criminal? If Urban's behaviour really was criminal, the
cardinals were right to oppose it—but not by electing an antipope,
for that in itself was a crime. Illustrating his arguments with quota-
tions from the Fathers, he concluded that contemporary canon law
did not draw the essential distinction between 'the church, the
congregation of all the faithful' and 'the church, the pope and cardinals'. The whole church could not commit a crime, but the pope and
cardinals could, and had demonstrably done so at various times in
the past. Therefore the church, the congregation of all the faithful
whose primary head was Christ himself, was superior to the pope
and cardinals, and could judge them. Obviously, it was impracticable
to bring all the faithful together for such a purpose. Their authority
would have to be delegated to bishops and secular leaders in a general council. The law ruling that such a council could be summoned
only by the true pope would have to give way to the common good.

In the following year, first an anonymous tract, the *Epistola Levia-
than*, and then a new, fully-reasoned treatise from Henry of Langenstein, the *Concilium Pacis*, repeated and strengthened these arguments.
Langenstein's conclusions were expressed unequivocally:

> If the cardinals have chosen a pope unpleasing to the church, she has the
> right to revise the work of her agents, and even to deprive them of their
> commission.... The criterion by which all acts of church and state
> are to be judged is that of whether they do or do not promote the
> common good. A prince who, instead of advancing the good of the state,
> ruined or betrayed it, should be resisted as an enemy. The same course
> should prevail in the church.

However, brilliantly though the German scholars argued their cases, it remained true that the proposals they made were actually illegal, and, as all mediaeval jurists believed that if the law were ignored, society would disintegrate, no one would take it on himself to act on their suggestions. Although they were revived from time to time during the next decade, it was not until the schism had been made permanent by the election of successors to both Urban and Clement that they began to receive the support they deserved.

It is noteworthy that although the Germans of Paris were willing to grant that Urban might be a criminal, none of them seriously considered the contention of the French Cardinals, that they had been free to elect a better pope on their own initiative. They regarded Robert of Geneva as an anti-pope, and the cardinals he created as usurpers. It was impossible for them to propound such views and remain in Paris. Like William of Ockham and Marsilius of Padua before them, and by whose teaching on the nature and distribution of authority they had been profoundly influenced, they found refuge within the frontiers of the Empire: Henry of Langenstein became Chancellor of the new University of Vienna, Conrad of Gelnhausen Rector of Heidelberg, and their followers at Paris teachers at several German universities. They all remained formidable opponents of the restored Avignon papacy until the schism was brought to an end.

The arguments of the *Epistola Concordiae* and *Concilium Pacis* were legalistic and closely reasoned; their form was determined by the type of legal and theological training their authors had received. But comparison of the direction their arguments took with the more popular doctrines of Wyclif in England, and the Beghards and Fraticelli still flourishing despite so many years' persecution in Germany, shows that the Paris jurists did not reach their conclusions wholly unaffected by the spirit of their times. The general reaction against the concept of universal sovereignty and even of hierarchical rule had influenced them, however remotely. So they must take their place as revolutionaries, beside the leaders of the popularist movements that brought civil war, and ultimate autocracy, to so many of the cities of Italy, and the Peasants' Revolt to England.

Unable to imagine a society without a supreme leader, the jurists of Paris made both the whole congregation of the faithful and Christ the ultimate authority in the church. They did away with the middlemen of ecclesiastical politics, the pope-and-cardinals. In England,

John Ball was entirely in favour of eliminating in addition the middlemen of secular politics, the lords and lawyers. The very battle-cry of the English rebels 'For King Richard and the True Commons!' reflected the same concern, and Wat Tyler, listing the rebels' demands at Smithfield, significantly began not with the demand for the ending of villeinage and the freeing of the serfs, but with a call for the suppression of all lords temporal except the king himself, and of all lords spiritual except one bishop to serve the ecclesiastical needs of the kingdom. Neither such a king nor such a bishop could be an effective sovereign: the real demand was for the supremacy of what Marsilius of Padua had called 'the human legis-lator', the body of the people itself—in ecclesiastical terms, the *Congregatio fidelium*: the congregation of all the faithful.

The popularist views of Wyclif's poor preachers and the leaders of the peasantry of England in 1381 were not, however, reflected in the official policy of the realm. From the outbreak of the schism onwards, the sole aim of the English court and parliament was to see the universal recognition of Urban VI as the true pope. England's standing quarrel with the papacy over the provision of benefices and the collection of church taxes sank into insignificance beside the great question of ridding the church of Frenchmen. At the beginning of the schism, in October 1378, Archbishop Sudbury examined the claims of both popes and advised the king and his ministers: 'You may receive Urban VI as the true pope'; then went on to attack the rebel cardinals in a sermon on the text 'I will set one shepherd over them'. The immediate result of his judgment was the passage of two acts by the Parliament of Gloucester, the first permitting the king to act against the agents of Clement VII, should any appear in the realm, and the second declaring that anyone who supported Clement in any way should be acted against as a traitor to the king. A month later, all customs and harbour officials were warned not to permit gold or silver to leave the country for any destination whatsoever, and Clement's emissary in England, Roger Foucauld, was arrested. In order to make doubly sure that no money from England should reach Clement, Parliament then ordered that all benefices held by foreigners should be confiscated and their revenues turned over to the king. At about the same time, Urban promulgated a bull ordering the alienation of all benefices held by the cardinals in England, and requiring that two-thirds of the income deriving from them should be remitted to him. At first this bull was ignored, but gradually, as it became possible to know friends from enemies, the benefices were transfered to Urban's nominees. As a token of his gratitude for English loyalty, Urban named William de Courtenay, the Bishop of London, as a cardinal, but three petitions from Londoners asking that he should be allowed to continue to live in England led the pope to transfer the nomination to Adam Easton, the abbot of a Benedictine monastery at Norwich. Easton went to Rome in 1379 and was known there as the 'Cardinal of England'.

The English enthusiasm for the Italian pope grew as relations with France and Scotland deteriorated. Not even the invasion of England by countless fraudulent missionaries and dispensers of indulgences could dampen it. The Dominican Martin Halcombe became so notorious a pardonmonger that Archbishop Sudbury was forced to arrest him; and in 1380, Urban wrote to England, exposing the sellers of bulls fabricated by 'the son of iniquity, Stephen de Cusa, falsely pretending to be the pope's secretary' and claiming to give dispensations for marriage within the forbidden degrees of kinship, the legitimizing of children and voiding of bequests, and granting special indulgences and blessings. Yet the trade went on, and soon was legitimately increased by the promulgation of two genuine bulls (*Dudum cum vinea Dei*, March 13, 1381, and *Dudum cum filii*, March 25, 1381), the first promising crusaders' indulgences to all who would take up arms against the schismatics of France, and the second granting the clergy themselves leave to desert their benefices in order to take part in the crusade. The bulls not only called for soldiers but also offered special indulgences to all who would help finance the fighting men.

The Peasants' Revolt delayed the publication of these bulls in England until 1382. Then, Archbishop Sudbury being dead, Henry Despenser, the fighting Bishop of Norwich who had crushed the revolt in East Anglia, published them on the doors of all the churches and ordered that parish priests should make a record of every parishioner and his subscription. Richard II granted permission for his subjects to join the crusade, and it became a popular national movement in 1383, after it was learned that, following a French victory at Ghent, some of the bishops of Flanders were giving support to Clement, and therefore to France. Strong English influence in Flanders was important to the wool traders of London: in February 1383, the merchants and financiers of London made large contributions to Bishop Despenser's treasury. Others followed their lead and, in the words of a contemporary chronicler, 'the said bishop collected an uncountable and unbelievable sum of money in gold and silver', much of it given by women 'to obtain the benefit of absolution for themselves and their dear friends'. All gave in proportion to their means 'for otherwise they would not be absolved'. By May 1383, Bishop Despenser was ready to sail for France, to re-establish the unity of Christendom and assure the future of the wool trade by 'the way of action'.

The English crusaders fought only one major engagement on continental soil, between Ypres and Flanders, then found themselves lacking both money and the will to continue. The real battles were fought after their ignominious return to England, when the bishop was deprived of all his benefices and an army of lawyers began checking the accounts of the numerous clerks of his treasury who seemed to have become suddenly rich.

It is doubtful whether this English intervention on the continent had any effect on the course of the Great Schism, but it may have reduced the number of troops the new French king Charles VI could spare to help his uncle, Louis of Anjou, to win his two Italian kingdoms of Adria and Naples. Certainly Louis's war, begun in 1382, proceeded badly, although the arrival of the French delayed the completion of Charles of Durazzo's conquests in Naples. Despite the invasion, Charles continued to support Clement VII against Urban, whose insults, compounded by war, were more unforgivable than mere political enmity.

The 'way of action' was a resounding failure. Throughout the eleven years of Urban's reign, war was epidemic in central Italy. Louis of Anjou was killed at Bari in September 1384, but his adolescent son was immediately proclaimed Louis II, and peace remained unattainable. Urban, at intervals between periods of governing what was left to him of the church, took the field himself, notably at Nocera in 1384. By this time, his rages had become so terrible that the cardinals he had created to fill the void in his administration left by the rebellion began to be afraid of him, and six of them—among them the Cardinal of England—decided that he must not be permitted to continue to rule the church. But was it possible legally to depose him? They took their problem to a well-known jurist, Bartolino of Piacenza.

Bartolino offered them one possible solution to their problem. In his judgment, the church was, in its terrestrial form, a corporation, and therefore normal corporation law could be invoked to save it from danger from mismanagement. As executive members of the corporation, the cardinals could constitute themselves into a council of government, and make their council legal guardian to the corporation's nominal but incapacitated head.

Despite its obvious dangers, this scheme might have been made to work, if news of it had not leaked out. When Urban learned of it, though, he naturally construed it as a plot. He arrested all six cardinals and put them to the question, and concluding that his closest enemy, Charles of Durazzo, must be involved in some way, excommunicated him. Charles replied to this sentence by besieging the pope at Nocera. Urban climbed up into the battlements and with bell, book and candle solemnly excommunicated the opposing army not once but three times. Rescued from Nocera by the Genoese, he sailed to their city, carrying his cardinal-victims with him. The Cardinal of England, Adam Easton, was released on the petition of Richard II and, although degraded from the Sacred College, was permitted to return home, but after enduring weeks of torture, Urban's five other prisoners mysteriously disappeared.

Describing Urban's behaviour during these months, Dietrich of Niem, a witness of the cardinals' agonies, paints a portrait which could only fit a madman even in that harsh age. He describes Urban walking in the garden, calmly reading his breviary, while the aged Cardinal of Venice, under torture by being raised to the ceiling and dropped to the floor of a nearby room, screamed through the window at the pope whenever he could get breath enough, 'Holy Father— Christ suffered for our sins!'

When the five cardinals disappeared, no one doubted that they had been murdered. Cardinal Aegidius of Viterbo said of this mass murder that it was 'a crime such as former ages had never heard of', but Urban was capable of worse. He had the Bishop of Aquila murdered and his body left by the roadside 'for the dogs'—as he put it—merely for complaining of discomfort.

Meanwhile neither Urban's curses at Nocera nor the Genoese victory there had settled anything in central Italy. Men were still fighting and dying for the notional Kingdom of Adria. In 1385, Charles of Durazzo left Italy for Hungary in pursuit of a doubtful title to the throne of that country, leaving his infant son Ladislas as the nominal ruler of Naples, with his mother, Margaret of Durazzo, and Cardinal Acciciuoli as regents. They continued the war, but lost the city of Naples to Louis II of Adria in 1386. That same year, Charles was killed at Buda.

Louis II's victories brought no relief to Urban. Nor did developments in the north of Italy, where a quarrel among the Viscontis which had kept them out of central Italy for some years was resolved by Gian Galeazzo's defeat of his uncle Bernabo in 1385. He offered Urban the support of all the vassals of the Visconti in exchange for the title King of the Lombards, but Urban refused it, and from that time on the Milanese supported Clement VII. Yet Urban did gain some minor successes. He managed to win control of Rome itself in October 1388, and to hold on to the city until he died, almost exactly a year later, on October 15, 1389.

His death solved few problems. On November 2, the fourteen cardinals who had been bold enough to accompany him to Rome elected the thirty-five-year old Cardinal of Naples, Pietro Tomacelli, to succeed him, and so effectively perpetuated the schism. He announced that he would be known as Boniface IX and immediately renewed the bull of excommunication on Clement VII—who reciprocated the courtesy. But Clement's real enemy had been Urban VI, and many thought that at that moment means other than the 'way of action' might have been found to restore the unity of the church if only concern for the spurious Kingdom of Adria had not perpetuated French interest in the politics as well as the religion of Italy.

Boniface IX was, however, too deeply involved in Italian affairs to have time for much besides. In 1388, Florence had formed a central Italian league against Gian Galeazzo Visconti, who in the previous year had advanced southwards to take Verona and Vicenza, and was, of course, now allied to Louis of Adria, firmly entrenched in Naples. Boniface, desperate for help, made peace with the regents of Ladislas in a treaty of friendship uniting them against Adria, and in May 1390 permitted a legate to crown Ladislas as King of Naples three years before he reached his majority, in token of the alliance between them. He proved an expensive ally, and his forces failed to win the victory the young pope was impatiently awaiting. There were other frustrations, too: Boniface spent much of his time trying to find the money necessary to restore order to the chaotic administration left by Urban, and a good deal more trying to win back the respect for the Roman papacy which Urban, by his inefficiency and cruelty, had dissipated. How far this weakening of respect had gone was made painfully clear in 1390, when Charles III of Navarre, after twelve years of careful enquiry, led his kingdom to the support of Clement VII.

Meanwhile Clement had let it be known that he would consider putting the whole question of authority in the church before a general council, provided the Roman pontiff claimed no more than to be the leading cardinal present. He thought that the head of such a council should be the King of France. It was an opinion that no one else would accept. Scholars of the University of Paris were discussing a new compromise solution to the problem of the schism which had first been authoritatively advocated by Pierre d'Ailly, who called it the 'way of cession'. Both popes, he proposed, should resign, and their two cardinalates should combine to elect a single ruler for the church. The question of who had been right and who wrong in 1378 should be forgotten: the only fact of real importance was that the church was suffering, and her suffering could and should be ended.

The proposal was a sensible one, but made little headway while Urban ruled in Italy. Yet continued pursuit of the 'way of action' by both popes brought no acclaim to either of them. It seemed to many that Clement's court at Avignon had all the vices of earlier papal establishments there. Clement was subject to the king of France; his thirty-six cardinals and numberless officials and dependents seemed to be slaves to luxury and avarice. An anonymous tract of the times, entitled *De Ruina Ecclesia*, said, with a sarcastic reference to the pontifical title 'Servant of the Servants of God':

> This pope [Clement] has indeed been a servant of all the servants—of the princes and lords of France! He has had to endure all kinds of scurrilous treatment from the hands of the courtiers. Multitudes of bishoprics and prelacies have been handed out to the benefit of unworthy young men. He has allowed himself to be drawn into enormous expenses to gain or keep the favour of the mighty. He has permitted all the exactions demanded by these people to weigh the clergy down. By bowing to their aims in this way, he has reduced the clergy to dependence on the lords temporal, so that to all appearances it is they, and not he, who exercise the papal power. Fifteen years have passed in this servitude . . .

Yet although pride, avarice and lust were said to have ruled the court at Avignon during those fifteen years, such was the ineptitude of the rival Roman administration that Clement appeared to be in a stronger position that ever when, at Epiphany 1391, Jean Gerson, the Chancellor of the University of Paris, a former pupil of Pierre d'Ailly, attacked the schism in a sermon preached in the presence of the king. Gerson came out strongly in favour of royal intervention— by the 'way of action' if need be—to put an end to the scandal.

That sermon was intended to be the first shot in a new war of words. After ten years the theologians and jurists had rediscovered Gelnhausen and the concept of the sovereignty of the congregation of all the faithful. Shocked by this threat to his pope, however, the king forbade the discussion of such a question at the university. The jurists obeyed, but the theologians, although they stopped making public pronouncements, continued to explore the possibilities of the 'way of cession' and the new theories about authority in the church, theories which led directly to 'conciliarism', the belief that a general council representing all the faithful is the ultimate source of authority under Christ. In June 1394, the supporters of these radical ideas at the university felt strong enough to ignore the king's ban, and they presented him with a set of proposals in support of cession. The leaders of the movement against Clement VII were now Gerson, d'Ailly, by then a cardinal, and Nicholas of Clemanges, titular Patriarch of Alexandria.

Recognizing the threat that these proposals represented to his authority, Clement VII tried to reach a reconciliation with the scholars, but their only response was a letter outlining the steps that should be taken to end the schism by the way of cession, and accusing the Spanish Cardinal Peter de Luna of working against the restoration of peace in the church. It had been Peter de Luna who, as Clement's ambassador, had persuaded first Portugal, then Castile and Aragon, and finally Navarre to decide in favour of the Avignon papacy. A few days after receiving the scholars' letter, on September 16, 1394, Clement VII died of apoplexy brought on, it was said, by his anger at its contents.

Immediately Charles VI heard of his death, he wrote to the cardinals of the Avignon curia, suggesting that for the sake of peace they should not perpetuate the schism by electing a new pope. Their sharp reply was to go into conclave and elect Peter de Luna as soon as it was canonically possible, on September 28, 1394. He announced that he would reign from Avignon as Benedict XIII.

Chapter IV

THE WAY OF CESSION

IN EARLIER centuries an affair like the Great Schism, so deeply affecting all Europe, would have evoked an immediate response from the Emperor of Germany. With the publication of the Golden Bull on German elections in 1356, however, the empire had as it were served notice that, temporarily at least, the German peoples were not prepared to involve themselves in the affairs of the south and west of Europe. German eyes were fixed on German affairs and especially the affairs of the eastern marches, Poland, Brandenburg, Bohemia and Hungary. Even the idealism of the Teutonic Knights was directed towards this Slavic frontier, rather than southwards, against the Turks of Rum. The Order, founded in the twelfth century for the defence of the Holy Land and first engaged in the battles of the Third Crusade, was now used to create and hold a group of states marking the north-eastern limits of German expansion: Pomerania, Danzig, East Prussia and Lithuania. Early in the fourteenth century, these Baltic lands had still been missionary areas, where the Order could claim to be exercising a function not unlike that for which it had been created, but gradually, as the primary tasks of the knights were fulfilled, nationalism took over from evangelism as the justification for continued German occupation of these areas, and local resentment against this occupation grew.

The difficulties experienced by the Teutonic Order in the northeast were matched by similar problems in the south-east, where royal rulers, as well as fighting one another, struggled against growing national awareness among the Bohemians and Czechs. The expedition of Charles of Durazzo to Hungary in 1385–6 in a vain attempt to win the crown was only one incident among many that marred the peace of the region in the years of the Great Schism.

When Charles IV, the 'priests' emperor' who had repudiated the pope's hold over him with the Golden Bull, died in 1378, he left Germany in a weak and divided condition. Two years before his

155

death, he had outwitted his rivals among the German princes, and brought sufficient pressure to bear upon the German electors, to have his son Wenceslas named as emperor-elect and King of the Romans during his own lifetime. Papal consent to the election was won from Gregory XI by the expedient of ignoring the terms of the Golden Bull and returning to the conditions of the oath Charles had taken to the papacy in 1346, by which he guaranteed papal possessions in Italy, and promised not to use the imperial power there— even to make a king of the Romans—without prior consent of the pope. The election of Urban VI and the death of Charles both occurring in the same year, it is tempting to see what followed as an exchange of diplomatic recognition: Wenceslas supported Urban against the rebel cardinals, while Urban confirmed the election of Wenceslas, despite German objections that it was invalid because it had been made during the lifetime of his father. It was, however, an exchange of recognition between men each weak in his own sphere. Wenceslas did not control the whole empire. He was only seventeen years of age at the time of his father's death, and not yet strong enough to force the Germans to accept his rule. Moreover, by Charles's will, Wenceslas inherited merely the title to Luxemburg and Bohemia; his younger brother Sigismund inherited Brandenburg, a third brother, John, the district of Goerlitz, and a cousin, Jost, that of Moravia. The history of the next two decades in the empire was shaped by the rivalries and reconciliations of Charles's heirs, and the plots of Germany's other princes to rid the world of them all. The Great Schism exacerbated an already difficult situation. The acceptance of the authenticity of Urban's election first by Charles and then by Wenceslas did not decide the question for the whole empire. In the absence of absolutely decisive proof in support of the claims of either Urban or Clement VII, conscience, political considerations and prejudices were all thrown into the scales. Although the majority of the most powerful rulers—Wenceslas himself, the King of Hungary and Poland, the Archbishops of Triers, Maintz and Cologne, and the Count Palatinate Rupert of the Rhine —all decided for Urban VI, the general situation was too uneasy for Wenceslas to take any practical steps to support him. Moreover, as the years passed, the situation worsened rather than improved. The continual strengthening of the generally anti-Roman and pro-French block of cities and territories lying between Germany and the Papal States and ruled from Milan by Gian Galeazzo Visconti, the war in Hungary precipitated by the attempt of Charles of Durazzo to seize the throne and ending with Sigismund firmly established there, and the unrest caused by the spread of Wyclif's teaching to Bohemia where it encouraged local national feeling—all these factors combined to keep Wenceslas out of Italy. Although he was recognized as King of the Romans, he was never able to make the journey to Rome for his imperial coronation, although both Urban VI and his successor Boniface IX urged him to do so.

In 1392–3, Boniface's need of imperial help was so pressing that he was willing to grant almost any concession to Wenceslas and overlook any shortcoming in him, if only he would bring 'the way of action' to bear against Louis II of Adria, and now of Naples, and Gian Galeazzo, Lord of Milan, who in the years since Urban had refused him the iron crown of the Lombards had swallowed up Verona, Vicenza and Padua. Wenceslas took what he could from Boniface, but gave him nothing except, admittedly a most welcome aid, regular remittances of the tithes and annates due to him. The year 1393 was made a period of special Jubilee in the empire, marking the mid-point between the centennial year of Jubilee 1343 and that expected in 1443. It was said that both emperor and pope drew large profits from the indulgences sold during the celebrations. Reversing centuries of papal policy, Boniface permitted the advancement of royal favourites to important posts in the church: the case of Wenceslas Kralik, who collected valuable benefices in every part of Germany, was a notorious, but not an isolated one. Yet the emperor neither led a crusading army into Italy to rescue the pope, nor even co-operated with the ecclesiastical authorities in German lands, unless it suited him to do so.

At the very time when the special Jubilee was being preached, Wenceslas's favourites embroiled him in several disputes with the Metropolitan Archbishop of his own Kingdom of Bohemia, John of Jensteyn, the Archbishop of Prague. The troubles began with the judicial murder of two priests, arrested on serious charges, but executed without proper trial and despite the laws of sacerdotal immunity. The archbishop summoned to his own court the royal official who had ordered the execution, and severely censured him. The emperor took this as a personal affront. When later in the year 1393 a fresh cause for a quarrel arose, no one was in a mood to overlook it.

The grounds for the new dispute was Wenceslas's plan for the endowment of a new bishopric in western Bohemia by transferring to it the estates belonging to the Benedictine monastery of Kladruby. For this to be done with even a semblance of legality, the monastery had to be suppressed by the monks themselves 'voluntarily' deciding not to elect a new abbot when their present ruler died. Pressure was brought on them to volunteer this sacrifice, but when the moment came, they elected a new superior, who was immediately confirmed in his appointment by Archbishop John, through his vicar-general, John of Pomuk. Wenceslas, still smarting under the archbishop's former slight, over-reacted to this new assault on his unstable authority, ordering the arrest of the archbishop himself, and three of his advisers, including the vicar-general. The archbishop was soon released, but the three advisers were put to the question, the vicar-general so severely that, when the king ordered their release if they would sign statements denying that they had been tortured, he was unable to write his name. His incapacity was taken for obduracy, and he was drowned in the River Vlata.* When the king's anger cooled, he did what he could to restore good relations with the archbishop, using the indulgences and penances of the jubilee year to prove his penitence, and inviting the injured prelate to negotiate reparations with him. But John of Jensteyn fled to Rome, where he laid charges against Wenceslas before Boniface IX. On the basis of the evidence, almost any other pope would have excommunicated almost any other emperor and declared him deposed, but Boniface needed the emperor's help more than he needed that of a single archbishop. John of Jensteyn waited until a rumour reached him that he was about to be deposed. Then, in 1395, he resigned.

Treating the archbishop so shamefully brought Boniface no reward from Wenceslas. In the year of the archbishop's resignation, Wenceslas made an alliance with the ambitious Gian Galeazzo Visconti of Milan, granting him the title Duke of Milan for a fee of 100,000 gold florins. It was an overtly anti-papal act, but there was nothing Boniface dared to do about it.

However, if Boniface IX had grave problems in Italy and Germany, those of Peter de Luna, Benedict XIII, in France were scarcely less oppressive. Elected on September 28, 1394, by the early months of 1395 he was already being pressed to accept the 'way of cession' and resign. A French national assembly, bringing together more

---

* During counter-reformation times, he was canonized as John of Nepomuk, and became central Europe's patron saint of bridges.

than a hundred prelates and jurists at Paris from February 2 to 18, voted for cession by a majority of more than three to one, and the Dukes of Berry, Orleans and Burgundy went together to Benedict's court at Avignon to tell him what was required of him. But Benedict refused to have anything to do with the idea of cession and the most the noble ambassadors could win from him was one offer to give up his rights in the Kingdom of Adria to its secular rulers (so surrendering a large part of the Papal States), and another to consider the possibility of some form of negotiation with Boniface, to end the schism by the 'way of discussion'.

The national assembly, however, frightened the cardinals who had so hastily elected Benedict the previous year, and they soon convinced themselves that they could no longer be sure that they had done their best for the church. Meeting at Villeneuve-les-Avignon on June 1 they concluded that in future they would work for the acceptance of the way of cession by both popes. A year passed in the 'way of discussion'. No kings except of France favoured the idea at first: if two popes, they asked themselves, one of whom must be the valid ruler of the church, can both be asked to resign, what security do other rulers have? Gradually, however, the arguments of the lawyers and prelates of France won acceptance in England and Castile.

Castile had looked with great disfavour on the schism from the first. Peter de Luna's mission to King John I, to persuade him that Clement VII was the valid pope, had been successful only after two years: even then, the king had insisted on the need to send a commission to Rome, Avignon and Naples to gather evidence, and allowing his clergy six months to debate its findings before offering the allegiance of his country to Clement VII. Now, in 1395, with Peter de Luna himself ruling at Avignon, John's successor, Henry III, was ready to re-open the debate, and see it settled by the way of cession, especially as Castile's newest ally England, although still nominally supporting the Roman pope, declared herself in agreement.

Richard II's parliament and advisers had tired of Boniface's attempts to restore his personal authority over the whole church as early as 1390. In that year the Statute of Provisors, directed against the papal court of 1351, was revised and strengthened to forbid 'reservation, collation or provision' to any 'archbishopric, bishopric, dignity or other benefice . . . by the court of Rome'. Three years later, a new Statute of *Praemunire* forbade any appeals from England 'in the court of Rome'. The new acts were applied vigorously to stop the flow of money from England to either pope or his supporters. But the new Statute of *Praemunire* also made it clear that the Lords Spiritual were not willing openly to deny that the pope—the legitimate pope—had spiritual jurisdiction over them: they were, however, as uneasy about the continuance of the schism as were Richard and his ministers about the influence of foreign churchmen in England and their maintenance from England.

In March 1398, an English ambassador met the King of France, an envoy of the King of Castile and Richard II's brother-in-law, Wenceslas of Bohemia, temporarily in exile, at Rheims, and on the 21st it was announced that their four countries would henceforward maintain a position of neutrality towards the popes and work for the acceptance of the way of cession by them both. Embassies were sent to Avignon and Rome: neither pope was ready to comply with the suggestions put to him. Benedict's reply to Pierre d'Ailly, the leader of the embassy to Avignon, was a simple statement of his faith in the justice of his cause: 'I have never accepted the way of cession, and I shall never accept it. I believe that if I were to follow that way, I should sin mortally.' In his own judgment, he was the true pope: to have denied the fact would have been to deny the gift of the Holy Ghost. Boniface IX was equally convinced of his own vocation.

For the moment it seemed that not only the way of cession but even the way of discussion was closed.

Jean Gerson and the masters of the University, powerfully assisted by Philip the Bold, Duke of Burgundy, set about convincing France that it was not so. A national assembly held at Paris in May and June 1398 was reluctantly led, by some very special pleading, to the conclusion that all support and obedience should be refused to both popes. Leaning too heavily on Marsilius of Padua and William of Ockham for any theologian in less desperate times to follow them, the scholars argued that to refuse obedience was merely to restore the ancient liberties of the national church. The president of the assembly and titular Patriarch of Alexandria, Simon de Cramaud, proposed the thesis that, 'As Benedict has shown himself obstinate by refusing [to restore peace by following the way of cession] it behoves us to consider whether the Church of France ought not reciprocally to refuse obedience to him, or at least partially to withdraw obedience, in order to make him reconsider.' Benedict's refusal to abdicate, it was argued, was tantamount to heresy—for which he could be deposed. The national church should have control over revenues collected from the nation and appointment to benefices or 'collations' supported by the nation.

Acceptance of these dubiously legal propositions had revolutionary effects, for they put the pope at the mercy of secular rulers and the lower clergy. Boniface IX, safe in Rome, ignored such parts of them as might have been said to apply to him. As early as March 1391 he had condemned the doctrine that a general council or any other representative body could be superior in authority to a pope. Benedict XIII, against whom they were primarily formulated, would have ignored them if it had been possible for him to do so, but at Avignon he was too close for comfort to the French court. The Royal Decree of August 8, published on September 1, giving effect to the proposals made by the assembly by voiding all the collations made by Benedict, and allowing diocesans the right to confirm elections without reference to him and to absolve all sinners again without reference to him, would have made his position untenable if he had been entirely without friends in France. As it was, its publication all but destroyed the administration centred on Avignon. Eighteen of Benedict's twenty-three cardinals put the Rhône between themselves and their pope as soon as they could, taking with them to Villeneuve the papal seal and, they claimed, the papal authority. Fighting broke out in the old town, and Benedict and his five faithful supporters disposed their forces for a siege. The eighteen hired the mercenary captain Godfrey of Boucicaud to fight their pope for them. But Benedict was a determined man, still convinced that he was right. Moreover, he knew that the decision behind the royal decrees had not been unanimous, and that many recognized its illegality. He waited. The siege dragged on through the winter, but in April 1399, it was lifted after Benedict had made the minimal concession of agreeing to think again about cession. He was still watched—and he still waited. Right was on his side; time would prove it.

The proof of his strength, if not of his rectitude, came quickly. A self-governing national church, if conceivable in later times, was certainly not practical in 1398–1400. The new-found freedom of the French church proved to be an intolerable burden on the French people. Its new masters, the royal favourites and the university, were infinitely worse than the old, because there was neither law nor tradition to limit their activities. Electors and collators soon found

that it was not they who were free, but royal and academic nomina-
tors. Aids, subsidies, tithes and annates were ruthlessly collected for
the benefit of the crown. Still Benedict waited. The Duke of
Orleans, hesitant from the first about accepting the decrees of 1398,
partly from conscience, but partly also because they were so warmly
championed by his enemy the Duke of Burgundy, made himself the
leader of lay opposition to the war against the pope. The Universities
of Toulouse, Angers and Orleans and many individual bishops and
priests decided that obedience could not legally be withdrawn from
Peter's successor. Opposition to the free French church was greatly
strengthened in March 1400, when Royal Letters made it quite clear
what categories of persons electors and collators were alone henceforward to be free to promote: the nominees of the king, the queen,
the dauphin, the king's brother and uncles, and the University of
Paris, in strict rotation. Meanwhile, among the territories Benedict
had ruled outside France it was, generally speaking, only those most
closely linked with the French crown that withdrew their obedience:
Naples and her tributaries, and the duchies and counties within
striking distance of French armies, Bar, Lorraine, Namur and Brabant. Henry III of Castile withdrew obedience at first, but found
himself under continual pressure from his own people to restore it,
and finally did so in 1402. Aragon, Benedict's home country, never
wavered in its allegiance to him. Provence, a fief of Naples, withdrew obedience at first, but restored it after only two years.

In short, by 1402, the royal policy lay in ruins. Benedict was
almost as strong as ever, but the somewhat unnatural alliance
between the court and the university had gained many enemies for both
parties. As it became clear how much damage 'liberty' was doing to
the church in France, Chancellor Gerson and d'Ailly began to have
second thoughts about the arguments for withdrawal of obedience.
Although the siege had been formally lifted, Benedict was not free
to come and go as he chose. In defiance of the terms of the truce of
April 1399, he was kept under house arrest at the papal palace, a
humiliation for which many found it difficult to forgive the king.
The agents of Louis of Orleans spun webs of intrigue so thickly
around both the royal and papal palaces that on March 11, 1403, it
became possible to smuggle Benedict out of Avignon into Provence,
where he was given sanctuary befitting the true head of the church at
Château Reynard.

His escape was a master-stroke of diplomacy. What opposition to him still lived in France collapsed as soon as news of it became known. On March 29 it was announced that his cardinals had returned to him, and that he had proposed a council to restore unity to the French church. Two days later the people of Avignon made their submission, and received his pardon. Although the Dukes of Berry and Burgundy at court, and Simon of Cramaud at the University, continued to oppose him, France itself submitted to him on May 28, on the sole condition that he would explore the possibility of healing the schism by the way of cession. Benedict moved in triumph to St. Victor's at Marseilles and from there, after a delay which was almost fatal to the new French loyalty to him, sent an embassy to Boniface IX in Rome in September 1404. The chief proposal which this embassy carried was that the two popes should meet at some neutral place and discuss the practicability of prohibiting their cardinals from electing a successor to whichever of them died first, so that within a few years the schism would be extinguished. But the Avignon representatives reached Rome a little too late to make Benedict sole heir to the see, for Boniface was already on his deathbed, and proper discussions were impossible. He died on October 1, 1404, but not before he had repudiated with scorn both Benedict XIII and his proposals. For him, there could only be one end to the schism, the submission of the Avignon rebels to Rome.

The conclave for the election of his successor was delayed for several days while his cardinals argued with Benedict's envoys, trying to convince them that it was their pope who should be forced to resign. It was obviously a good moment to put cession into operation, but Benedict's envoys could not be brought to doubt his title. When they had left the city, refusing to pass on the Roman proposals, the conclave was sealed amid civil disturbances reminiscent of those which had marred the election of 1378. The new Roman pope was proclaimed on October 17: Innocent VII, formerly Cardinal Cosimo Migliorati and Archbishop of Ravenna in the Kingdom of Adria, and by birth, again, a Neapolitan. Before his election, Innocent had sworn to restore the unity of the church by lawful means, through a general council summoned by himself. But continued revolutionary tumult in Rome made it impossible for him to take immediate steps to fulfil that promise. He had inherited a very uncomfortable throne. In 1398, Boniface IX had persuaded and bullied the Romans into surrendering the republican commune by which they had ruled themselves for many years, but they had never fully accepted papal government, as these new disturbances showed. Needing an immediate ally, Innocent chose Ladislas of Durazzo, summoning him to Rome and giving him the fulsome title 'Defender, Preserver and Standard-bearer of the Church'.

Ladislas had for several years been the most powerful ruler in central Italy. His rivals, Louis of Anjou and Gian Galeazzo Visconti, were both gone. Louis, driven out of Naples by Ladislas himself in 1399, had lost faith in the Kingdom of Adria and returned to France. Gian Galeazzo had died in 1402, when he had seemed on the point of smashing the last resistance to his dream of a united kingdom of Italy centred on Milan, and his successor had proved incapable of holding what he had won. There was no one except Ladislas to whom Innocent could turn.

The new Defender of the Church made immediate use of his powers, but was careful to see that only he himself profited from them. His clumsy attempts to pacify Rome in co-operation with the pope's nephew and captain in the city, Luigi Migliorati, provoked fresh risings in the Spring of 1405. The rioters were massacred, and, blamed on all sides, Innocent fled to Viterbo.

Benedict XIII chose that moment to sail from Marseilles to Genoa, expecting to be hailed as the saviour of the church as soon as he set foot on Italian soil. He landed at Genoa, then held for the French crown by Boucicaud, the mercenary who had besieged him at Avignon, on May 16, 1405, and announced that he was prepared instantly to proceed to Viterbo and confer with Innocent. As he must have known, it was no time for conferences. The offer was not accepted, and when plague broke out at Genoa, he made it an excuse to sail back to France.

Innocent VII was personally more interested in scholarship than in political and religious intrigue. In quieter times, he might have made an ideal pope. His dream was to re-establish the University of Rome, first founded a century earlier by Boniface VIII. His bull on the subject, dated September 1, 1406, showed that he longed to make it a centre for the study not only of theology and canon and civil law, but also of medicine, philosophy, logic and rhetoric, and lastly 'in order that our institute shall lack nothing, there shall be there even a master who will give the fullest instruction in the language of Greece, and in its authors'. The work of Michael Chrysoloras was already bearing fruit. Innocent gave employment at the papal court to several men who were to be remembered for their

Renaissance-style humanism, notably Leonardo Bruni, Poggio and Vergerio, all of whom had studied under Chrysoloras at Florence. In 1406, Vergerio, a former lecturer in logic at Padua, became secretary to the Roman curia. His influence over Innocent VII was immense, and great changes were anticipated at Rome when suddenly, on November 6 of that year, Innocent died of apoplexy.

There were thirteen cardinals at Rome to attend the papal funeral and the subsequent conclave. Before the voting, each of them took an oath that, if elected, he would work solely for the reunion of the church, accepting the way of cession if need be to bring it about, and creating no new cardinals during his reign, so that there would be no new generation to perpetuate the evil of schism.

On November 30, the conclave unanimously elected Angelo Correr (or Corrario), who announced that he would rule as Gregory XII. He was eighty years of age and already believed to be feeble. Describing the election, the ambassador of Rupert of the Palatinate, Emperor-elect of Germany since a successful rebellion against Wenceslas in 1400, reported hearing the Cardinal of Palestrina ask the Cardinal of Florence, 'What do you think of that old man?' and the reply, 'Even if he wanted to be corrupt, he is too old and weak; he will not live long.' But the new Roman pope was still sufficiently alert to know his own mind. He declared that he was determined to keep the oath he had taken: 'I will hurry to the place of reunion, by sea, in a fishing boat if necessary, or by land, with a pilgrim's staff in my hand . . . '. In a bull addressed to Benedict XIII only ten or twelve days after his election, he announced his coronation to the French church and underlined his determination to follow the way of cession, if the Avignon cardinals would join with his own to elect a new pope to rule the whole church. He was, he said in a letter accompanying the bull and probably written for him by Bruni the humanist, ready, like the woman who repudiated her child at the judgment-seat of Solomon, to surrender his own child, the church, rather than see it torn in two.

At that moment, Benedict XIII was more inclined than he had ever been to come to terms with Rome. The failure of his mission to Italy in 1405 had lost him credit with the University of Paris, and discussion had begun again around the idea of withdrawing obedience from him. By November 1406, the talk had crystallized into definite proposals, and on the 18th of that month, the University, the king and the clergy of France, sitting in a general assembly, heard Simon

of Cramaud and Jean Petit propose that the king should make himself sovereign in his own dominions, obeying neither the pope of
Avignon nor the pope of Rome. At this assembly, Pierre d'Ailly
spoke strongly in support of papal authority and Benedict's right to
wield it, citing the canons to prove that a pope could be condemned
only for a recognised heresy, and arguing that to withdraw obedience was to transfer the authority of the church from her heart
to her outlying members. He was supported by Guillaume Fillastre,
who was soon to become one of Benedict's cardinals. Against the
opinion currently gaining ground, Fillastre argued that no person or
group of persons, not even a general council, had the right to judge
and condemn a pope. These arguments carried weight with the
assembly. When its resolutions were published, it emerged that the
clergy were unwilling completely to withdraw their obedience from
their pope. His spiritual authority was to remain unimpaired, but
'the ancient liberties' of the church of France were to be restored.
Henceforward it would be illegal for the pope to collate benefices,
prelacies, or any other dignities, or to collect annates or tithes in
France, unless a general council decided otherwise.

These compromise decrees were dated January 7, 1307. Within
weeks of their publication, Benedict had agreed that a meeting
between himself and Gregory XII might have valuable results. For
his own part, he still favoured the way of discussion; but the subject
of cession might be raised in the course of conversations between
the popes, if the times seemed propitious.

Chapter V

THE COUNCIL OF PISA

DIPLOMATIC EXCHANGES between Gregory XII and Benedict XIII in 1406 and 1407 finally brought them to the point of a reluctant agreement to meet at Savona on St. Michael's Day, 1407. Savona was a small city, lying on the coast some twenty-five miles west of Genoa. It was not a neutral place for, lying within the frontiers of the fief of Genoa, it was subject to the French crown under the government of Boucicaud the mercenary captain.

The full weight of the authority of the French king and of the University of Paris had been needed to force the popes to agree to meet. Simon of Cramaud led a solemn delegation consisting of himself, two archbishops, five abbots, three knights, and twenty scholars, first to Avignon, then to Rome, to impress upon the two popes that, whatever their feelings, the schism was not going to be allowed to continue. In Rome, the delegation promised that whoever was pope after the conference should rule the church from St. Peter's, a French concession reassuring to the Romans, but not to Gregory XII. Many flowery compliments were exchanged, but neither pope could be persuaded to accept the principle of cession for himself.

Benedict XIII actually arrived at Savona on the appointed day. There was, however, no sign of Gregory XII. Although Gregory had declared himself ready to hasten 'with a pilgrim's staff', if need be, to the place of reunion when there had been little chance of his being called on to do so, now that the moment had come he was unwilling to enter French territory and meet the formidable Benedict face-to-face. By St. Michael's Day, he had advanced northwards only as far as Siena, well inside the frontiers of friendly Tuscany. Heartened, perhaps, by his obvious hesitancy, and certainly urged on from France, Benedict moved his court from Savona to Porto Venere, the easternmost harbour in the fief of Genoa. Not to be outdone,

Gregory moved on, but only from Siena to Lucca, in northern Tuscany. By January 28, 1408, the popes were only forty miles apart—but still worlds away from one another.

'If one advances,' a member of Gregory's party said, 'the other retreats. One is a sea-beast that would die on the land; the other a land-beast that would drown in water. So, for the sake of what little life and power remains to them, these senile priests imperil the peace and salvation of the Christian world.'

In all probability, that was the truth. Their consciences apart, although the schism had been a great blow to papal prestige, they both had a great deal left to lose, as also did the members of their courts. Gregory was certainly under pressure not to meet Benedict. His chief lay supporters—Sigismund of Hungary and Ladislas of Naples among them—were most anxious that there should be no compromise with the French, and the clerics of his following, led by his nephew Antonio Correr and the Archbishop of Ragusa, urged him to surrender nothing that had been given him by God.

On the other hand, Benedict XIII, whatever his personal convictions and those of his closest advisers may have been, was under increasing pressure early in 1408 to arrive at a quick agreement with Gregory. While he had still been at Savona in November, his most vociferous supporter at the French court, Louis of Orleans, had been assassinated. On January 12, the king of France announced that he would hold himself totally free of any obligation, temporal or spiritual, to either pope unless some measure of union had been achieved by the feast of the Ascension. Benedict's reply to this ultimatum was ambiguous: he demonstrated his eagerness for union by moving to Porto Venere, and emphasized his firmness in a letter reminding the king of the spiritual penalties of refusing to obey the true pope. There was nothing more he could do to bring Gregory to a meeting, except leave French territory and go himself to Lucca— and that he either would not or could not do. Realizing that Benedict no more wanted a settlement than he did, Gregory next half-heartedly proposed meetings at several places within Tuscany, including Pisa and Leghorn. Tempers began to fray. The Italians turned against Gregory as the French had done against Benedict. In April, sensing an opportunity to win a decisive advantage, Benedict despatched galleys down the coast of Italy, as far as the mouth of the Tiber, hoping that they would be received with rejoicing. The

Italians, seeing them as the heralds of a French invasion, did not welcome them, but Ladislas made their coming an excuse to seize not only Rome, on April 25, but also the eastern Papal States as far north as Umbria. Such disturbing news from his Roman headquarters made it unnecessary for Gregory to go on with the pretence of willingness to meet Benedict, a circumstance so providential that he has often been accused of having pre-arranged it. In the absence of hard evidence it is, however, unnecessary to accuse him of such a depth of double-dealing. Ladislas was ambitious enough, and sufficiently afraid of renewed French influence in Italy, to have grasped the potentiality of the situation for himself.

Less than a fortnight later, Gregory took a step which almost proved fatal to his cause. On May 4, he announced from Lucca that under no circumstances would he voluntarily renounce his pontificate.

Why he made so public a pronouncement is obscure. He may have believed that Benedict's attempted 'invasion' of the Patrimony had been a final throw of the dice by a man virtually at the end of his resources. He may even have had prior notice of the debate that was to take place at the University of Paris on May 21, and end with the total withdrawal of obedience to Benedict in France, expunging all his acts and legalizing the persecution of his remaining adherents. On the other hand, he may have been thrown into senile panic by the northward advance of the Neapolitans. For whatever reason he acted as he did, however, he miscalculated the temper of his cardinals. The consistory at Lucca on May 4 was a stormy one, and at its conclusion he found it necessary to forbid the cardinals to leave the city or have any dealings with emissaries from the other side. Heated argument continued for five days, then, on May 9, Gregory told his court that, as cession was forever out of the question, he would increase the number of the cardinals from twelve to sixteen. The new appointments were to be filled by his nephew, Antonio Correr, Gabriel Condulmar (later Eugene IV), the Protonotary Apostolic Giacomo of Udine, and Domenici, Archbishop of Ragusa. Both the fact of these promotions and the names on the list scandalized the cardinals. They had not forgotten the promises Gregory had made at his election, and they knew that all the new men were strongly opposed to cession and conciliarism, and violently anti-French. Despite Gregory's ruling, seven of them left Lucca before the consistory on May 11 at which the bulls of appointment were read and the red hats bestowed. As two cardinals were legitimately absent from Lucca on papal business at the time, there were only three old men to watch the ceremony.

The seven rebels went only as far as Pisa, a dozen miles away, before they halted to issue two statements, one addressed to Gregory, the other to the Christian princes of Europe, explaining what they had done and excusing themselves for having done it. In their letter to Gregory, they informed him that they were appealing 'from the *papa* ill-informed to the *papa* better-informed', from Gregory himself 'to Christ, to a General Council and to the future pope'.

Both popes were now in real difficulty, for both had lost their home bases. In France, new laws closed all channels of income to Benedict. Ladislas's forces in the Papal States made it impossible for Gregory to return to Rome, unless he would go as a virtual prisoner. After some days' delay, while everyone wondered what was to come next, four of Benedict's cardinals sailed to Leghorn to meet six of Gregory's rebels who, as a consequence of their revolt, felt safe to enter the city, even though it was being held for Genoa, and so ultimately for France, by Boucicaud. Both parties of cardinals found themselves, much to their respective masters' dismay when they heard of it, united in the view that only a General Council could save the church. They decided that Gregory and Benedict must both be forced to abdicate. After further deliberation, they announced to the world that a council would be held at Pisa, beginning on March 25, 1409.

Neither Gregory nor Benedict welcomed the news. Both announced general councils of their own, Benedict's to take place at Perpignan, a city then subject to the King of Aragon, from November 1, 1408; Gregory's either at Ravenna or Aquileia, but certainly in the eastern Papal States, from Pentecost 1409. No sooner had they made these pronouncements than each left for a safer place: Benedict, deserted by most of his cardinals and fearing that Boucicaud might have secret orders to force cession on him, sailing for Perpignan, and Gregory, with only five of his cardinals still loyal to him, travelling to Siena, where he hoped the Florentines would protect him.

The moral pressure on the Western world to accept 'the way of the council' intensified all that summer. Among the first to succumb were the Florentines. In September, when Gregory created ten new cardinals, so making unmistakable his intention to perpetuate his court and pontificate, they repudiated him and announced their decision to accept whatever the Council of Pisa should propose. Gregory promptly left for Rimini in the Romagna, and the protection offered to him by Carlo Malatesta.

In that same September, France made final the break with Benedict. At a general assembly of the clergy and nobility, lasting from the 5th to the 11th, it was decided vigorously to apply the decrees passed in January and May. Henceforward it was to be illegal to obey any command issued by Benedict or send any money to him. All his bulls dated after May 16, 1407 were declared void, and all legal cases awaiting hearings in papal courts were transferred either to local penitentiaries or to episcopal courts. The measures taken by this assembly were closely parallelled in those countries dependent on France and hitherto subject to Benedict. The result was that when his council opened at Perpignan on November 1, although about three hundred delegates were present, it could not be called an oecumenical council. Most of the delegates came from the countries traditionally loyal to the non-Roman pope, Scotland, Savoy, Lorraine, Castile and Aragon, although a few prelates from France defied the royal ban to attend. From Benedict's point of view, the council was a failure. The prelates disagreed so violently that many left before any resolutions were taken. The rest begged him to negotiate while he still had time; he should, they said, send legates to Pisa with his offer to abdicate, if Gregory would do the same. Still convinced that it would be sinful for him to follow the way of cession, he at last agreed to abdicate on the day when he learned that Gregory had effectively done so, a day which he could confidently expect would never come. His only other concession to the prevailing desire for an end to the schism was to give reluctant permission for delegates from countries obedient to him to attend the council at Pisa. It was little more than a face-saving gesture, for they would probably have attended whether he had sanctioned such a move or not. Only Scotland, Aragon and Castile were still solid in their adherence.

Gregory XII was on the whole more loyally served, despite the defection of the Florentines. But Henry IV of England announced complete neutrality, as an agreement with the French bound him to do. So too did Wenceslas, who was still technically King of the Romans, though he had only functioned as king in Bohemia since the

German revolution of the year 1400, and even there was in serious trouble with Hussite heretics and political rebels. Many of the lesser princes of Europe also decided in favour of neutrality and of the Council of Pisa, among them the rulers of Lorraine, Holland, Poland, Austria, Navarre, Portugal, half of Romagna and Cyprus, together with the Electors of Cologne and Maintz, the University of Bologna, and Louis of Anjou, speaking as claimant to the thrones of Naples and Sicily. But impressive as this list appears, Gregory still had massive support, most notably from Rupert of the Rhine, emperor since 1400, five of the electors and most of the lesser princes of Germany, Ladislas—still occupying Rome and the southern Papal States—and the kings of Scandinavia.

Although some, especially among the rulers, probably allowed political expediency to determine their attitude towards the rival popes and the proposed council, for others the choice was a hard one. In their opinion, wide acceptance of the proposal for a council first made by Gelnhausen and Langenstein more than twenty years earlier did not make it any less illegal and revolutionary than it had been at first. Although such revered scholars as Gerson, d'Ailly and Cramaud had found arguments to support the view that authority in the church resided ultimately in Christ himself on the one hand and the whole body of the faithful on the other, the final sources of that opinion remained as suspect as ever. Canon law and the collections of decretals still spoke of the Supreme Pontiff 'who can be judged by no one', as they had for a thousand years. Although such advocates of conciliarism as the canonist Francis Zarbarella maintained that the word 'church' can mean only 'the congregation of the faithful' in contexts where no other definition is specifically mentioned, there were in fact several other meanings with which it was commonly endowed; and even Zarbarella himself used the phrase 'the mystical body' to mean both 'the congregation of all the faithful' and the unitary organism which came into legal existence when a bishop and his canons met in chapter.

The kind of interior debate in which those with tender consciences, and an awareness of political realities, found themselves immersed in the winter of 1408–9 is vividly illustrated by the footnotes made on a copy of the cardinals' bull convoking the council by an unknown scholar, probably from Heidelberg, some time before the council met. He realized that there should be reforms, but not, in his judgment, 'in the constitution of the church'. The canonists were going too far: their conciliar theory overthrew the foundations of the church:

> One must submit unconditionally to the pope, however wicked he may be. Gregory XII is the true pope. Hence it is unlawful to deny obedience to him, and one cannot damage him in any way, no matter what good may be the purpose of it. The cardinals' withdrawal of obedience, made without any semblance of due form, is invalid; the arguments made in support of this action carry no weight. It is impossible to say that Gregory has committed a heresy by being involved in the schism . . . The pope will have to give account to God for the vows he made to bring unity to the church; no mere human being has any right to judge him in respect of them, nor has an assembly of bishops, and still less one of the cardinals . . . (*To let them decide the church's future would be to make them the vicars of Christ*) . . . In any case a union of the two colleges cannot be acceptable (*because one of them must be illegal, and the other cannot legalize it*) . . . They are trying to force the hand of the Holy Ghost! The whole affair has been arranged to put the contrivances of the French into effect with some semblance of regularity . . .

His doubts were shared by most of the Germans, but he was less than fair in attributing responsibility for the whole affair to the machinations of the French. It would, perhaps, be truer to say that canonists such as Gerson and Zarbarella were ready to use French national ambitions to win what they considered the most important of prizes, the unity of the Church. Dietrich of Niem, who was with the Roman curia through most of the years of the schism, expressed their attitude most bluntly in his treatize 'On uniting and reforming the church by the way of a general council', written, probably, in 1410 after the Council of Pisa had failed: 'The end of unity sanctifies all means: craft, deception, violence, bribery, imprisonment and death. For all law is for the sake of the whole body, and the individual must give way to the general good.' This was the doctrine of expediency in its most pernicious form, as only despairing men would dare to express it. But the jurists were in despair, and, despite the protests of the Germans, preparations for the council went ahead.

When the delegates assembled at Pisa in 1409 they made an imposing array; there were twenty-two cardinals, drawn from both camps, four patriarchs, eighty bishops in person and the delegates of two hundred more, eighty-nine abbots, forty-one priors, the heads of four religious orders, representatives of more than a hundred cathedral chapters, more than three hundred canonists and jurists, and official envoys from almost every state in Europe. The president was the aged Cardinal-Bishop of Palestrina, Guy de Malesset, the Cardinal of Poitiers who thirty years earlier had helped vote Urban VI to the papal throne. Now, at the first session of the Council of Pisa on March 25, it was his duty in the council's name solemnly to summon Angelo Correr and Peter de Luna to stand forth for judgment. Naturally, neither Gregory nor Benedict was at the self-styled council. De Malesset had their names called at the doors of the church of St. Michael, where the council fathers were assembled, heard preliminary arguments for their deposition as contumacious heretics, and suspended judgment for a week, so that he could hear arguments as to why they should not be condemned.

Gregory had powerful advocates among the assembled noblemen and prelates. Rupert of the Rhine and Carlo Malatesta both spoke strongly in his support, arguing that he could not attend the council because the Florentines were now among his bitterest enemies. When these arguments were rejected, the Bishop of Worms, with the agreement of all the imperial party, presented the council's fourth session with a document listing twenty-four legal arguments against the legitimacy of the council itself. The arguments were very similar to those of the unknown canonist in his gloss on the cardinals' bull: the true pope could be judged by no one except for heresy—and schism, even if it could be proved against him (which it could not, for how can the pope separate from himself?), was not heresy—and as there could be no true council without the pope at the head of it, the combination of the two cardinalates must be invalid. The twenty-four charges against the validity of the council were answered point by point at the seventh session, with a great wealth of argument drawn from canonists past and present. But the weakness of the cardinals' case could not be concealed: it suffered from the same disabilities as the case made by the ultramontane cardinals at the beginning of the Great Schism, the unwillingness of early canonists to consider situations in which it might be necessary to depose a pope. Although the charges were answered, the critics of Pisa were not convinced. Fundamentally the argument turned on the acceptance or rejection of the concept of the church as a corporation, a minority opinion, first put forward by the canonist Hostensius, and finding wide support only during the period of the Great Schism itself, when the older and sounder opinion, giving absolute sovereignty to the pope unless he was a proven heretic, became too uncomfortable to sustain. The Council of Pisa itself recognized the weakness of the position it had adopted, and in an attempt to strengthen it, passed a resolution at its eleventh session declaring and defining its own powers: 'This council is a General Council . . . representing the whole Catholic Church, and has the right, as the supreme judge on earth, to take cognizance of, decide and determine' the case against Gregory XII—and so also against Benedict.

Having voted itself competent, the council then set itself to its real task: the deposition of two popes and election of another, whatever the opposition. The trial of Gregory and Benedict occupied six full sessions, and as neither was guilty of any known offence against the faith, a new 'heresy' had to be invented with which they could be charged. The crime chosen was the heresy of schism. It was argued that by not ending the schism, although they had both promised to do so, they had denied faith in the 'one, holy, catholic and apostolic church' of the creeds and so were worthy of condemnation as obdurate heretics. The charges were a fabrication, and everyone knew it; but popes could be deposed only for heresy so there was no other approach possible. Both Benedict and Gregory were duly condemned at the fifteenth session of the council on June 5, in the most solemn terms:

> Having invoked the name of our Lord Jesus Christ, this Holy Council, representative of the Universal Church, recognized as having competence and authority in the matter, pronounces, defines, declares and decrees [Angelo Correr and Peter de Luna to be] notorious schismatics . . . and heretics . . . who are by that fact rendered unworthy of all honour and dignity, including that of the pontificate.

Having resolved that trifling difficulty—the whole council was a farce, although one most solemnly played—the delegates next turned their attention to the less open-and-shut matter of who should be their puppet-pope.

The man longing to be chosen was Balthazar Cossa, a Neapolitan nobleman who, after an early career as a sea captain—some said a pirate captain—had turned to the church and been made a cardinal in 1402. It was he who, as Gregory's legate in the Papal States, had been chiefly responsible for the failure to prevent Ladislas of Durazzo annexing their largest part the previous year, and so involved Gregory in the shame of having to offer 25,000 florins to buy them back. He was said to hate his former master and did nothing at Pisa to allay the rumour that he longed to supplant him. But at the time he was unsuccessful.

The council decided that the united cardinalates alone should vote for the new pope, and that to forestall any dispute after the election, the successful candidate must have two-thirds of the votes of each cardinalate separately. In law, the only man among them indisputably entitled to vote for anybody—if the papal throne was indeed vacant—was Guy de Malesset, the sole surviving cardinal, apart from Peter de Luna, of Gregory XI. The council hoped that, by delegating all its powers to the cardinals, it would validate the votes of the invalid cardinals appointed by the still unidentified anti-pope, and that the world would accept their unanimous choice.

They were vain hopes, as subsequent events proved. The conclave itself was a long and stormy one, lasting from June 15 to 26. It elected as its pope Cardinal Peter Philarges, who called himself Alexander V.

Peter Philarges, known as Peter of Candia, was a native of Crete, and so a citizen of Venice. He was a Franciscan who had studied law at Padua, Oxford and Paris and, following tradition, had written a commentary on the *Sentences*. After brief appointments as a missionary in Lithuania and a teacher of law at Pavia, he had entered the service of Gian Galeazzo Visconti and, in 1395, had conducted the negotiations which had bought him the title Duke of Milan. In 1420, Gian Galeazzo had made him Archbishop of Milan, and, after the duke's death, he had been a member of the council of regency. Innocent VII had appointed him to the cardinalate in 1405, and he had since been a prominent advocate of the conciliar movement at Rome. Gregory XII hated him: so also, once he had been elected, did Balthazar Cossa. But the council recognized him as the only true pope, and he in his turn recognized the council, making his first pontifical action the authentication of all its proceedings so far. However, although France and England and their allies claimed that he was the saviour of the church, neither Benedict nor Gregory would treat with him, and the last sessions of the council were devoted to plans for eliminating them and reforming the church through regular councils. Oaths of allegiance to the new pope were required from all suspected of favouring anyone else.

The loyalty of the Dominicans was of special concern. Unless their Order, which still supplied the majority of the church's inquisitors,

agreed to the Pisan pope, there was little hope of his general acceptance; and their loyalty was in doubt, for the Archbishop of Ragusa,
the prelate most outspoken in Gregory's support at Pisa, was himself a Dominican. To ensure that there would be no wavering in the
ranks of the Order, every suspect Dominican was required to recite a
long oath of allegiance to Alexander, specially composed to leave no
loopholes. It opened uncompromisingly:

I, N., professed in the Order of Friars Preacher, having been made aware
of the divisions and schisms by which I was ensnared into believing in,
supporting and clinging to those foster-children of hell Peter de Luna
and Angelo Correr, who were known to those of their obediences as
Benedict XIII and Gregory XII, relinquish both them and all others
believing in and supporting them, and those also adhering to their
supporters and defending them or compliant to them, or accepting
help or privilege from them, and therefore, drawn thereto by my own
resolve, I do now and forever, by my free and spontaneous will, and the
grace of God, return to unity with the Holy See, publicly confessing my
error, and by my present action do adhere to the Catholic Faith, and do
believe and hold whatsoever is believed and held and taught by Holy
Mother Church, presided over by our Lord, the Lord Alexander, by the
providence of God the fifth of that name, and [I do further believe and
hold] that the same Lord Alexander was and is now the true Roman
Pontiff, and true Vicar of Christ and successor of Peter, canonically
elected, enthroned and crowned as Roman Pontiff by the cardinals
whose right it was to enthrone him on the vacant apostolic throne, and
crown him. . . .

It was all very dramatic, but not markedly effective. Both Benedict
and Gregory were still free. While the council was still in session,
Benedict was laying plans for a future under the protection of Martin
I of Aragon and Sicily, and Gregory was scheming for the downfall
of both his rivals at a council of his own.

After much hesitation, he had decided that it should be held at
Cividale in Friuli, in the far north-east of Italy, as remote as possible
from the French, Balthazar Cossa, Alexander V and Benedict XIII.
Unfortunately for his reputation, it was not a success. Although
Rupert of the Rhine sent delegates, it could not be called a 'general'
council. Gregory presided at the first session, on July 6, by summoning both Benedict XIII and Alexander V to appear before him,
and putting himself immediately under the protection of Ladislas of
Durazzo, whose quarrel with the Roman papacy it would now be the

work of Alexander V and Cardinal Cossa's mercenaries to resolve. Then his affairs took a grave turn. His own native Venice transferred its obedience from him to Alexander, and when he tried to depose the Archbishop of Aquileia for this betrayal, the people rose against him. On September 6, he was forced to flee in disguise. One of Ladislas's galleys carried him to Ortona and from there he made his way to Gaeta, to prepare for war.

He was not the only pope in difficulties. Alexander V had been forced to accept the protection of Cossa, and was shut up in Bologna, while Cossa, its *Vicarius* and military commander, planned the reconquest of the Papal States with Louis II of Anjou (whose enfeoffment with Naples had been revived and confirmed by the Council of Pisa), and the Florentines.

An error of judgment on Ladislas's part gave this new alliance some quick victories. Misled, perhaps, by the ease with which Genoa threw off French rule in September 1409, he underestimated Louis's military capacity and, almost contemptuously, chose this moment to go to Hungary in an attempt to overthrow Sigismund and so seize the throne that his father had died trying to claim. In his absence, Paolo Orsini betrayed Rome to Louis on January 3, 1410, and although Naples stood firm and Gregory XII remained safe at Gaeta, the western Papal States were lost. His return to Italy steadied his remaining allies, but all seemed set for the triumphal entry of the Pisan pope into Rome when, on May 3, it was suddenly announced that Alexander had died at Bologna.

As his death was sudden, it was naturally said that he had been poisoned. Many declared that they knew the poisoner: Balthazar Cossa, the Cardinal-legate and Vicar of Bologna, his rival at Pisa, against whom he had recently issued a bull naming him the father of an illegitimate son and daughter. Bologna was so convinced of the truth of this rumour that it never forgave the cardinal, even after he had been elected pope there on May 17.

Later in his career, almost every imaginable crime was to be alleged against him. He was almost certainly guilty of simony at his election, buying the papal throne with promises of money and promotion, reinforced with threats. A cardinal-deacon at the time of his election, he was ordained priest on May 25 and crowned the following day as Pope John XXIII. His election and consecration exposed to the world the futility of the proceedings at Pisa. Before the council, there had been two self-perpetuating administrations in church. Now there were three. To the advocates of conciliarism, the situation was disastrous. As one of them wrote, 'the infamous duality had spawned an accused trinity'.

The council had demanded not only unity, but also reforms from its popes. The primary aim of these reforms was to be the restoration of the (largely imaginary) 'ancient liberties' of colleges of electors and individual bishops and collators, by the decentralization of the administration of the church and the dismantling of the elaborate machinery for collecting money and information set up at Avignon during the previous century, and now imitated by all three popes. John XXIII was quick to learn that it is impossible to fight a war without money. Despite the objections of those who longed for an end to papal wars, he restored old forms of taxation and invented new ones to keep his armies together. Much later, he declared, 'They say I have a pliable conscience—but I have done more than any other pontiff for the Papal States.' He had in fact reconquered them. By April 1411, he was able to enter Rome and take possession of the visible signs of pontifical authority, the palaces and basilicas of the city. The following month, his ally Louis II heavily defeated the Neapolitans under Ladislas at Roccasecca, within the frontiers of Naples and only a few miles from Gaeta, where Gregory had believed himself safe. But that summer, good fortune deserted him. Bologna rebelled and other cities rumbled with discontent. The strongest of the mercenary captains deserted him for Ladislas, and Louis II failed to take advantage of his initial victories. John announced a synod at Rome to put into operation some of the reforms demanded by the council, and preached a crusade to raise money for the war against Gregory and Ladislas, offering huge and very expensive indulgences to the faithful throughout the Western world.

The dignity of the synod was spoiled at the beginning, it was maliciously said afterwards, by a large owl which flew out from behind the altar at the inaugural Mass of the Holy Spirit, and fixing its eyes on the pope, sat screeching at him, until the cardinals, flapping at it, drove it away. The money raised for the crusade was added to the income from the new taxes and offered as an inducement to Ladislas to change his mind about the Council of Pisa and transfer his allegiance from Gregory to John.

Secret negotiations for this betrayal occupied the first half of 1412. But by October, everything was arranged. Ladislas gravely

announced that he thought it might not be good for his soul to go on
supporting Gregory. John returned the compliment by stating that a
treaty had been drawn up between himself and the loyal Gonfalonier
of the Church, Ladislas of Durazzo, King of Naples and Sicily,
Lord of the hitherto-papal cities of Ascoli, Viterbo, Perugia and
Benevento. Ladislas locked 120,000 gold florins away in his treasury
and thanked the pope for promising to maintain a thousand cavalry-
men to help in the subjugation of the Aragonese King of Sicily. At the
same time, John made public plans for a proper council of Rome to
implement the decisions of Pisa, and named several new cardinals,
among them the chief advocates of conciliarism at Paris, Pierre
d'Ailly, Francis Zarbarella and William Fillastre.

By the end of the month, Gregory had fled from Gaeta to his last
ally in Italy, Carlo Malatesta, Lord of Rimini; and Louis of Anjou
had crept away to France.

John seemed to be on the point of total victory. But two factors
were working against him: his unpopularity with his closest subjects,
the Italians, and the depth of the conciliarists' distrust for the papacy,
a distrust not eliminated by the canonists' promotion. These factors
were not unrelated, for it was the arrogant use of papal power that
alienated both the people and the new cardinals.

The canonists saw the dangers of that arrogance: the people
experienced them. At Rome, papal taxation to meet the costs of the
new alliance with Ladislas raised the price of all basic commodities
disastrously: the price of wine, for example, rose nine-fold in
1412-13. Moreover, the alliance itself was mistrusted. Ladislas had
sacked the city only four years earlier, and Antonius Patri spoke for
many when he told John, 'We Romans would rather eat our children
than have that serpent as our Lord.' But John was not interested in
their opinions.

The real thoughts of the canonists continued to be those savagely
expressed by Dietrich of Niem in 1410. They wanted a proper
council, representing the whole church and given full powers to force
unity on the popes. Dietrich himself actually called for the transfer
of all papal authority to such a council. Of what use, he asked, is a
chief shepherd who thinks of nothing except making money out of
his flock, 'who passes his time living in luxury, who loves simony,
sells benefices, steals through subsidies and continually makes new
laws and regulations to heap up more money in his treasury?' The
first act of a real council 'if it truly desired to see complete unity and

the wiping-out of schism' would be 'to limit and put an end to the coercive power usurped by the popes'.

Dietrich, who over more than thirty years with the Roman curia had seen so much to distress him, had lost his faith in the papacy. But if the papacy would not reform itself, who could force reform on it? The failure of the Council of Pisa had shown that the 'local' authority of kings did not command enough respect. To be effective, a general council to control the popes would have to be summoned by someone with equal, if different, authority. There was only one possibility: the hero of the old Roman dream, a king of the Romans who would prove himself a fit emperor for the world by the firmness and justice of his action in ending the schism for the common good and in fulfilment of the common will. 'Unless there is an emperor, or a just King of the Romans, a stern man, universally acknowledged, the schism will not only persist but, we are bound to fear, will become ever worse.' What was wanted, in fact, was the benevolent dictator, described philosophically by Marsilius and William of Ockham, and poetically by Dante and his followers.

The difficulty in 1410–11 was that there was no emperor, nor even a universally acknowledged King of the Romans. Rupert of the Rhine had died, leaving to claim the throne the three heirs of Charles IV, Wenceslas of Bohemia, Sigismund of Hungary, and Jost, Count of Luxemburg and former Elector of Brandenburg.

The seven electors could agree only that Wenceslas of Bohemia should not be restored. The princes had forced his abdication as King of the Romans in favour of Rupert a decade earlier, and no one was willing to risk putting power back into his hands, although he tried to claim it by virtue of his former election. Two elections in 1410—one on September 20, the other on October 1—produced two Kings of the Romans, Sigismund and Jost. For a year it looked as though Germany was on the verge of a schism as obdurate as that in the papacy. Then Jost died and Wenceslas, lacking firm support and in difficulties with nationalists and heretics in Bohemia, submitted to his brother Sigismund.

Sigismund's chief concern throughout his adult life had been the safety of the eastern frontiers of the empire and the stability of his own kingdom of Hungary. His loyalty in the Great Schism had always been that which he had inherited from his father, the Emperor Charles IV, to the pope of Rome. His three most significant contacts with Italian politics had all been unfortunate. Twice the Durazzi had tried to seize his throne, and at the Council of Pisa his arguments in support of Gregory XII had been brushed aside as irrelevant. The question in 1412 was whether or not he would be willing for the sake of the church to involve himself in Italian affairs again. And if so, would he still feel loyalty only to Gregory XII?

The canonists were not alone in asking these questions. John XXIII was also awake to the possibility that here was a new ally. He welcomed Sigismund's election, and when he announced plans for the council to begin in Rome on April 1, 1413, revealed that he was deeply concerned over the problems of Germany. The main subject of debate would be the Hussite question, and Sigismund's co-opera-tion would be most cordially welcomed.

Chapter VI

THE POPE OF ROME AND THE PREACHER
OF PRAGUE

IN PLANNING to discuss Hussitism at the Council of Rome in
1413, John XXIII and his cardinals have sometimes been
accused of having deliberately turned their backs on the real
problem of the day, the schism in the papacy. But although it may
seem to us, from our vantage point in time, that the most obvious
subjects for discussion were the proper relations between popes,
cardinals, national churches and scholars, Hussitism and the control
of the empire may well have seemed genuinely more important at the
time. If John could have won Sigismund and controlled the Hussites,
not only his own position, but also that of his conciliarist cardinals,
would have been immeasurably strengthened. Moreover, there was
no doubt at all that the total repudiation of the papacy and the
hierarchical church preached by the Lollards of England and the
Hussites of Bohemia was a growing threat to the whole church.

It is not certain how far towards denying papal authority Wyclif
himself went in his preaching. The propositions attributed to him
and condemned at London in 1382, two years before his death,
denied the authority of sinful bishops and their ability to administer
valid sacraments, condemned the doctrine of transubstantiation and
the sacrifice of the Mass as unscriptural, and agreed with the earlier
Poor Men and Fraticelli that 'it is contrary to Holy Scripture that
ecclesiastics should possess anything'. Before his death, Wyclif had
denounced both Clement VII and Urban VI as antichrists and
servants of the devil, and agreed with Gelnhausen and his Parisian
followers that only a general council could save the church. All this
went far enough, but before the end of the century Lollard teaching
had become much more extreme.

The *Lollard Conclusions* of 1394 claimed that 'our common priesthood, which started at Rome . . . is not the priesthood that Christ
ordained' and argued that priests, being bound to celibacy, must in

the nature of things be sodomites, and nuns, also forbidden to marry, must practise bestiality, abortion and infanticide. They denied the value of all the traditional practices encouraged by this evil priesthood, including every sacrament except baptism, and all exorcisms, pilgrimages and prayers to the saints, declaring them idolatrous and worse than useless. Indulgences, they said, were founded on fraud, and auricular confession was no more than an opportunity for sexual intrigue. For good measure, the *Conclusions* also denied the ultimate authority of the state, claiming that it had no right to wage war because Christ had taught 'a man to love his enemies, and show pity to them, and not to kill them'.

To replace both the hierarchical church and the traditional state, the Lollards called for the establishment of an ideal realm of faith, hope and love, where everyone would have enough of the simple necessities of life, and the 'unnecessary arts' of such craftsmen as armourers and goldsmiths would no longer be practised.

The principles of Lollardy were probably carried to Bohemia by members of the household of Richard II's Queen Anne, the sister of Wenceslas. They took firmest root there among the fervently nationalist Czechs, neither the German nobility nor the Slovenes being deeply infected for some years. From the beginning of the fifteenth century onwards the centre from which Lollard teachings spread was the Bethlehem Chapel, founded in Prague in 1391 with a constitution requiring its administrators to arrange for two sermons to be preached there in Czech every feast day. Bethlehem's most celebrated incumbent was John Hus, who began to preach church reform in the Czech language just at the time when Czech-born doctors of theology first outnumbered the Germans at the University of Prague. Hus's attacks on abuses were in the tradition of Wyclif and earlier reformers: his most frequent targets were simony and clerical luxury. The violence of his denunciations led to his suspension from preaching by the Archbishop of Prague for a short time, but during his early years at Bethlehem he was not noted for being an extremist, except in his manner. Lollard teachings in their most stringent form, denying the efficacy of the sacraments and condemning the clergy, were proposed to Prague University for condemnation in 1403 and again in 1407. On the first occasion, the masters refused to go further than to rule that Wyclif's doctrines ought not to be taught; on the second, they actually condemned the heresy contained in forty-five propositions, but not the fundamental

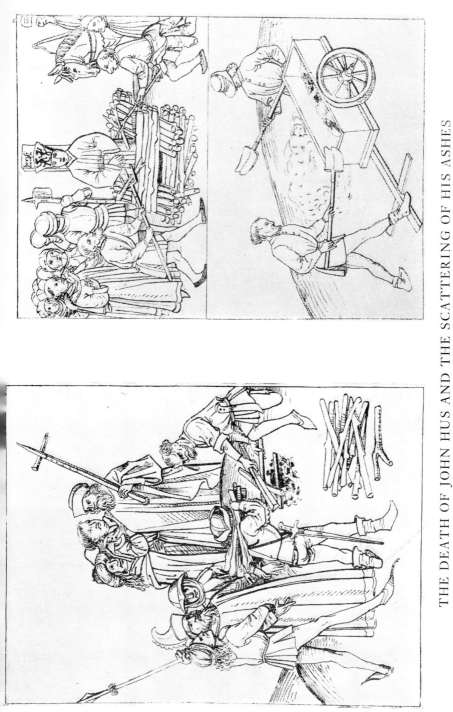

THE DEATH OF JOHN HUS AND THE SCATTERING OF HIS ASHES

From Ulrich von Richental's Chronicle of the Council of Constance,
a facsimile of the 1465 edition

PETER DE LUNA
(BENEDICT XIII)

thinking on which they were based. Hus was among the professors who refused to condemn Wyclif and was warned to think again. Complaints against his own preaching were constantly made to Archbishop Zybnek, and in 1408 he was deprived of his licence to preach.

It had been one of Wyclif's earliest unorthodox theories that no one needs a licence to preach: God alone gives the power and authority to do so. Faithful to his master's principles, Hus continued to preach both after his suspension, and after an excommunication pronounced against all Bohemian followers of Wyclif in the year 1409. By then, he was an undisguised rebel, and he spoke so plainly against the archbishop that after one of his sermons the mob sacked the archiepiscopal palace. Archbishop Zybnek felt compelled to leave the city, although he gave it out that he was going voluntarily to attend the Council of Pisa, where he switched his allegiance from Gregory XII to the conciliar pope Alexander V.

Alexander owed his elevation to the papacy largely to the universities' support for conciliar theory. Hence it was with considerable optimism that the doctors of Prague appealed to him against their archbishop's rulings on Wyclifitism. But the anarchy of Wyclif's system was unacceptable to the new pope. He banned preaching by any but licensed preachers in licensed chapels and ordered the destruction of Lollard texts. In January 1410, Archbishop Zybnek burned Wyclif's writings at Prague and excommunicated Hus and his adherents. This sentence was followed by riots in the churches and streets of the city, and the university announced that Hus would be the main speaker at a disputation in defence of the teachings of Wyclif. The archbishop thereupon pronounced a second excommunication against Hus, and the new pope of Rome, John XXIII, summoned him to the city to answer charges of heresy before a commission presided over by Cardinal Odo Colonna. He refused to make the journey, and succeeded in convincing King Wenceslas that his theories were advantageous to the state, and that he therefore deserved royal protection.

There matters rested until the pardoners preaching John's crusade against Ladislas of Durazzo and Gregory XII reached Bohemia in the spring of 1412. Although Hus's protector Wenceslas and the professors had pronounced themselves in favour of the crusade, Hus denounced the proffered indulgences so fiercely that Bohemia was brought close to revolt. When three of the noisiest opponents of the crusade and of the government were arrested, summarily executed and buried in the Bethlehem Chapel, the Czechs began immediately to speak of them as national martyrs. Hus hesitated at first, but soon he too was preaching about the martyrs of Prague. Wenceslas withdrew his protection and set himself to destroy the heretical movement, and with it Czech nationalism. In July 1412, at his insistence, a synod at Prague uniting the city clergy and the doctors of the university condemned fifty-one Wyclifite propositions, but Hus chose to defend five of them which he said were capable of orthodox interpretation, and argued against the burning of Wyclif's writings, on the grounds that unless students were permitted to read them they would never understand what was wrong in them. Meanwhile, new complaints against Hus had been sent to Rome. After studying them, Cardinal Colonna again summoned the preacher to appear before his commission, and when Hus gave no sign of intending to do so, he was condemned *vitandus* on July 29. In theory, this form of excommunication was especially harsh, amounting to a form of ecclesiastical outlawry. Everyone was forbidden to hold any intercourse with the excommunicate person, and if he was given shelter anywhere, the whole district was put under an interdict.

The sentence of excommunication *vitandus* against Hus reached Bohemia in September, but Hus continued to preach openly in Prague for another month. Then he went underground, re-appearing from time to time to preach, and publishing numerous treatises in defence of Wyclif and Czech nationalism, much to the chagrin of the authorities, who regarded him as especially dangerous because of his subtlety as a disputant and magnetism as a demagogue.

Thus when John XXIII announced the Council of Rome for April 1413, Wyclifitism was a real threat to the authority of the church in Bohemia, as well as in England, where Oldcastle was bringing Lollards to the point of revolt against the Prince of Wales, soon to be Henry V, the chief persecutor of their sect under the Statute *de Haeretico Comburendo*. The fact that John concerned himself with Wyclif and Hus during the period of preparation for the council has sometimes been represented as a deliberate (and, by implication, unworthy) attempt on his part to divert attention from his own shortcomings as the pope of unity that conciliarists wanted him to be. But there is evidence that Cardinals Colonna and d'Ailly were both anxious for him to act against the heretics. They were a real danger, and besides, d'Ailly and his fellow-conciliarists, notorious reformers and former professors themselves, may well have believed that they were all in danger of being identified with the extremists of Prague, and liable to fall under the same condemnation, unless they dissociated themselves publicly from the Wyclifite movement. When, on February 2, 1413, John condemned all the writings of Wyclif and his followers, and called on Sigismund to help him put down heresy and restore the unity of the church, he was following the advice of his cardinals as well as the inclinations of his own conscience.

Wyclifitism would have been the main subject of discussion at the Council of Rome if it had ever taken place. But at the beginning of March, it became obvious that the time was not ripe for a council. The new King of England was not yet crowned. The old King of France was suffering from one of his periodic bouts of insanity and his country was seething with rebellion. Bohemia was in confusion, and the infection seemed likely to spread to Germany, where Sigismund's control was not yet complete. In Italy itself, Gregory XII was still receiving protection from Carlo Malatesta at Rimini; there were rumours of war from the Tyrol, where Frederick of Habsburg, Duke of Austria, had for a decade been trying to extend his power into the Swiss Alps; and Ladislas of Durazzo, although bought so expensively for John's party the previous year, was threatening not to go and conquer Sicily but to destroy John himself if the pope did not withdraw his appeal to Sigismund, the enemy of the Durazzi for thirty years. On March 3, therefore, John announced that the council must be postponed until December, when it might be possible to convene a more representative assembly.

This announcement did not satisfy Ladislas. His always uncertain temper and judgment were now damaged beyond repair by the mental effects of the syphilis which was to kill him the following year. He suspected a plot against his rule in Naples, especially as John gave no sign of breaking his agreements with Sigismund. In June, he mounted a ferocious and devastating attack against the Patrimony, and drove John out of Rome, putting him to flight together with his cardinals and the Byzantine Manuel Chrysoloras, who had been at the papal court for discussions intended to lead to reunion between the Latins and the Greeks.

John fled north. Both Florence and Milan, torn by internal discord, refused him more than minimal aid. His only hope was Sigismund, who was in Lombardy, trying to bring order to the

Tyrol. At the end of August, John, settled uncomfortably at Sutri, sent an embassy to him consisting of Cardinals Zarbarella and Challant, and Manuel Chrysoloras, seeking his immediate aid, and promising to summon a truly general council as soon as he was safe. The embassy met Sigismund at Teserete in the Duchy of Milan on October 13: on the 31st, without waiting for confirmation from John of the agreement reached in their talks, Sigismund announced to the world from Cremona that a general council would begin just a year later, on November 1, 1414, at Constance, a city then under his personal jurisdiction. It was not until December 9, after John had met Sigismund in person at Lodi and received something of an ultimatum from him, that the pope of Rome himself promulgated a bull summoning all the prelates and princes of the world to meet him and 'his son' the emperor-elect at Constance, and confer with them on the future of the church.

Sigismund's precipitancy reflected both his decisive character and the advice it may confidently be supposed that he had received from Chrysoloras and the conciliarist cardinals. In the East, the authority of the emperor to summon councils had never been successfully challenged, and it is difficult to imagine that Chrysoloras would not have reminded Sigismund of the power he was said to have inherited. Zarbarella had been teaching before the Council of Pisa that the authority of a general council flows not from whoever summons it, but from those attending it: anyone could summon a council, and as long as it really was general when it met, it would speak with the authority of the whole church, the 'University of the Faithful'.

The news of the proposed council was welcomed wherever conciliarism, loyalty to Sigismund or fear of Ladislas was strong. Sigismund's allies, the kings and princes of the eastern marches of Germany and Henry V of England, immediately signified their willingness to sent delegates, as also did most of the lords of northern Italy. Bologna relented towards John, and offered him protection until the council met. France, at war again with England and internally divided, received the emperor's proposals less warmly, although the University of Paris and most French prelates promised to attend. Gregory XII and Benedict XIII, each with his party of faithful adherents, denounced the whole idea. Spain, Sicily and Scotland, firmly loyal to Benedict, refused to send delegations: for them, the true council had opened and closed at Perpignan in 1408.

During the months of John's stay at Bologna, he seems gradually to have realized how close he was to disaster. But everyone treated him with decent respect, and his principal enemy, Ladislas, was still almost universally hated. The Neapolitan threat to northern Italy increased daily during the first half of 1414, and became acute when, in June, Ladislas forced Florence to accept a treaty of alliance. But then, in camp at Narni, he suddenly became too ill to carry on. He was taken back to Naples, and died there on August 6, leaving as his heir his ineffectual daughter Joanna II.

His death made central and northern Italy safe, and permitted John to see the real feelings of those around him. With Ladislas no longer menacing the peace of Europe, preparations for the council quickened, and John realized that he was likely to be its first victim. When he rode out from Bologna at the beginning of October, he knew that he was once again in urgent need of a respite and an ally. He tried to persuade the nine cardinals of his escort that they should turn south and retake Rome, but they made it clear to him that soldiering was no longer his business. The cavalcade turned north, towards the Tyrol and Switzerland.

It was in the Tyrol, at Meran, in mid-October, that he found his ally, in the person of Frederick of Habsburg, Duke of Austria.

Frederick presented himself to the papal party as a noble mountain guide, proposing to lead it in person over the passes of the Arlberg. By the time the pope and the duke could look down on to the lake of Constance, they were firm friends. The alliance cost John the promise of six thousand florins a year to his newly-named Captain-General of the Armies of the Church.

Seeing the lake spread out before him as the party descended the passes, John is said to have murmured, 'So that is the net they have spread for foxes!' Although the authenticity of this remark has been questioned, it reflects what must have been his thoughts, for he was being universally blamed for the failure of the policies of the Council of Pisa. He admitted openly that the council was none of his choosing: 'But what can I do?' he asked Bartholomew Valori, 'when my fate drags me along . . .'

However unwillingly he followed his destiny, it dragged him into Constance on October 28. He was among the first of the important delegates to arrive, but the city was already crowded with lesser prelates and masters of theology and their numerous dependents, mercenary soldiers, hucksters and mountebanks, pickpockets and prostitutes. John took over the bishop's palace, and renamed it the Apostolic Palace for the occasion. He was regally treated by the city fathers. It was announced that the emperor would arrive at Christmas and that the council was expected to sit until Easter. On All Saints Day at the cathedral of Constance, John celebrated Mass and preached the sermon formally inaugurating the council. Cardinal Zarbarella read the bull of convocation of 1413, and the date of the first working session was fixed for November 3.

In fact, however, the only important event on that day was the arrival of John Hus in Constance. Lured out of hiding by the temporary lifting of the ban against him, protected by three Bohemian noblemen nominated by Sigismund and the promise of an imperial safe-conduct, he rode in with an escort of thirty horsemen and eight personal servants in two carriages. His accusers from Prague were already in the city, armed with their own arguments and a legal opinion obtained from Jean Gerson of Paris earlier in the year, ruling that Hus's teaching on the sacraments and grace was heretical. While Hus made his domestic arrangements, settling his people in a lodging in the Paulsgasse, both his noble protectors and his accusers went to the Apostolic Palace to inform John of his coming.

His arrival, and the failure to appear of so many men important to the success of the council, led to the postponement of the first session to November 5, then to November 16.

Meanwhile, Hus's imperial safe-conduct had reached Constance. On the 9th, the Apostolic Palace informed him that he could now regard himself free from the ban of excommunication; he might say Mass privately, but was not to preach before the hearing of the charges against him. The pope let it be known that he wanted to talk personally to Hus, but Hus, fearing a trap, said that he would meet the pope and cardinals only in the presence of the whole council.

On the same day at Aachen, Charlemagne's capital, Sigismund was at last crowned King of the Romans, so that on his entry into Constance he would be clothed with the highest secular authority.

Five days later, those doctors already at Constance presented the pope with a memorandum reflecting the ambiguity of the conciliarist attitude towards the papacy. While addressing him as the only true successor of St. Peter and declaring that his two rivals ought to be deposed, by force if need be, they remarked that 'in every body the limbs must restrain the head if it is given to tyranny and frenzy' and demanded the appointment of procurators charged with the duty of ensuring that no proposal was overlooked and no delegate prevented from speaking in the council by intimidation.

Although John would have liked to hurry matters on while there was still an Italian majority at Constance, the session on November 16 decided nothing. The following day, Cardinal Pierre d'Ailly reached the city with a mixed company of French and English delegates to the council, the representatives of the University of Vienna and the Dominican Cardinal Domenici, the former Archbishop of Ragusa, delegate to the council of Pope Gregory XII.

The second plenary session of the council had been provisionally announced for December 17. It was now postponed again until Sigismund could attend. During the month's delay, the delegates were far from idle. The memorandum of November 14 had been a straw in the wind, the significance of which might have been missed by traditional papalists. After Cardinal d'Ailly's arrival, however, no one could have had any doubts about which way the wind was going to blow. D'Ailly took up the demand made in the memorandum for the appointment of procurators and with the enthusiastic support of English and German conciliarists expanded it in a period of some two months into a scheme for the organization of the council which denuded the pope and cardinals of almost all their traditional power.

At the Council of Pisa, following common practice at the universities, the delegates had spoken and voted as members of the four nations present, France, Germany, Italy and England. No pope had been present at Pisa, so there had been no complications. But John's presence at Constance necessitated a variation of the Pisan scheme, to ensure that the aura of papal power did not overawe the delegates. The scheme proposed that, at Constance, each 'national' delegation, however few its members might be, should be taken to represent the whole nation from which it came. Every topic would be debated by each nation separately until agreement on national policy had been reached. Then at general sessions the conclusions reached nationally would be discussed and voted upon conciliarly in an atmosphere of freedom, with no group interest dominating the debate.

This proposal for voting by nations was totally destructive of both papal and cardinalate authority, signifying in essence that John and his allies could vote only as simple delegates of the Italian 'Nation'.

They were as little satisfied as the representatives of the more populous nations are with the voting procedure at the General Assembly of the modern United Nations Organization. But in the twentieth century, the idea of 'national' voting is a familiar one and therefore seems tolerable to many. In the fifteenth, it was revolutionary, and intolerable. D'Ailly's scheme did not find universal and immediate acceptance, and John's degradation to the status of a mere delegate might never have been accepted if he had not shown himself as guileful yet inflexible as ever by arresting John Hus.

Hus was seized in spite of his safe-conduct just before dark on the afternoon of November 28. Invited to explain his beliefs to the pope in person by an apparently honourable delegation composed of the Bishops of Augsburg and Trent, the Prince of Baden and the Burgomaster of Constance, he voluntarily left Paulsgasse in its company and, attended by the Knight of Chlum, one of the Bohemian noblemen nominated by Sigismund to protect him, went to meet John.

He was examined first by the cardinals under Odo Colonna, the special commissioner for heresy, then by a Franciscan renowned for his skill in disputation. He parried questions concerning his doctrine of the eucharist and the church, but was unable to deny that he had taught that the papacy was unnecessary. Even so, he defended himself skillfully, arguing that the 'rock' on which the church is built is not Peter but Christ himself, and that there had been many 'unholy and defiled popes'; one had only to think of 'Joan of England', the Agnes of whom a legend universally believed in the fifteenth century said that she had reigned in the year 885, and had given birth to a son in the middle of a papal procession, whereupon she had been stoned to death and buried on the spot. Jean Gerson himself had used Joan as an example in an appeal to Benedict XIII in 1403, and she was to appear again in argument before the council at Constance was over.

Papal authority, Hus said, was an invention of the Emperor Constantine. The church was older than the papacy and could exist without the pope.

The cardinals, conciliarists though most of them were, could not accept so radical an argument. None of them objected when John announced that for the future welfare of the church, Hus would be kept under arrest until his trial. The Knight of Chlum protested, and John replied that the cardinals would not permit him to let Hus go free.

His imprisonment was mild for the first week. Until December 6, he was merely required to live under the ward of a canon of the cathedral, and was attended by John's personal physician, but on that day, having denied again that he had ever taught any of the forty-five propositions of Wyclif, six of which he had publicly defended at Prague since 1412, he was moved to a small and unhealthy cell at the friary of the Dominicans.

Hus's arrest and imprisonment, supported although it appears to have been by the cardinals, severely weakened John's position at Constance. Chlum complained vociferously and found many to agree with him. Even before Sigismund reached Constance on Christmas Eve, the Roman party had few friends left in the city.

At the midnight Mass of Christmas, however, all appeared to be well. John sang the Mass and Sigismund attended wearing the imperial dalmatic and crown (although his coronation as emperor was not to take place until 1433), and sang the Gospel, as he alone among laymen was entitled to do. But throughout January the net for foxes tightened around John.

Sigismund did not disguise his anger over the matter of the safe-conduct he had given to Hus, and although he was persuaded that Hus was a danger to the church, he insisted on removing him from Constance, giving him into the charge of the bishop of the city and ordering that he should be taken to the episcopal castle at Gottlieben, where he would be safe.

Another blow to John's authority was the council's decision to admit John Domenici, Gregory XII's legate, as a cardinal equal to any other, although the Council of Pisa had declared Gregory himself to be deposed and excommunicate. Then, in the course of a sermon, d'Ailly made it plain that the pope would be expected to accept the council's decisions, no matter what they were. At Sigismund's suggestion, the second session was postponed again, until February 7, to allow time for the arrival of more delegates from Benedict XIII and Gregory XII. When they did enter Constance towards the end of January, both delegations showed themselves inflexibly inimical to the pretentions of 'Balthazar Cossa', and Sigismund was disquietingly ready to listen to their arguments. Boniface's legates announced that their master was prepared to meet Sigismund at Nice, providing that John remained in Constance. Gregory's embassy promised that their pope would submit himself to Sigismund's judgment, provided that 'Cardinal Cossa' was not present at the interview and could be forced, together with 'Peter de Luna', to resign his claims.

Nor was this all. Before the month was out, the scheme for voting by nations was brought a step nearer to acceptance, and Italian influence further reduced, by a German proposal that full voting rights at plenary sessions should be granted to the delegates of bishops and abbots not personally present, to all doctors of theology and the delegates of all universities, cathedral chapters and princes. This was conciliarism in an extreme form. At earlier councils of the Western church, no one but bishops and mitred abbots had been permitted actually to vote, although others had been allowed to express their views. As a conciliarist proposal in the tradition from Marsilius to Langenstein, it was warmly supported by d'Ailly, and when it was accepted, together with the scheme for voting by nations, on February 7, the power of the Italian majority was finally eclipsed.

At about this time, with John's personal influence at its lowest ebb since his election, an anonymous tract appeared charging him with every crime he had ever been accused of committing from his days as a corsair onwards. Its demands for an enquiry, and if necessary a trial, found support especially among the English and Germans. John, in desperate straits, let it be known that he would plead guilty on some counts, if the most serious were dropped. He was frequently urged to abdicate, and on February 16 at last agreed to do so.

That evening an unofficial session of the council heard Cardinal Zarbarella read a document embodying John's offer to resign—if 'Peter de Luna and Angelo Correr, condemned as heretics and schismatics, and deposed by the Council of Pisa' would do likewise. The delegates, a pack in full cry against the pope, rejected the document as too harsh against John's rivals. Two other formulae were composed, one by the commission set up to solve the problem of 'extirpating' the schism, the other, at Sigismund's wish, by d'Ailly. On March 1, John read this second formula to the council as though it were his own: on the following day, he was forced to repeat it before a plenary session of the council, humiliatingly kneeling before the altar, while Sigismund and the delegates looked on and, one suspects, gloated: 'I vow and I swear . . . to give peace to the church by genuine cession from the papacy.' When he had finished Sigismund and several of the cardinals knelt and kissed his feet, in token of the church's gratitude for his generosity. But they still did not trust him. Five days later, the formula of renunciation was published in a bull entitled *Bonum Pacis*, 'for the perpetual memorial of the matter'.

Even so, Sigismund continued openly to show his distrust, and the call for the arrest and trial of the pope grew louder. He was warned that there was a plot to kill him. Sigismund, on the point of leaving for Nice and conversations with Benedict XIII, urged him to appoint a legate procurator, preferably Sigismund himself, to resign in his name at Nice if Benedict would also accept cession. Delegates from the French court, who had arrived at Constance with Jean Gerson during the previous week, urged immediate abdication on him, or at least the acceptance of Sigismund's proposals. It was rumoured in the city that John and the Italian cardinals were on the point of denouncing the council and fleeing to Italy. Sigismund ordered a guard to be maintained on all the city gates.

In his despair, John turned to his expensive friend, Frederick of Habsburg. The duke did not fail him. On March 20, although it was the Wednesday of Passion Week when the Lenten fast was reaching its climax, he staged a magnificent tournament under the walls of Constance, for the entertainment of the emperor and the ambassadors to the council. The whole town turned out to watch, and not surprisingly the system of guards broke down. Just after dark, when the confusion was at its height, with the narrow streets around the gates crowded with excited people, 'our Lord the Pope . . . fled from the city of Constance, and, dressed in peasant style, went to Schaffhausen, which lies within the diocese of Constance, four German miles from the city, and is a property belonging to the illustrious Prince Frederick, Duke of Austria'.

His relief at reaching the castle safely is clear in a note he wrote to Sigismund, dated the Friday of that week:

John XXIII to our most dear son Sigismund, King of the Romans:
Most beloved Son—
Here we are, by the mercy of God Almighty, in the free and salubrious air of Schaffhausen. We came to our agreeable son, the Duke of Austria, not because our mind turns from those things which, by our renunciation, we promised to do for the peace of the Holy Church of God but so that we might perform in personal freedom and safety those actions which we still certainly intend to take.

Although he sent similar letters to the cardinals, the council and the princes, insisting that he still intended to resign, the council did not believe him. A committee of two cardinals and an archbishop, sent to interview him on March 23, defected to him: the following day, six more cardinals joined him. He then wrote to the universities, complaining that there was no real freedom in a supranational council divided into and voting by nations: it was no longer supranational if national delegates were given equality with himself, whose powers came from beyond this world. Meanwhile at Constance, the nations quarrelled with the cardinals, only two of whom, the conciliarists Zarbarella and its president d'Ailly, attended the third plenary session on March 26. Neither of them protested when the council voted itself a legitimate body, legally constituted, whose authority was in no way diminished by the absence of the pope or anyone else. Four days later, on Holy Saturday, a plenary session presided over by Cardinal Orsini accepted Zarbarella's version of a decree outlined by the German, French and English nations, maintaining its own authority against John, forbidding him to attempt to interfere in its operations, to act pontifically without its agreement, or to order his cardinals and officers to follow him to Schaffhausen.

In fact John, was no longer at Schaffhausen. The previous night, warned that Sigismund had ordered a mixed force of Germans, Hungarians and Swiss to bring in the rebel Duke of Austria, he had left with his faithful cardinals for Lauffenberg, thirty miles further away from Constance. From there, he sent messengers to emphasize that he was still prepared to abdicate, if his personal safety could be guaranteed. The pursuit continued, and when it began to look as though he were being persecuted, several more members of the curia left Constance secretly to rejoin him.

The result was that schism threatened the council itself. Sigismund and the conciliarist cardinals saved the situation by firm action. Calling the delegates together at the cathedral on April 5, the emperor had read to them a summary of all the negotiations with John thus far, put together in such a way as to reveal him in the worst possible light. As a consequence, the next day the fifth plenary session of the council assumed complete responsibility for the government of the church, ignoring the ancient rights of the pope and cardinals:

This Holy Synod of Constance, constituting a General Council, legitimately met in the Holy Spirit . . . for the extirpation of the present schism and for the union and reform of the Church of God *in its head and in its members* . . . advices, defines, decrees and declares as follows:

Firstly, that this synod legally assembled in the Holy Spirit, constituting a General Council and representing the Catholic Church, holds its power directly from Christ; every person, whatsoever his degree or his dignity, even though this latter be pontifical, is bound to obey it in everything relating to the faith and the above mentioned schism. . . .

In the whole of papal history in the West, no council had ever claimed so much. It seemed that conciliarism could go no further. The 'head' had become subject to the 'body': the plenitude of power, with which popes for more than two centuries had believed themselves endowed, had evaporated. The congregation of the faithful—the 'human legislator' in its religious aspect—was claiming for itself infallibility in ending the schism.

It used its infallible power to crush its acknowledged pope. Day by day, the nations of the council plunged deeper into rebellion. At the sixth session on April 17, it was actually proposed that all the cardinals should be banned from any part in the work of the council; but at the same time, Zarbarella and Fillastre were ordered to seek out John and command him to present himself for judgment. They traced him to Brisach, but he left the town before they could see him, moving into Burgundy.

Duke John the Fearless was afraid to help him. John was obliged to turn back into the empire, and finally granted the cardinals an interview at Freiburg on April 27, offering once more to abdicate, but only if his own safety and that of Duke Frederick, now Sigismund's prisoner, could be guaranteed.

His terms were refused. At the seventh session of the council, on May 2, after the proposal to strip the cardinals of their right to vote except as members of their respective nations had been accepted, John was cited to appear within nine days and answer charges of heresy, simony and schism. A week, and three sessions, later, a force of three hundred troops was sent to bring him in. There was now no question of reconciliation between him and the council on anyone's terms. Within twenty-four hours of being set up, a commission appointed on May 13 had produced a list of seventy-two charges against the pope, and the council, at its tenth session, had found him guilty of them all, including the murder by poison of Alexander V, and declared 'the said Pope John XXIII suspended from all pontifical authority, both spiritual and temporal'. He was taken under guard to the castle of Rudolfzell and imprisoned there.

Just as when Alice was tried in Wonderland, the trial came after the condemnation. Only fifty-four of the original seventy-two charges survived the scrutiny of ten days of hearings. John was given a list of them on May 25 and told to prepare his defence.

There is no evidence that he was ever called upon to make that defence, or thought it worth while to attempt to persuade the council that he ought to be allowed to do so. The council was quite satisfied with its own appreciation of the truth. On May 29, at its twelfth session, having greeted with acclaim its own ruling that no one was to be elected pope in future without its consent, it proceeded in the prisoner's absence to declare 'having examined the clauses in the indictment of the Lord Pope John XXIII' it had reached the following conclusions:

> That the flight of the above-mentioned Pope John XXIII from the city of Constance and from the general council of Constance, clandestinely, at night, at a suspicious time, disguised in an unseemly garb, was and remains an act harmful to the Church of God, notoriously scandalous towards the said council, disturbing and delaying to the peace and unity of the said church, perpetuatory of an obdurate schism, contrary to the vow, promise and oath given by the same Lord Pope to God, the church and the holy council . . . that the same Lord John has been and is a notorious simoniac . . . that having notoriously scandalized the church of God and the Christian People by his life and detestable and dishonourable morals both before his election to the papacy and afterwards, until this present time, he has given scandal and is now scandalous to the Church of God and the Christian People by reasons of these facts . . . that the necessary and charitable warnings having frequently been given to him, and several times repeated, he has obstinately persevered in the above-mentioned sins, and in his arrogance, and so has shown himself notoriously incorrigible, and . . . that therefore, on account of the above-mentioned crimes, and of others referred to and proved against him in the process of the said trial, he, being unworthy, useless and dangerous, should be removed, deprived and deposed from the papacy and from all administration, both spiritual and temporal.

The decree continued by freeing all Christians from allegiance to John and handed him over for safe keeping to 'the Most Serene Prince and Lord Sigismund, King of the Romans, of Hungary, and of other places' for 'as long as it shall please the said General Council'. His seal was taken from him and broken, and the sentence having been confirmed at the thirteenth session on June 15, John, now once more Balthazar Cossa, was taken from Rudolfzell to the bishop's castle at Gottlieben, where John Hus also lay, to await the pleasure of this undeniably self-satisfied council.

While dealing with its right wing, in the persons of the pope and the Italians largely loyal to him, the council had not forgotten that on its left lay a large body with opinions that could be equally destructive of its authority, the Lollards of England and Hussites of Bohemia, whose doctrine of domination by grace was, in its mildest form, so similar to the ecclesiology of extreme conciliarists.

Jean Gerson in particular was firmly determined that Hus should be condemned. Even during the exciting weeks following John XXIII's flight to Schaffhausen, the question of his heresy was being investigated by commissions of the council set up under Cardinals d'Ailly and Fillastre. John Wyclif, and forty-two propositions said to have been taught by him, were formally condemned at the eighth session of the council, on May 4, and sentence was pronounced against him:

> The Holy Synod declares, defines and pronounces that the said John Wyclif was a notorious and obstinate heretic, and that he died in heresy, anathematizing himself thereby and condemning his memory: it decrees and ordains that his body and his bones, if they can be distinguished from those of other faithful persons, should be exhumed and cast out from church burial, in accordance with the canonical sanctions approved by the law.

This sentence was actually carried out only thirteen years later, in 1428, when Bishop Fleming of Lincoln ordered Wyclif's bones dug up, burned and thrown into the river near his home.

The preparation of the case against Hus continued simultaneously. The fact that it was John XXIII, now himself disgraced, who had arrested him, was ignored. In April, his fellow-reformer, Jerome of Prague, arriving at Constance with a safe-conduct to answer charges of heresy concerning the Eucharist, was arrested and imprisoned. Hus was questioned almost daily. He was no longer charged with having taught Wyclif's condemned propositions, but with having expressed false doctrines of his own account, notably in *De Ecclesia* and in sermons. The formal hearing of the case against him began on June 5 in the presence of Sigismund, with d'Ailly as prosecutor, at the Franciscan monastery in Constance, and continued there on the 7th with a searching interrogation of the prisoner; but it was not until the 8th that he was presented with a list of thirty-nine propositions on which he was to be tried. Almost all of them attacked the doctrine of the papacy still being officially taught although denied in practice by the council itself: that unworthy popes and prelates are not true popes and prelates but antichrists, that Peter was not made head of the church by divine election, and so on. Hus defended himself by denying that he had taught that unworthy popes could not rule. They had manifestly done so. He had only discussed the implications of the unworthiness of such figures as Pope Joan and Pope John XXIII. At the end of this session, Sigismund is said to have remarked that any one of the propositions alleged against Hus would, if it were proved, be enough to burn him, and added, 'And mark you, even if he promises to retract, or does apparently retract, there is no need to believe him. For my own part, I shall not believe him, because when he goes back to his friends in Bohemia, he will teach his falsehoods all over again.'

With the key-figure of the emperor so prejudiced against Hus, there was little hope for him, any more than there had been hope for John XXIII once Sigismund had rejected him. But his physical danger was greater than the pope's had been. John XXIII had been cited but not tried or condemned, for heresy. John Hus was tried on the thirty-nine propositions, and condemned for heresy, a crime worse than murder, because it was reckoned to threaten the whole fabric of the world. On June 27, his books and his body were ordered to be condemned.

Hus continued until the end to maintain that he had never taught the errors alleged against him. Both d'Ailly and Zarbarella went to ingenious lengths to find formulae that would save him, but he refused to abjure what he had not taught. As he wrote to friends at Constance on July 5: 'I refuse to confess that I have taught, preached or held the propositions attributed to me by false witnesses. So I cannot bring myself to abjure them, for fear that by so doing I shall perjure myself.'

He was formally condemned the following day, in the most solemn of ceremonies, in the presence of Sigismund, sitting crowned in the midst of his nobles. The ceremony began with Mass. Then two hundred and sixty propositions of Wyclif were read and attributed to Hus himself, and after them, the sentence, identifying him as an 'obstinate and incorrigible heretic' and decreeing that

the same John Hus should be deposed from the priesthood and from all the orders that he has received. [The Holy Synod] entrusts to its Fathers in Christ the Archbishop of Milan, and the Bishops of Feltri, Asti, Alexandria, Bangor and Lavour, the care of proceeding regularly with the said degradation, in the presence of the said Most Holy Synod, and in accordance with the canons. And understanding that the Holy Church can have nothing more to do with him, the Holy Synod of Constance abandons John Hus to secular jurisdiction, and decrees that he should be handed over to a secular tribunal.

He was degraded on the spot, his tonsure deformed by irregular cutting and a paper cap put on his head, bearing the words: 'Behold —the Heresiarch'.

The secular arm did not waste time trying him. He was given an opportunity to recant, and refusing, was burned that same day, at Constance, in a fire supposedly made merciful by the addition of gunpowder.

John Hus died for heresy, condemned by lawyers and bishops defending the papacy, while the pope against whom he had chiefly offended lay imprisoned by the order of the same lawyers and bishops for defending himself.

Chapter VII

THE POPES OF ROMAGNA AND SPAIN

WHEN THE Council of Constance opened, Gregory XII was in an undeniably difficult position. In his own mind he was convinced, despite the deposition pronounced against him at Pisa, that he was the true pope. He had, however, been deserted by everyone except a handful of cardinals, most of them related to him, and the dependents of Carlo Malatesta, Duke of Rimini. Moreover, Malatesta was being pressed to recognize that the schism and conciliarism had swept away the world in which his family had taken oaths of allegiance to Gregory and his predecessors, and to remember that the lesser lords of the Papal States owed a traditional loyalty to the emperor.

Induced by Malatesta, Gregory sent the ablest of his loyal followers, John Domenici, 'the Cardinal of Ragusa', to Constance as his observer. The cardinal reached Constance on November 17, 1414, the same day as Pierre d'Ailly, and so witnessed at first hand the struggle for the subjugation of the Italian majority to the nations and of the papalists to the conciliarists and imperialists. Although personally gratified by the council's decision to accept him as a cardinal equal with those of John XXIII's curia, he continued loyally to send reports to his old master, and his master's ally Malatesta. The main stumbling-block in the path of what Gregory saw as the natural alliance between himself as true pope and the traditional defender of the faith, the King of the Romans, was the usurper John XXIII: the opening of the case against John with Sigismund's approval was a sign to Gregory that fruitful negotiations between himself and his 'loyal son' were now possible, and he set the Cardinal of Ragusa to make approaches on his behalf.

John was formally deposed at the twelfth session on May 29, 1415: the same session also declared that neither John himself, 'Balthazar Cossa', nor either of his two rivals 'Peter de Luna' and 'Angelo Correr' should ever be elected pope again. Notice of these two

202

decisions was immediately sent to Rimini and on receiving it, Gregory decided that he could accept cession after all.

On June 15, Carlo Malatesta arrived at Constance, offering fealty to his lord Sigismund, and presenting letters of credence showing him to be the plenipotentiary of the Lord Pope Gregory in negotiations with the King of the Romans. The letters ignored the existence of the council, except in as much as it was an advisory body called into being by Sigismund himself. To Gregory, John had always been a schismatic, and his bull summoning the council had been meaningless.

Throughout the rest of the month of June, while in public the nations debated the question of heresy in England and Bohemia, and the problem of justifiable tyrannicide (a side-issue to most, but a burning question to Gerson, who had been faced with it in Paris), private negotiations continued between Malatesta and Sigismund, with Domenici of Ragusa as the acceptable ecclesiastical expert.

Gregory had now dropped his demand for the resignation of both his rivals simultaneously with himself. John was no longer a danger, and was soon to be handed over for safe keeping to Lewis of the Palatinate, his sworn enemy, who would keep him imprisoned at Haussen near Mannheim, until he eventually accepted a ransom of 38,000 florins after a quarrel with Sigismund in 1419. Nor could Benedict be expected to hold out indefinitely, for Sigismund was determined to go himself to Nice and bully or cajole him into repudiating his claims. All that Malatesta and Domenici were now asking was that the old pope, now in his late eighties, should be treated with respect. After the commission for the restoration of unity had discussed the questions involved at length, a special session was called for July 4, at the opening of which Sigismund would preside, so that there could never be a suggestion that the envoys of Gregory XII had in any way 'submitted' to the representatives or appointees of John XXIII. When the session opened, bulls were read before it naming Malatesta and the Cardinal of Ragusa plenipotentiaries of 'our Most Holy Lord, the Lord Pope Gregory XII' to the assembly now in being at Constance—the origins of which were carefully left undefined. It then heard the Cardinal of Ragusa solemnly convoke a general council at Constance in the name of the said Lord Pope Gregory and of the Most Holy Trinity:

By the authority of [the said pope's] commission and command, I, John, by the mercy of God Cardinal Priest with title at St. Sixtus, called John of Ragusa, speaking in my own name and in the name of all those my colleagues belonging to my party . . . and in the name of the Father and of the Son and of the Holy Ghost, on the authority of our Lord Pope, inasmuch as he is concerned for the most effective unity, reform and extirpation of heresy, so that, by the grace of God, disunited Christians, professing the faith under various pastors, may be united again in the unity of our Holy Mother the Church and by the bond of charity—convoke this Holy General Council, in the form and manner prescribed. . . .

Letters from Gregory were then read, in which he recognized John's cardinals as true cardinals, and so effectively united the two obediences. Sigismund surrendered the chair to the elected president, the Cardinal Bishop of Ostia, who immediately called for a statement of the actual powers given to Malatesta. As everyone knew, they were unlimited.

Once Malatesta had been acknowledged as Gregory's legate at the council, it was expected that he would abdicate immediately in Gregory's name. But his first act was one in keeping with his master's life-long reputation for the diplomatic use of delay. He tried to postpone the moment of cession by asking if renunciation might not be put off until there was news of successful negotiations with Peter de Luna.

The idea of further delay was anathema to the council and the delegates insisted on immediate abdication. Malatesta then agreed to read the document of cession as soon as decrees guaranteeing Gregory's own future had been promulgated. Nine in all, they were presented and adopted that same day. Their most important effects were to confirm Gregory's acts and appointments: 'everything canonical or reasonable done, either directly or indirectly, or caused to be done, or ordained, commanded or granted by dispensation or indult, with apostolic authority by him who is called Gregory XII within the region effectively under his obedience, and everything that would have been done, etc., within a month but for his renunciation' was to remain undisturbed. Gregory himself was appointed Cardinal Bishop of Porto, and freed from the fear of persecution by a restatement of the decree against his re-election in a form relieving him of blame for the schism: 'the decree or ordinance formerly made,' the council explained '. . . was not made on account of any incapacity of the same Lord Gregory, as though he were not worthy of the papacy, but for the good of the peace of the church . . .'

Gregory's own future and the fortunes of those appointed by him having thus been secured, Malatesta at last read his act of cession, and the whole assembly sang *Te Deum laudamus*.

Gregory lived only two years after his renunciation of the papacy, ruling Ancona as cardinal-legate until his death at the age of ninety. In official Roman succession-lists, he is regarded as the only legitimate pope between Innocent VII and Martin V, who was elected at Constance in 1417, two years and five months after his abdication, but less than a month after his death. During those two years, it is reckoned, the see was vacant, and the council ruled the church. But Peter de Luna would have disagreed.

When Gregory abdicated, Sigismund and the enthusiastically co-operative council had disposed of two popes in little over a month. Only Benedict XIII still held out against them. The council left him to Sigismund, while it turned to the consideration of necessary reforms. Just over a fortnight after Gregory's renunciation, when it had become clear that there would be no unfavourable reaction in Venice or Romagna, the King of the Romans went to the cathedral at Constance to hear Jean Gerson preach a sermon of farewell and god-speed to him before he set off to crush the last enemy of unity in the West.

Gerson took as his text the words 'the God of our salvation will make our journey prosperous'. They were taken from Psalm 68, which, as he pointed out, began 'Let God arise, and let his enemies be scattered'. The emperor was going, he said, to negotiate as the representative of them all. His journey would take him personally to Nice, but lead the whole church in the way of God's commandments. For a long time, that way had been 'blocked by a huge and horrible monster, frightening by reason of its sheer size: Pride and the daughter of pride, the frightful and terrible Lust for Power'. The General Council had been called into being to destroy this monster in all its manifestations, and in the course of the ensuing struggle, twelve rules had emerged by which the future of the church would be guided. Gerson's rules and his illustrations of their operation were all extremely conciliarist in tone, the keynote being determined by the first of them, which was in fact a restatement of the decree passed on April 5: 'A general council holds its power directly from Christ: everyone, whatever his degree or dignity, even if it be papal, is bound to obey it.'

The second law was: 'A general council may not only lead, by way of counsel, but also compel, by way of authority, him whom it regards as Sovereign Pontiff to offer his resignation, or it may dismiss him . . .' and the third began: 'A general council is above the pope.' Thus Gerson claimed plenitude of power for councils. But in compensation he also promised every Christian, of whatever degree, the right to be heard at councils, and proposed the perpetuation of popular dominance over the church by decrees ordering councils 'to meet more frequently than in former times—for example, at intervals of ten years—a law being passed compelling the Sovereign Pontiff to attend them'. In other words, Gerson was proposing a parliament for the church, legalized under the familiar name of a general council.

Armed with the seemingly formidable authority claimed for the general council in these 'laws', Sigismund left Constance on July 21 for his encounter with Benedict. He was accompanied by an expert committee of sixteen prelates and learned doctors, and an armed escort of four thousand troops. It was an imposing cavalcade. But it was not imposing enough to overawe Benedict XIII, successor to Clement VII, and so ultimately, in his own judgment, to Peter, the Prince of the Apostles himself.

He chose not to be at Nice when Sigismund arrived. The legates he had left there were without authority to speak for him on any important matter. Sigismund rode on into Provence. Delay was made the prelude only to more delay, while political trouble between France and England weakened the unity of the council, and so Sigismund's authority.

Two days after Gregory's renunciation and on the very day that John Hus was burned, Henry V of England had declared war on France. English troops landed in Normandy on August 13 and laid seige to Harfleur. France was weakened by internal division, and there was always the possibility of treachery in the south, where fiefs such as the County of Foix and the Viscounty of Narbonne were anxious only to preserve and increase the measure of their independence. Some of these fiefs were ecclesiastically subject to Benedict XIII: others were divided in their allegiance. While Sigismund made slow progress along the French coast, Ferdinand of Aragon, Benedict's strongest supporter, worked to delay the inevitable meeting between pope and emperor for as long as possible, to give this situation time to ripen. It was not until September 18, four days before the English took Harfleur, that Sigismund was at last permitted to meet Benedict at Perpignan, from where the pope had ruled a fifth of Western Christendom since before the Council of Pisa.

It was immediately clear that Benedict was as intransigent as ever. Years earlier he had said that for him to renounce the papacy would be mortally sinful. Fundamentally, he still believed that to be true, but as a great concession to the needs of the church, he agreed to abdicate on three conditions: firstly, that the decrees of Pisa against him should be annulled; secondly that all the faithful should agree to recognize the new pope, and thirdly that the new pope should be elected in accordance with canon law.

These conditions look reasonable, but they made agreement impossible. 'Canon law' as Benedict understood it had not been amended by the Council of Constance, for he did not recognize that there was such a council. Under the old law, only cardinals appointed by legitimate popes were entitled to take part in conclaves. In Benedict's eyes, after he had accepted the hated 'way of cession', he himself would be the only true cardinal in the world, for he was the only survivor of the Sacred College as it had existed under Clement VII and Gregory XI. He alone, therefore, would be responsible for electing the new pope—and, under the second of his conditions, the world would be bound to accept his choice, even if he should vote for himself.

While, away in the north, the English marched to Agincourt and at Constance the nations argued out the problems of the heresy of Jerome of Prague, who wanted to give holy communion to the faithful in both kinds, and the treachery of Frederick of Austria, who had rebelled against Sigismund's sequestration of his property for aiding John XXIII, the obstinate old pope at Perpignan fought on for what he believed. Forced to make concessions by the fear of losing support if he did not, he withdrew his first conditions for abdication and substituted others: his own cardinals should elect six arbitrators, who would meet eight or even twelve of the cardinals from Constance at a neutral city and there elect a pope by the two-thirds rule of canon law. These terms were still unacceptable. The arguments went on until mid-November when Sigismund, convinced that nothing was to be gained by continuing them, left Perpignan and returned to France. Fearing that, when he returned, Sigismund would be ready to kidnap or even to kill in order to gain what he wanted, Benedict also left the city and, on November 21, reached the safety of the fortress of Peñiscola, from where his family had long ruled vast estates in Aragon. The only way of winkling him out was by war, a risk which Sigismund was not willing to take, although Gerson's sermon had assured him of the council's support for the use of force. Instead, ignoring the problem posed by Benedict himself, he initiated negotiations at Narbonne intended to subvert his supporters, the Kings of Castile, Navarre and Aragon, the Counts of Foix and Armagnac, and the legates of the Scots. This policy was partially successful. On December 13, an agreement in twelve clauses was signed by the princes and legates and the Archbishop of Rouen representing the King of France on one side and by Sigismund and his negotiators from Constance on the other, by which, without prejudice to Benedict—or so it was alleged—those of his obedience pledged themselves to meet certain other persons at Constance and hold a council there, to discuss a papal election, heresy and other matters important to the future of the church. The problem of the authority claimed for itself by the council then sitting at Constance was solved, as Gregory XII had solved it, by ignoring its existence. Benedict would be canonically deposed after a council had been convoked, although with no reference to the Council of Pisa, and the problems caused by the appointments he had made would be solved as they arose.

Whatever the kings and legates may have believed, this agreement was, of course, wholly prejudicial to Benedict's position. In fact, it was a total betrayal. This was made clear on January 6, 1416, the Feast of the Three Kings, when the eloquent Vincent Ferrer, who was later to be canonized for his missionary work, but had hitherto been famous for his brilliant advocacy of Benedict's cause, allowed himself to be persuaded by the king to read and preach on the edict withdrawing Aragonese obedience from its native pope. As the King of Aragon was also Lord of Catalonia, Valencia, Majorca, Sardinia and Sicily, and had a claim to the throne of Naples, his defection was a serious matter. A few days later, the King of Castile followed Aragon's example, and at intervals through the year, Scotland, Portugal, Naples, Foix, Navarre and Armagnac all announced that they too would accept the Convention of Narbonne.

At Constance, the news of Aragon's surrender to the council was greeted with the joy it deserved. At a special meeting on February 4 (not called a session, so as not to offend the Spaniards, for whom the council did not yet exist), the convention was ratified and formal invitations were issued to all Benedict's former adherents in Spain and to the Counts of Foix and Armagnac, to come to Constance.

Sigismund's vision, of which he had often spoken, was the old German imperial dream of uniting the whole world under himself and a true pope, and driving the Turks and Saracens out of the Holy Land, so that Christendom would be one and at peace again. After Narbonne, it seemed that the fulfilment of his vision was much nearer. While the Aragonese were preparing to go to Constance, Sigismund himself went to Paris and London in an attempt to end the Anglo-French wars and bring political unity to the West. He made an ally and personal friend of England's Henry V. They were men of similar character facing similar problems: Henry's kingdom was still riddled with Lollardy and there were disturbances on the Scottish borders; while the whole empire seemed threatened by the formation of a Hussite League among the Bohemians to whom the dead John Hus was already a martyr, and there were border troubles also in the Baltic lands where the Poles, among whom Hus had preached, were trying to throw off German influence and expel the Knights of the Teutonic Order. It is on record that Sigismund liked London, but Paris, the mad King Charles, and the faction-fighting between adherents of Burgundy and Armagnac that surrounded his court, were not to the emperor's taste, although he faithfully carried out promises he made to the French of mediation in England to end the wars. Meanwhile, mixed news reached him from the council. Late in March, the reunion of Christendom seemed suddenly closer, with the arrival of a delegation from Constantinople to join the Eastern Emperor's cousin, Manuel Chrysoloras, in discussions intended to lead to the reunion of the churches and the mounting of a united crusade. But Benedict XIII proved himself still able to delay the unity of the West.

In the summer of 1416, the Count of Armagnac and the Regent of Scotland, Robert, Duke of Albany, were still completely ignoring the Convention of Narbonne, while the Archbishops of Toledo and Seville were actively working to make good the damage done to Benedict's prestige by its first acceptance in Spain. Ferdinand of Aragon was dead before his example in renouncing Benedict was followed by Navarre in July and the County of Foix in August. By that time, Sigismund's alliance with England had earned him the distrust of France and the hatred of the anglophobic Count of Armagnac. For a while it seemed that France might even withdraw from the council altogether. But the new King of Aragon, Alfonso V, was loyal to the agreement his father had made and, on September 5, his ambassadors reached Constance, together with those of Joanna II of Naples, with whom he was endeavouring to make an alliance.

How sadly the conciliar and conciliatory spirit of the early days at Constance had deteriorated, as a result of political unrest in Europe and Sigismund's failure to play the mediatory role assigned to the emperor by the students of Marsilius, was revealed by the reaction of the four nations when, at the twenty-second session of the council on October 15, it was formally proposed to admit Aragon to the council and unite her with Portugal to form the fifth 'Spanish' nation.

The Portuguese immediately objected that they were already a nation, not subject to Aragon. Their politico-rationalist argument was echoed by the Sicilians who, although subject to Aragon since the massacre of the Sicilian Vespers, still regarded themselves as worthy of independent consideration and felt threatened by the alliance between Aragon and Naples. The French then raised the question of Sigismund's partiality. All summer they had been showing signs of willingness to do whatever would hurt his interests most, drawing closer to the Italians who, from the beginning of the council, had opposed its most conciliarist and anti-papal decrees, and during 1416 had fought so successful a rearguard action against the commission for reform set up to reduce the power of the papacy that its work had come to nothing. In this matter, the Spanish were the natural allies of the Italians, for, with Clement VII and Benedict XIII, they had lived under popes claiming and exercising the plenitude of power. The decay of conciliarism among the French was counterbalanced by an increase of the influence wielded by the cardinals. While the scandals of the court of John XXIII were fresh in men's minds, and while Sigismund was at Constance, the cardinals had been treated almost with contempt; there were even attempts to deprive them of their right to vote. But in July 1416, d'Ailly and Fillastre had been appointed proctors at Constance for the French crown. The new weight which these appointments gave to their voice in debates they used in support of Italian views of the papacy in opposition to the English and Germans. In the month that the Aragonese arrived in Constance, the debate about the future of the papacy was given a new direction by the General of the Dominicans, Leonard Statius, speaking with such force and conviction in support of papal plenitude of power that the cardinals' party took new heart. From the moment the Aragonese were admitted as the fifth nation, and lent their support to the papalists, the old dominance of the universities and the nations over the council was doomed. When the Spanish themselves demanded more power in the council than the English, whose nation never numbered more than twenty at the council, they were strongly supported by d'Ailly, even though it was he who at the beginning of the council had been the chief architect of the system of national representation. Times had indeed changed.

However, despite the shifting balance of power and opinions within the council, its work did proceed. Although only a fraction of the whole Spanish people was represented at Constance, it was now possible to claim that the world was united against Benedict XIII. A case was opened against him on November 5, the charges being essentially those raised at Pisa, seven years earlier, schism and heresy consequent upon schism. Attempts to prove other charges of the criminal kind that had enlivened the case against John XXIII failed for lack of evidence. The hearings went on for three weeks and on November 28 a summons was issued, ordering Benedict to appear before the council as a heretic and schismatic. Legates were sent to Spain to deliver it, but discovering that Peñiscola was impregnable without a siege, instead they nailed copies of the summons to public buildings in the nearby town of Tortosa and returned to Constance. Doubtless Benedict was later shown this document as a curiosity, but publicly he ignored its existence.

Further action against him was delayed by a dispute over the future direction of reform and the national factionalism of the delegates at Constance. The arrival of representatives from the County of Foix on December 14, and from the Kingdom of Navarre on the 24th, passed almost unnoticed, but Sigismund's return to the city on January 27, 1417 was marked and marred by demonstrations of distrust so open that the council almost collapsed. The ring-leader of this anti-imperial agitation was d'Ailly, a cardinal-convert to both papalism and nationalism. The council could make no progress until the suspicions of the nations against him and one another had been dispelled. It had even become a matter of dispute as to who should vote first.

The cardinals alone seemed to prosper in this atmosphere. The continuing revival of their influence was marked by a decree ruling that their agreement must be obtained before any act of the council could take effect. February 1417 passed with little accomplished except the condemnation of Frederick of Habsburg, who had again revolted against Sigismund. But the envoys of Castile, reaching the city at the end of March, fourteen months after their king had accepted the Convention of Narbonne, found themselves thrust immediately on to the centre of the stage when they enquired—as they had been commanded to do by the council of regency now ruling Castile —under what conditions a new pope would be elected, and refused to join the Spanish nation before they had received a satisfactory reply.

It was an awkward moment for the council to be asked so delicate a question. Everyone knew that the Castilians themselves, the majority of the Italians, and many of their allies, favoured a traditional election by the cardinals, of whom there were now more than twenty, of mixed provenance, at Constance. No one else would agree to excluding all the doctors and all other prelates from the voting. Moreover, Peter de Luna was still gloriously reigning at Peñiscola, a symbol of the council's failure. The case against him had been re-opened on March 8 with his condemnation for contumacy. Further evidence was heard two days later, and a day or two after the Castilians reached Constance, but before they had presented their credentials, he was condemned again, at the thirtieth session, on April 1. But he was their old master. To convince them that he deserved condemnation and hasty deposition, and that a new pope elected by this council would be a better man, was not an easy matter.

From April to the middle of June, confusion reigned at Constance. Gradually, however, conciliarists and traditionalists alike brought themselves to accept a formula proposed by d'Ailly, in the name of all the cardinals, in a treatise entitled *Ad Laudam*, suggesting that an electoral college should be formed by the college of cardinals and an equal number of other council members, a two-thirds majority from each party separately being required for election. By June 18, the Castilians felt that the council would prove able to elect a pope, and they signified their willingness to be enrolled in the Spanish nation. The necessary decrees were passed that same day.

Even then, however, the council's troubles were not over. Sigismund's Anglo-German party was now heavily outnumbered, and his lack of tact in pointing this out gave the united Latins a fright. They refused to go on to the next essential piece of business, the formal deposition of Benedict, until the emperor promised to protect not bully them, and permit them to speak freely in debate. When he did so, the cardinals conceded that reforms might precede a papal election, and general, although purely temporary, unity was demonstrated by a series of national and conciliar votes for the deposition of Peter de Luna. The final decree against him was promulgated at the thirty-seventh session on July 26: the only significant charge was that of heresy against unity, invented by the Council of Pisa, although a great deal was made of his obduracy and the council's patience. 'Peter de Luna, called Benedict XIII' was, it said, 'a source of scandal to the universal church, author and propagator of an obstinate schism . . . a man troublesome to peace and unity, a schismatic and heretic, outside the true faith, a confirmed violator of the article of faith expressed in the words *unam, sanctam, catholicam ecclesiam*,' and declared him divested of all the powers he claimed and exercised, forbidding anyone ever to obey him in the future.

The unity induced by the fear of Benedict's continuing influence lasted only until this sentence had been approved. Within two days of its promulgation, the delegates were at loggerheads again over the dominance the Aragonese claimed in the Spanish nation, the arrogance of Sigismund, and the question of whether reform should precede or follow the election of a pope.

Sigismund, the cardinals complained, was behaving 'as though he were Master and Lord of the whole council' in his anxiety to see reforms made before any election took place. If the council elected a pope, most of the Western world would obey him, whether he reformed the church or not. Reform, therefore, had to come first in Sigismund's view. The cardinals of John XXIII's former curia took the opposite view: in their opinion, it was for the pope to reform the church. Sigismund, the English and the Germans fought hard to reduce the influence of John's cardinals, and to prevent agreement between them and the majority of the nations on any terms except those he dictated. On one particularly difficult day, fearing imminent defeat for his policy, he sent soldiers with threats to arrest the whole commission for reform as it tried to force its way into the cathedral, the doors of which he had ordered to be locked to prevent the delegates from meeting.

In September, both sides in the dispute suffered major losses. Cardinal Zarbarella died, to the dismay of the Franco-Roman party. But so too did Sigismund's most influential adviser, Robert Hallam,

Bishop of Salisbury. Immediately after Hallam's death, the English nation deserted Sigismund's party to join that in favour of an election before reform. Their change of allegiance swayed the Venetian Cardinals, Antonio Correr and Gabriel Condulmar, against the imperial view, which they had hitherto supported, partly at least from dislike and mistrust of John's former curia.

It appears probable that the English changed sides because Henry V had sent them instructions to do so. Their defection would almost certainly have resulted in an inglorious defeat for Sigismund at the next general session of the council, if the whole situation had not been changed by the arrival in Constance of the English king's uncle, Bishop Henry Beaufort of Winchester.

Beaufort was supposedly on pilgrimage, going to Jerusalem, and it was given out that he was merely breaking his journey at Constance to carry his nephew's good wishes to the emperor and renew old acquaintances. It is likely, however, that Constance was his real goal, and that he was carrying both reassurances and warnings from the king to Sigismund. If the council broke up, so would Europe. The English had joined the cardinals' party, because the church and the world urgently needed a pope, as a sign and centre of unity. Therefore the council's first aim must be to elect a pope, binding whoever was elected to undertake such reforms as the nations agreed unanimously must be made, and leaving disputed matters until after unity was assured.

Although malicious gossip at Constance said that the only pilgrimage a man like Bishop Beaufort would take at the beginning of winter was one in search of the papal tiara for himself, his compromise found general support. Sigismund and the Germans agreed to a conclave being held as soon as the commission for the election of a pope could decide who had the right to vote, while the Franco-Roman party agreed to work on reforming decrees. Within a fortnight of Beaufort's arrival, problems that had seemed insoluble for months had been resolved. On October 9, five reforming decrees were unanimously accepted. They were all designed to limit the powers of future popes in ruling the church and collecting taxes.

The first of them—the decree *Frequens*—embodied the essence of conciliarist theory in a modified form of the proposal for frequent councils made by Gerson in his sermon before Sigismund's journey to Nice and Perpignan. Its fundamental principle was succinctly expressed in its opening sentence: 'The frequent celebration of general councils is one of the best ways of cultivating the vineyard of the Lord' and the rules it laid down were equally unambiguous: 'We decide, decree and ordain that general councils shall be regularly celebrated, the first following the end of this present council after five years, the second after this present council seven years after the first, and then others at intervals of ten years.' It permitted the pope, acting on the advice of the cardinals, to bring a council forward, but not to delay its opening, and laid down principles for the popes to follow about announcing the dates and places of councils well in advance.

The other decrees passed the same day ordered that a general council should be convened within one year of any further outbreak of schism, bound popes on their election to profess the faith in the tradition of the apostles, fathers and first eight general councils, from Nicaea to Vienne, forbade them to translate bishops from see to see without the agreement of the cardinals (so preventing, it was hoped, either promotion or punishment by papal whim) and, restoring powers of procuration and collation to diocesan bishops and colleges of electors, declared it illegal for popes to claim the feudal fines known as *spolia* traditionally paid at the deaths of prelates to their leige-lords.

Once these decrees had been passed, only one important problem remained, the election of the pope who was to rule under them. The compromise on the composition of the conclave suggested by d'Ailly some months earlier had lost support; it had been realized that the Italians would inevitably dominate an election in which there would be no German or English cardinals, and only one Spaniard, but fifteen Italians and seven Frenchmen. Meetings of the commission for the conclave were stormy. According to Cardinal Fillastre's account, every nation was suspicious of all the others, and the only point on which all the cardinals agreed was that a German pope would be a tragedy. At last, fearing that Sigismund might impose such a disaster on the church, they agreed on a compromise suggested by the French. On October 30 it was decreed that the twenty-three cardinals should be accompanied into the conclave by six prelates or doctors from each nation—thirty in all—and that at least four votes from each nation individually would be required for election, in addition to a two-thirds majority of the whole conclave and the two-thirds majority of the cardinals required by canon law. Thus any three national electors could prevent an election.

The members of the conclave nominated by the nations were formally elected to serve by the council's forty-first plenary session, on the morning of November 8, 1417, and led in solemn procession to the city exchange, where they were ceremoniously locked in. A guard of German noblemen, provided by Sigismund, stood sentinel over the building, and the rations were supervised by two bishops.

Contrary to general expectations, the conclave was a brief one. Although Fillastre had noted in his journal, 'No one except the Italians wants an Italian', a few hours short of three days after the conclave was sealed it was announced, at ten o'clock on the morning of Thursday, November 11, 1417, that Odo Colonna, Cardinal-Deacon of St. George in Velabro and president of the council's first commission for heresy, had been elected, and, this being St. Martin's feast, would be known as Martin V.

The new pope was fifty years of age. He had been made a cardinal —although then only a sub-deacon—by Innocent VII in 1405. His family connections and the skill with which he had kept himself out of damaging disputes at Constance had earned him election. His appearance in the streets of the city, in procession to the cathedral, was greeted with wild scenes of joy. He was made deacon on Friday, November 12, ordained priest on Saturday, consecrated bishop on Sunday—the day he celebrated his first Mass in the presence of the King of the Romans and a hundred and forty mitred bishops and abbots—and received homage as pope and oaths of fidelity on Monday. The following Sunday, November 21, he was crowned amid general rejoicing.

By then he had already been at work for nine days undoing as much as he could of the council's work for reform by the reduction of papal power. On the day after his election, he had already prepared and presented to the cardinals rules for the administration of the papal chancellory claiming more personal authority for the pope than any hitherto seen. Significantly, the publication of these rules was held up for three months while the council, now unmistakably senile and dying of old age, went through the familiar motions of debate and voting on reforms. In these last stages of the great debate, national differences overshadowed every other consideration and it was easy for the pope to divide the nations and prepare to rule them. General reform being out of the question, it was decided that specific reforms should be guaranteed by concordats between the papacy and individual countries. The Italians, the Spanish and the English

THE MONUMENT TO MARTIN V BY DONATELLO AND MICHELOZZO
IN S GIOVANNI IN LATERANO, ROME

BONIFACE VIII ANNOUNCING THE INDULGENCE
OF THE JUBILEE YEAR 1300

From the fresco by Giotto in S Giovanni in Laterano, Rome

(protected already by *Provisors* and *Praemunire*) now discovered that there were no practicable reforms of special interest to them and the concordats they signed with Martin might well have been agreed in pre-conciliar days. Thus, for instance, that drawn up between the pope and Henry of England and concluded, without urgency, only in July 1418, provided for the control of the sale of indulgences and dispensations, and for the promotion of Englishmen to offices in the curia. The French and the Germans, however, insisted on clauses restricting provisions and reservations and reducing annates. But their concordats were to run only for five years, until the next council, announced, under the terms of the decree *Frequens*, for Pavia in the year 1423. In practice, the concordat with France lasted only six months, when opposition to it in that country led to its unilateral repudiation.

Futility was the keynote at Constance in 1418. Everything that could be postponed was postponed, even the discussions with the Byzantines, which were reduced merely to an exchange of sermons and a promise to meet again. The only point on which the whole council was united was the opinion that Hussites were undesirable people. A bull promulgated on February 22, 1418 entitled *Inter cunctos* laid down specific tests to be applied to suspected heretics. They were to be asked under oath whether they believed in the Council of Constance and supported its action against Wyclif, Jerome of Prague and John Hus. *Inter cunctos* and related decrees put a powerful weapon into Sigismund's hands in the battle for the East, but the council refused to decide the Polish question for him. It might well have shown more concern with the affairs of eastern Europe if it had foreseen the terrible Hussite Wars that lay only two years in the future.

At the last session of the council, the forty-fifth, held on April 22, 1418, the pope swore to 'hold and observe inviolate each and every point that had been conciliarly defined, concluded and decreed with respect to the Faith by this present council', Sigismund said a few words of thanks, an indulgence was announced benefiting all those who had attended the sessions, and after the delegates had been bidden to 'Go in peace' Martin V was free to devote himself to the real work of his rule, rebuilding the authority of the Sovereign Pontiff.

At that moment, however, he could not even return to Rome. The city was being held by Sforza Attendolo for Joanna II of Naples—

almost the last of her father's conquests still in Neapolitan hands. Martin V spent eighteen months at Florence, negotiating with the captains of the Great Companies and with Louis III 'of Anjou and Adria' to win back control of the Papal States and the city. Although most of his actions in the course of these months were successful, his interest in Naples and the south of Italy aroused first the suspicion and then the enmity of Alfonso V of Aragon, and consequently almost brought the Great Schism back to life again.

For the truth was that the schism was not over, although the council called too end it had dispersed. At Peñiscola, Benedict XIII was still in power.

His condemnation and deposition by the Council of Constance in July 1417 had no immediately discernable effect on him, although it did serve to justify in their own eyes those who had already withdrawn obedience and were witholding the taxes they had promised him. He continued to issue bulls and make appointments from his castle until his death on May 23, 1423, acting always as though he were the true pope, as indeed he was, if the election of Urban VI in 1378 was invalidated by the cardinals' fear of the Roman mob. During his later years, however, he was of international significance only because King Alfonso of Aragon chose to use him as a threat to hold first over the Council of Constance, then over its pope Martin V. Early in 1418, approaches were made to attempt to persuade him to accept the realities of his situation before the council ended, but although two of his four remaining cardinals deserted him, he continued to rule large parts of Aragon with the more or less open support of Alfonso. A little later, Cardinal Adimaro, sent to Spain as Martin's legate to persuade the clergy to end the schism, succeeded only in antagonizing them at a synod held at Lerida.

Loyalty to Benedict was not limited only to the clergy of Aragon. Count John of Armagnac—the man Sigismund had offended by his partiality towards the English in 1416—continued to maintain a Vicar General named by Benedict, a certain Jean Carrier. Shortly before Benedict died, he nominated Carrier to the cardinalate, together with three other priests faithful to himself, and bound them by an oath to elect a successor to him after his death.

On June 10, 1423, after a conclave conducted with all due formality, the Sacred College of Peñiscola elected Gil Sanchez Munoz, the Provost of Valencia, to rule the church. He took the name Clement VIII and received the homage of most of those faithful to Benedict's memory. He also inherited the authentic papal tiara of Sylvester I, which Clement VII had carried to Avignon, and Benedict XIII had worn on ceremonial occasions throughout his long reign. However, Carrier was not satisfied with this election. On November 12, 1425, having meditated for two years on what action he should take, he held a secret conclave with himself, and in his wisdom elected a certain Bernardo Garnier as anti-pope to Clement VIII.

Garnier called himself Benedict XIV. The proclamation of his 'election' roused a storm of protest in Spain, and his cardinal-elector Carrier fled to Armagnac, leaving him to make the best he could of an untenable position. Benedict's solution was flight on his own account: he followed Carrier to Armagnac.

Alfonso remained loyal to Clement VIII, whom he was using to embarrass the Roman Pope Martin in Sicily. In the year of the counter-election, 1425, Martin sent a new legate, Cardinal Pierre de Foix, to negotiate an end of the schism with Alfonso, but the king refused to meet him declaring, in April 1426, after keeping him waiting for a year, that Martin V was not the pope, and so had no authority to appoint or need to send legates anywhere. To drive home his point, he then arranged for the solemn coronation of Clement VIII, a ceremony which had been constantly postponed until then, in case it became politically expedient to repudiate him.

Crowned and enthroned, Clement VIII was immediately recognized by John of Armagnac, who was already sheltering 'Cardinal' Carrier and 'Pope' Benedict XIV.

By this time, however, Europe was tired of the schism. The threat of an interdict from Rome, which would have brought Aragonese overseas trade to a standstill as well as causing internal religious conflict, made Alfonso think again. He offered to receive a legate from Rome, and the Cardinal of Foix made the journey back to Spain. By the following year, the basis for an agreement between the king and Martin V had been established, and at long last, on July 26, 1429, with the promise of a pension from the 150,000 florins with which the Romans had bribed his king, Clement VIII repudiated his claim to the throne of Peter and a solemn conclave at Peñiscola elected Odo Colonna to rule as Martin V.

Even that was not quite the end. Benedict XIV continued to rule the church in make-believe from Armagnac, with the support of Count John. The count was, however, quickly persuaded by bluff and threats to give up this strange allegiance, and a Synod at Tortosa in 1430 finally reunited the Western Church, fifty-two years after the beginning of the schism.

But the archives of Armagnac reveal that, thirty-seven years later, fanatics in the county were still waiting for the day when Benedict XIV would come into his own. In 1467, he anointed a new king of France, a certain Charles, whose name and future office had, he said, been revealed to him in a vision.

PART FOUR

AUTHORITY AFTER THE SCHISM

Chapter I

REBUILDING THE CITY OF GOD

CATHOLIC THEOLOGIANS and historians have never found it difficult to demonstrate the legality of the Council of Constance, and it appears in histories of the Western church as the fourteenth oecumenical council. Yet it was never demonstrably oecumenical even in the limited sense in which that word was used in the West after the definitive break with the Eastern churches in the eleventh century. If Benedict XIII was the legitimate pope all the time, the Council had no standing, and the church was without a true pope at the head of its affairs—and indeed treated its true pope, Clement VIII, as a schismatic—until the conclave at Peñiscola elected Odo Colonna as Martin V in July 1429. Moreover, at no stage did all Western bishops and theologians accept the council's legitimacy. At the outset, perhaps two-thirds of their total welcomed the summons either of Sigismund or of John XXIII to attend at the council. After Gregory XII had joined in its convening, approximately four-fifths accepted its authority. Before it was finally terminated, nine out of ten realized its expediency and acquiesced even in the questionable procedure by which it found a pope; but it was still not fully representative.

The general revolt against papalist theory at the universities and against papal administration and taxation at royal courts and in national assemblies during the fourteenth and early fifteenth centuries was a measure of the damage done to papal prestige by the Avignon Captivity and the Great Schism. It was not, however, papalist theory alone that had been called into question, but the whole theory and practice of mediaeval government in western Europe, the vision of the unitary City of God, in which the political nation states of the continent were merely Christendom in its secular aspect—the Kingdom of Christ in this world under his Vicar Plenipotentiary, the pope.

The revolt against this theory opened the way for the triumph of

Renaissance humanism in the church and of nationalism in the world, and so ultimately to the splitting of the church from the world begun in Protestantism and completed by the secularist revolutions of the eighteenth and nineteenth centuries in so far as these were successful.

Nor did the effects stop there. Reasoned nationalism and conciliarism were, at least at the time of the Council of Constance, phenomena of the upper levels of society, but their impact was felt at every level. The majority of the eye-witness accounts already quoted come from kings, bishops or professors because the ill-educated and frequently unconsidered masses left few records behind them but their bones and their children. Yet the readiness with which the Lollards and the Hussites found recruits and the ease with which nationalism, and its most striking early manifestation in the north, national Protestantism, spread across Europe are proof of the magnitude of the injury which the papacy inflicted on itself in the schism.

Throughout his reign Martin V worked continually to minimize the effects of this wound. Whether or no he was in fact the legitimate pope before 1429, he believed himself endowed with the plenitude of papal power from the moment of his election at Constance. He accepted the realities of his situation. It was no more possible for him to ignore the strength of the conciliarists and the effects of the decree *Frequens* than it was to close his eyes to the presence of Neapolitan troops under Attendolo Sforza in Rome and of Hussite rebels in Bohemia. He faced all these threats to his power and overcame them pragmatically.

Martin's most urgent problem, being unwilling to make himself the slave of the conciliar movement, was to put himself out of reach of the conciliarists and their powerful allies, in particular Sigismund. He was careful never to ratify outright any of the decisions made by the council before his election. The council's 'questions to be put to Wyclifites and Hussites', which he approved, asked if they accepted the Council of Constance as a general council 'representing the whole church', but no one appears to have put the same question to Martin. He accepted those parts of the council's work that he chose to accept, like the condemnations of Hus and Wyclif secured by his own commission when a cardinal, but ignored the rest, sheltering under a casuistic distinction between what had been done *conciliariter*, by the whole church in council, and what had been done by the Nations or by partially representative commissions. In his judgment, nothing had been effected by the *whole* church in council before he became pope, since while the Holy See was vacant the church was not complete.

While defensible in theory, this distinction was not always easy to draw in practice. The fourth and fifth general sessions, in March and April 1415, which ended with the declaration of the superiority of general councils over popes, presented special difficulty even before the council ended. To papalists, they were not genuine sessions. To conciliarists, they were the most important sessions of all. There were other arguments against their legality besides the fact that the pope had not been present. They had been riotous in character and, after the fourth session, the cardinals had been deliberately excluded from voting, a circumstance which led d'Ailly, once a conciliarist himself, to claim later that 'this debate . . . would clearly appear not to have been a debate by a general council conducted *conciliariter*'. With such disputes already in the air before the council closed, there was plenty of room in which Martin could manoeuvre, even after he had made such apparently unequivocal statements as the one he made at the last session, when he 'approved and ratified everything that had been done *conciliariter* with regard to the faith, but not what had been done otherwise and in a different manner'. By this statement, although it was welcomed by the delegates, he was actually reserving the right to ignore anything that he had not done himself.

He could not ignore *Frequens* and its call for recurrent general councils. There was, however, much that could be achieved before the council called for Pavia in 1423. The first question that had to be settled was that of where the pope was going to live. Sigismund offered a German city. The French suggested Avignon. Determined to establish his independence, Martin went first to Mantua, then to Florence, while working for an ultimate return to Rome. From Mantua, he visited Milan, where he dedicated the high altar in the magnificent Visconti cathedral, but failed to make a friend of Filippo Maria Visconti, who had begun determinedly to reconstruct the vast duchy his father had ruled and his brother dissipated. At Florence, he received Balthazar Cossa and reinstated him to the Sacred College as Cardinal-Bishop of Tusculum on June 23, 1419, only to hear of his death two days before Christmas that same year. He remained in Florence for nineteen months, until September 1420, and during that time he laid firm foundations for the future.

While at Constance, he had cultivated the acquaintance of Louis of Anjou and reawakened in him dreams of an Italian kingdom centred on Naples. With that card already in reserve when he reached Florence, he next set out first to make peace with Joanna II of Naples and Count Sforza, her commander in Rome, so regaining the right to enter the city, and then to win control of the Papal States and the rents and taxes they paid.

Within a month or two of reaching Florence, he had achieved the first of these aims. Sforza agreed to hold Rome for the pope, but his occupation of the city was not undisputed. It had not been continuously in Neapolitan hands since the flight of John XXIII but, after the death of Ladislas of Durazzo, had fallen, together with most of the central Papal States, into the hands of a Perugian *condottiere* named Braccio di Montone. Sforza had retaken Rome for Joanna, but Braccio still claimed it, and was prepared to back his claim with force of arms. While fighting continued around the city, Rome was of no use to Martin, and as Braccio proved too strong to be defeated in war, the pope won him by diplomacy, calling him to Florence and, after discussions early in 1420, announcing that he would from then on be Papal Vicar in Perugia and Assisi, controlling in the pope's name the all-important highway across the centre of Italy. Within a few months of his appointment, Braccio had forced Bologna back to her allegiance. As part of the agreement stipulated that he must leave Sforza in peace, there was now nothing to prevent Martin's return to Rome. He made a solemn and dignified entry on September 30, 1420, to find the city in ruins and its life almost at a standstill. It was impossible even for him to occupy the papal palace and he went to live at his family home near the Church of the Twelve Apostles while commissions he had appointed began the rebuilding of the city. He proceeded to devote himself largely to political affairs, although it was by his direct intervention that several Tuscan painters, Masaccio among them, were commissioned to decorate the restored churches.

The territories held by Sforza and Braccio di Montone were only a small part of the whole Papal States. Martin wanted all that he could legitimately claim. Rebellion by the eastern states under Malatesta warned him that he could trust only his own family. In the course of the next few years he endowed his relations with castles and estates throughout central Italy, won for them by police marriages—his brother married the heiress of Urbino, and from her castles brought

Malatesta to heel—and by war. Soon the Colonna were more powerful even than they had been before Boniface VIII had humiliated the
Savage, at the end of the thirteenth century.

It was easier to restore Rome and the Papal States than to rebuild
pontifical authority in the West. The most intractable of all the
problem states proved to be Aragon, relations with whose king,
Alfonso V, were made more complicated by his possession of Sicily and
his claim to the throne of Naples. Louis III of Anjou, Alfonso's cousin,
invaded Naples a month before Martin entered Rome. Alfonso's
forces, with Joanna's consent, occupied the Castel d'Uovo and the
city itself in September 1420. In the course of the next four exceed
ingly turbulent years, Martin allied himself in turn with Joanna
against Louis III, then with Louis against Joanna and Alfonso, and
finally with both Joanna and Louis against Alfonso and his son Peter
of Sicily. At the end of the war, both Sforza and Braccio were dead
and Aragon had renewed its allegiance to Benedict XIII: but the
pope was supreme ruler of central Italy, overlord and acknowledged
friend of all his nearest neighbours.

Further afield, Martin also had to re-establish his authority in
Germany, France and England. The main problem in the empire
was the Hussite League, and the struggle against heresy in Bohemia
had degenerated into a war before Martin left Florence. Following
riots on July 31, 1419, and further outbreaks in mid-August of that
year after the death of Wenceslas IV, Sigismund, his heir, requested
and was granted bulls promising crusader indulgences to anyone
who would fight heresy in the empire. In reply, the Hussites promulgated 'The Four Articles of Prague', defining as their principles
freedom to preach without ecclesiastical license, freedom to receive
Holy Communion in both kinds, the abolition of large ecclesiastical
estates, and the fitting punishment of all sins especially that of
simony, irrespective of the nominal standing of the sinner. For these
reforms, they were willing to fight and if necessary die. They found
a military leader in the person of John Zizka, and for some time their
armies enjoyed widespread successes against the best troops that
Sigismund could find. If Sigismund could not help Martin, neither
could he interfere, forcing unwanted reforms on the pope. Although
papal plenitude of power was only theoretically re-established in the
empire, none of Martin's actual authority in those regions was
surrendered during the time of crisis.

In France it proved impossible to regain much of what had been lost. The death of Charles VI in 1422 did little to ameliorate the generally bad condition of a country which had been at war for a century and ill-governed most of that time. English victories after the invasion of 1416 and disunity among the French nobility had reduced the area under royal officers to a small fraction of the whole country. Henry VI of England, succeeding to his father's throne in that same year of 1422, was proclaimed in France almost simultaneously with her own king Charles VII. The country was in ruins and it can scarcely have mattered to most Frenchmen whether Martin V or anybody at all ruled the church. Yet the University of Paris, the mainspring of the conciliarist movement, continued to concern itself deeply with Martin's affairs. Its main fear was that he would attempt to evade the requirements of the decree *Frequens* and his undertaking to hold a council at Pavia in 1423. A year before the council was due to begin, it sent a deputation to him, under a Dominican confusingly named John of Ragusa, to remind him of his duty and draw his attention to a list of reforms it wanted passed to limit the power of the pope. He did, perhaps reluctantly, issue bulls for the council on February 22, 1423, asking prelates, doctors and princes to meet four legates named by him two months later at Pavia or such other safer place as they should decide. Pavia was in Visconti territory, and Visconti was on the point of conflict with Florence, the pope's ally. Martin had no intention of running the risk of personally becoming a prisoner of war.

In the event, only four Germans, six Frenchmen and a handful of Englishmen felt it expedient to be in Pavia for the council on the day of its opening, April 23, although the papal legates tried to form an imposing assembly by persuading the local clergy to attend later meetings. In the middle of June, plague broke out and Visconti's suggestion that the delegates should leave the city met with their warm support. The council was moved south into Tuscany, to the city of Siena, and the pope requested to meet it there, when it reassembled on July 21. By that date, enough delegates had come together for nations to be formed, but still the pope remained in Rome. Alfonso V sent ambassadors to complain about the pope's interference in his plans to take over Naples. Summer and autumn wore away while the delegates waited for the pope to come and answer these charges, but still he did not arrive. At last, on November 8, the council was solemnly inaugurated in the presence of only two cardinals, twenty-five mitred prelates and single representatives of the University of Paris and the King of England. The main work planned for it had been discussion of the progress made in talks with the Greek church, begun at Constance and continued until his death by Cardinal Domenici of Ragusa and then by Antonio da Massa at Constantinople. Da Massa's delegation had, however, reported failure. The delegates at Siena had nothing to interest them but the powers and reported misdeeds of the pope, and of heretics. At their second session, they confirmed decrees already made by Martin against Benedict XIII and the heretics of Bohemia. The National Concordats signed at Constance had recently expired and the French, despite the fact that they had repudiated theirs six months after its signature, devoted themselves to seeing them renewed in forms that would reduce papal powers to a minimum, by blocking papal appointments and rights of taxation. Several schemes were put forward to this end, each more overtly anti-papal than the last. Within a few weeks, it became obvious that Martin's legates were doing their best to end the council before it could vote for the virtual abolition of the papacy except as a conciliar appendage. Although the French were divided on many points, they were agreed that the papal legates should not be permitted to decide the council's future. By persuading the nations to the task of preparing schemes of reform, they kept the council in being until more delegates of the University of Paris, together with the Archbishop of Rouen Jean de la Roche-taillée, representing the English council of regency, reached Siena on February 12, 1424, and then united themselves under the archbishop, electing him their president. An open clash between the united Anglo-French nations and the papal legates seemed inevitable. The only point on which there was agreement was the future application of the decree *Frequens*: on February 19, the whole council approved a proposal that Basle should be the site of its successor, in 1431. As every other suggestion on any subject met with objections, the futility of the proceedings soon became obvious and delegates had begun to quit the city even before March 7 when the papal legates withdrew, leaving behind them a bull signed by Martin ten days earlier declaring the council closed.

The Abbot of Paisley, representing Scotland and the Benedictines, protested vigorously. So also did the traders of Siena. They persuaded the city fathers to lock the gates in an attempt to prolong the council by force, but in vain. The first battle on the terms of the decree *Frequens* had gone to Martin.

Realizing that he had been victorious, he took the initiative with a demonstration of his own good will towards the idea of reform. He instituted, or rather revived, a moribund commission of three for the reform of the curia, placing it under Cardinal Giordano Orsini. This body had limited terms of reference, which did not include discussion of papal authority. In a letter to Archbishop Dietrich of Cologne, dated March 12, 1424, calling on him to institute reforms in Germany, Martin wrote with undisguised pride of having 'deputed in our own curia certain of our venerable brethren from among the cardinals of the Holy Roman Church—the most prudent and wisest of men—to do this kind of thing here'. A constitution he published on May 16, 1425 to bring their reforms into effect shows how wise they were in the ways of their pope. Aimed at reducing clerical luxury and ensuring that everyone from the cardinals down did the work he was appointed to do, the proposals included nothing that had not been the subject of canons and decrees before the conciliar movement began. Moreover, limited though they were, they were never put into effect in Rome, but were used only to urge similar reforms on other parts of the world. It has since been argued that Martin was too busy regaining the Papal States and rebuilding the city of Rome to reform what he already held in Italy; but the whole history of his reign shows that he could be energetic enough to do several things at once when it suited him.

In one respect, that concerning the composition of the Sacred College, he did bow to the views of the councils, probably because those attitudes seemed sensible to him rather than from any fear of conciliar censure. The Council of Constance had asked that the Roman curia should be internationalized. When Martin came to choose cardinals, he picked them from all over the West. There is evidence that, before the death of Henry V, he wanted to make Henry Beaufort cardinal-legate to England in recognition of his services to the Council of Constance, but the king forbade the appointment. His first four appointments, made at secret consistories on July 23, 1423 and May 24, 1426, were of a Spaniard, Domingo Ram, and three Italians, Domenico Capranica, Guiliano Cesarini, and his own nephew Prosper Colonna: these names were not announced until 1429, but the consistorial document listing them made it clear that the new cardinals were to be allowed to vote if a vacancy occurred before its publication. The names of ten other new cardinals were published in May 1426: they included Henry Beaufort of Winchester, Jean de la Rochetaillée of Rouen, two other Frenchmen, a German, three Italians and a 'Greek', Hugo de Lusignan, brother of the King of Cyprus, who until late in the schism had given his allegiance to Benedict XIII.* With these ten names, Martin also published new rules ensuring effective papal control of the Sacred College, restricting the cardinals' dress as well as their behaviour.

The Sacred College so produced was a well-balanced body, including conciliarists as well as papalists—and Martin held the balance so well that no further reforms, in the sense that conciliarists understood that word, were possible for the remainder of his reign.

Attempts were made, notably by the French, to persuade him to surrender his privileges and to call the Council of Basle earlier than *Frequens* required. Where his powers were limited, however, it was not with his consent but against his will. So, for instance, Cardinal Beaufort was still not accepted as legate in England even after the publication of his appointment, and the statutes of *Provisors* and *Praemunire* were rigidly enforced by the council of regency for Henry VI to prevent papal appointments and taxation in England. Martin worked hard to have *Provisors* repealed, but without success. In 1427, he suspended Archbishop Chichele of Canterbury, alleging that he had not been doing his best to help in the campaign, and threatened to put an interdict on the whole country. The following year, Chichele asked Parliament to repeal the act, and so earned his own reinstatement, although his appeal failed. That same year, Cardinal Beaufort was permitted to enter England, but only to preach a crusade against the Hussites and on condition that he would enroll no more than half the men the pope had asked him to recruit. When he had succeeded in this task, he was not permitted to take them to Bohemia. By 1429 the French revival inspired by Jeanne d'Arc had made the position critical for the English armies in France, and the cardinal allowed himself to be persuaded to lead his men to France as reinforcements. Martin, whose relations with the French were already strained to the point of breaking, repudiated the cardinal and never trusted him again.

Martin's sudden death on February 20, 1431 was as timely as had been many of the actions of his life.

There was never any real evidence that he intended to avoid the

* Later in his reign, Martin appointed another French cardinal and another Spaniard; at the time of his death, there were nineteen living cardinals, from several countries.

Council of Basle, as he had indisputably avoided the Council of Siena. Yet there was little doubt in anyone's mind that, as the Dominican John of Ragusa said, 'he held the very word council in horror'. The horror was creeping very close to him when he died. Already in 1429 the University of Paris had reminded him in outspoken terms that the work of asserting the supremacy of councils over popes was not yet complete, and Sigismund, frequently defeated by the Hussites, had called for a general council to end the wars. In 1430 it was rumoured all over Europe that the pope intended to evade fulfilment of his obligations. Protests reached Rome from universities in many countries, and on November 8 a manifesto purporting to have been prepared by two German princes, one of whom may have been Frederick of Hohenzollern, the Elector of Brandenburg, was posted on several public buildings in Rome calling on all Christian princes to withdraw their obedience from Martin if he did not submit to a council the following March. The manifesto reasoned that councils had put down heresy in the past and that a new council was needed to put down the Hussite heresy before it was too late. This proclamation had the effect of redoubling the volume of rumour antipathetic to the pope and strengthening the hand of Roman conciliarists. By the end of the year, Martin had been forced to establish a commission to draw up a scheme of reform for presentation to a council. On New Year's Day, 1431, he named Cardinal Cesarini, a noted conciliarist, as his legate in a new crusade against the Hussites and on February 1 as his legate-president at the Council of Basle, with permission to proceed immediately to Basle and do whatever was necessary to ensure a successful council. Even now the pope was not willing to expose himself to the indignity of bowing in person to the will of a council, but he was under great pressure to do so when a cerebral haemorrhage ended his life before Cesarini had much more than set out on the road to Basle. He died as he had lived: still the supreme ruler under God of the Roman Church.

When the cardinals assembled on March 2 to elect his successor, Domenico Capranica, one of the two cardinals Martin had named at his first secret consistory, was refused admission to the conclave on the grounds that he had never received public acknowledgement of his appointment by the grant of the insignia of the office, the red hat. Capranica, still only thirty years of age, was related to the Colonna, and had been a favourite of Martin's, for whom he had governed

Perugia. It had been disturbances in Perugia that had prevented him from being in Rome on the day late in 1430 when Martin had given red hats to Ram, Cesarini and Prosper Colonna. His exclusion from the conclave was actually an act of panic on the part of the Sacred College, afraid of permanent Colonna domination.

The day after the conclave had been sealed, a new pope was announced, Gabriel Condulmar, who had once been an Augustinian hermit before Gregory XII had made him a cardinal in the days before the Council of Pisa. As a member of the Sacred College at Constance, he had supported Sigismund's demands for reform, and Martin V had used him as his ambassador at Constantinople. In spite of a full life, he was still only forty-eight years of age. On his election, he announced that he would be known as Eugene IV and that the Council of Basle would meet according to plan.

The next day, Capranica went to ask him for the red hat. After consultation with the other cardinals, Eugene refused it. Capranica declared that he would appeal to the Council of Basle. Rumour in Rome said that the Colonna were trying to bring the pope into subjection to their family, and attacks were made on their property within the city. From the Colonna castles with which Martin had ringed the area for his own protection, Colonna armies advanced to surround Rome. Eugene had an apoplectic seizure from shock, anger and frustration, and for several months he lay partially paralyzed and speechless while others strove to restore order. It was an inauspicious beginning to a pontificate which has since been both extravagantly praised and unwarrantably attacked.

While Eugene lay paralyzed, Basle prepared to welcome its distinguished visitors. On the day originally fixed for the opening of the council, however, it seemed that those preparations had been made in vain. The only delegate to have arrived was the Abbot of Vezelay. A month later, a bishop, an abbot and three Parisian doctors reached the city. On July 23, John of Ragusa and John Palomar, holding joint powers of proxy from Cardinal Cesarini, formally convoked the council, although the cardinal himself did not appear until September. By November, Eugene, recovered from his sickness and already tasting the bitterness of the life of a pope in thrall to reformers, thankfully decided that it was safe to put an end to the council as long as he did it tactfully. In a bull entitled *Quoniam alto* and dated November 12, he gave Cesarini permission to transfer the council to Bologna at a date in the summer of 1433. Meanwhile, however, the council had invited the Hussites to an open debate on their case at Basle. When news of this reached Eugene in December, he had *Quoniam alto* redrafted in more peremptory terms and promulgated it immediately over the signatures of ten cardinals, led by the hereditary rival of the Colonna, Cardinal Orsini. During the two months it took to carry messages from Rome to Basle in midwinter, the council went on with its business, reissuing *Frequens* and calling for the eradication of heresy and the reform of the church by the 'rooting out' of 'the weeds and thorns of vice' from the vineyard of the Lord. When the first version of *Quoniam alto* reached Cesarini, the council courteously replied that Basle was a convenient place for negotiations with Sigismund and the Hussites, and informed the princes of Europe that it intended to remain where it was. The second version, arriving at the end of January 1432, provoked first a storm of protest, then a revolt. The council would not be dissolved, and declared that it could not be without its own consent. In mid-February it adopted as its own the decrees passed at the fourth and fifth sessions of the Council of Constance, declaring the supremacy of councils over popes and curial officials, and approved a statement to the effect that it 'was not, is not and will not be possible, either in act or fact, to dissolve, or transfer to another place, or prorogue to a later date, by any authority whatsoever, even that clothed with pontifical dignity, this Holy Council of Basle, legitimately assembled in the Holy Spirit, except after discussion by and with the consent of the above-mentioned Synod of Basle'. Later in the month, demonstrating how firm it was in its determination to carry on, it divided itself not into nations, but into four deputations (equivalent to the Commissions of the Second Vatican Council) responsible for the Faith, Reformation, Peace and General Business. Each deputation was made up of equal numbers of prelates, doctors and national delegates, and a two-thirds majority in the deputation was required before a subject could be brought to the notice of the whole council in plenary session.

Boldly as the council spoke in that winter of 1432, it was still actually a very small and unrepresentative body. Sigismund expressed approval of it, partly because it was helping him out of difficulties with the Hussites, but less than forty prelates were present when in its third plenary session, on April 29, it showed its animosity towards the pope by 'most respectfully begging' him to recall *Quoniam alto* and to come himself to Basle within three months, failing which, it would feel compelled to take on itself the burden of 'the needs of the church, and act in a way equally befitting divine and human law'. It also summoned the cardinals.

Its sentiments towards the pope had hardened because the delegates had heard Capranica's story of his treatment at the hands of the non-Colonna cardinals and Eugene IV. Reduced to extreme poverty by the circumstances of his flight from Rome, it had taken him a year to reach Basle, but once there he was among friends. As a youth, he had studied under the same master as Cardinal Cesarini, as had two other noted young humanists, both admirers of the late pope, in whose company he reached the council, Nicholas of Cusa and Aeneas Silvius Piccolomini, the future Pope Pius II. The delegates heard his complaints against Eugene, and finding them to confirm their opinions of popes unrestrained by councils, recognized Capranica as a cardinal, and became more fierce than ever against Eugene. The combination of angry conciliarists and astute Colonna partisans at Basle made the council a much more formidable opponent than its size would suggest. The threat in the 'most respectful' appeal of April 29 was one that needed to be taken seriously.

Eugene reacted by forbidding his cardinals to leave Rome, but several of them nonetheless slipped away and others wrote to the council, encouraging it to continue its work despite *Quoniam alto*. Temporarily defeated, Eugene sent proposals to Cesarini for a new council of reform, the date and place of its assembly to be decided by the delegates at Basle. The wording of this document was as significant as the chief concession it offered, for it spoke, in the language of the Council of Constance, of the need to reform the church 'in its head and in its members'. Eugene still refused to go to Basle; the council still refused to meet anywhere else. On September 6, its sixth plenary session, attended by three cardinals and thirty-three mitred prelates, heard Eugene cited for contumacy. A few days later, his four personal representatives fled, but Cesarini allowed himself to be elected president of the whole council. In December, what was represented as a final summons was addressed to the pope, calling on him to surrender to the council and answer the charges against him within sixty days, an impossible task unless he had already started for Basle before the summons was issued. The summons was accompanied by threats: unless he appeared at Basle, any appointment he made during his sixty days of grace, or any arrangement he entered into for the disposal of ecclesiastical property, would be declared void. Officials of the curia would be stripped of their benefices if they did not acknowledge the lawfulness and authority of the council, and the whole church would condemn any other council meeting anywhere while the Council of Basle was in being.

It was a measure of the power of the combination under Cesarini that continually more people were accepting the authority of the council, despite the bull ending it. Fearing a conciliarist and Colonna victory over the pope, two more cardinals left Rome for Basle. A delegation of Hussites seeking peace went not to Eugene (although before his election he had been known as a reformer, if of the mild school) but to Cesarini. Eugene offered further concessions, but they were brushed aside as claiming too much power for the papacy. The long-distance wrangle continued throughout the first half of 1433, without any major change in the attitude of either pope or council, although Eugene went as far as to issue a bull validating the council's acts from February of that year. No further advance was possible, but political events were in train which were to have profound effects in the future.

Although Sigismund was deeply involved in the affairs of Germany, he had not been able to give his whole attention to the wars north of the Alps. In 1426, he had set the seal of imperial approval on Filippo Maria Visconti's power in northern Italy by granting him the title Duke of Milan, but Visconti had inherited his father's vision of a Visconti Kingdom of Italy and, not content with what he already had, forced war first on Venice then on Florence. Sigismund went to Italy to bring peace, but by 1433 had succeeded only in complicating the war. Following traditional Milanese policy, Visconti supported the council against the pope, whose temporal authority in the Papal States was a permanent block to Visconti's advance southwards. His encouragement of the most extreme conciliarists was another cause of anger to Sigismund, who had himself several times asked the council to moderate its attitude to the papacy although he had always supported its refusal to be removed from Basle, an imperial city. In 1433, after he had actually been besieged for some time in Siena by Milanese forces, Sigismund decided that he could no longer support any institution favoured by Visconti, and he opened negotiations with Eugene for a better accord between them. They agreed so well that, in May, he went to Rome and was crowned

Emperor of the West. He remained in Rome, apparently on the best of terms with Eugene, until the end of that summer.

Meanwhile the Council of Basle continued its work. In January 1433, it wrote to the emperor and the Patriarch of Constantinople inviting them to send a delegation to Basle to carry on the discussion begun at Constance and continued by Martin V on reunion of the Western and Eastern churches. In the same month, it received a deputation of Hussite Czechs. In April, it passed further decrees asserting its own authority, and in May sent delegates to Prague to make peace. In June, it refused to acknowledge the authority of any of the six presidents Eugene had proposed to it, and in July, at its twelfth plenary session, deprived the pope of most of his powers of collation and provision and all of his income except what the council itself saw fit to vote to him 'for the government of the church, and the maintenance of the cardinals and other officials necessary to the Holy Roman Church'. After this last decree had been passed, the papal legates gave up all hope of ever coming to terms with the council. Five of them left Basle that day, July 13, and only Cesarini, whose name Eugene had included among his list of six presidents acceptable to him, remained in the city.

Once again, the physical distance between Rome and Basle led Eugene to weaken his position through ignorance. When, on July 1, he promulgated a bull authorizing the council which he had convened in February to discuss faith, heresy and reform, but not ecclesiastical administration, he did not know that it had just rejected his list of presidents. Nor, on August 1, did he know that his presidents had already left Basle when he published another bull— *Dudum sacrum*—revoking his earlier dissolution of the council in *Quoniam alto* and legalizing all its actions from the beginning as long as they were within the terms of reference he had defined on July 1.

When *Dudum sacrum* was despatched from Rome, it seemed to Eugene that he had sent an offer of all but total surrender and to Sigismund that they were in sight of a victory for compromise and common sense. When it reached Basle, however, it read like a shifty evasion of the real points at issue and certainly an insufficient answer to charges of contumacy. In September, before it reached the council, the delegates had been diverted from declaring Eugene deposed only by eloquent pleading on the part of some national delegates whose principals, the secular rulers of Europe, feared a new schism. Eugene had grudgingly been granted another thirty days' grace.

Meanwhile he had heard at the beginning of August of the council's rejection of his presidents and had reacted in angry letters addressed to all the courts of Europe. When copies of his letters reached Basle, not long after *Dudum sacrum*, the case against him seemed plainer then ever.

To make matters worse, on the day that the council granted him thirty days' extra grace, Eugene signed a bull entitled *In arcano* suppressing the council's decrees limiting his income, passed in July. Copies went round the world accompanied by a spurious bull entitled *Deus novit*, written by an advocate to the consistory named Antonio di Roselli. This forgery was a skilful and vigorous refutation of all the principles of conciliarism. Everyone took it to be a true expression of Eugene's own opinions, and it did his cause widespread harm.

On the day that the period of extra grace granted to the pope expired, October 11, 1433, Sigismund himself entered Basle to attend sessions of the council. Although he was now universally believed to be the pope's ally, he still commanded respect as emperor, as champion of the church against Hussitism, and as an experienced leader of the reforming party. Basle welcomed him. But when, within a few days of his arrival, the contents of *In Arcano* and *Deus novit* became known, the anger of the delegates turned against him as well as the pope, and he could win nothing for Eugene except first an additional ten days' grace and then an extra week. Those seventeen days were enough, however, for the first anger of the delegates to cool. On November 7, Sigismund presided in imperial robes over a plenary session of the council attended by delegates from almost every country nominally subject to the pope, including even his native Venice, and heard it concede him a last ninety days in which to revoke his bulls against it and recognize the restrictions it had laid on his powers.

If the council alone had threatened him, Eugene might have stood firm. But his stroke had left him weak and gout had attacked his hands; Visconti had invaded the Papal States and the *condottieri*, as always in times of crisis, were seizing what they could. He was no longer safe in his own palace. The cardinals faithful to him urged him to make peace with anyone who would help him. At last, on December 15, 1433, he signed a formula prepared at Basle, in which he was made to declare that the council had been from its beginning a legitimate body 'for the eradication of heresy, the peace of the people of Christ, and the general reform of the church in its head and in its members and for everything relating thereto', and that therefore it should continue on its own terms. Three cardinals signed this shameful surrender with him. Its immediate effect was to destroy Eugene's prestige among his people. When Visconti's troops advanced again in the spring of 1434, the people of Rome revolted against their pope, and, barely escaping with his life, he was driven to seek refuge in Florence.

At Basle, the news that he had signed the formula of capitulation was greeted with the ringing of church bells and the singing of a solemn *Te Deum*, as though it were a great victory. Eugene, however, had already convinced himself that what he had done was invalid and so meaningless. 'We would rather renounce the tiara and abandon this life,' he wrote to his ally in the war against Visconti, the Doge of Venice, 'than bear the guilt of letting the pontifical authority be made subject to the council—a thing contrary to all the canons.' He had surrendered only on paper, not in person, and only for as long as was needed to regroup his forces. The fight was to continue.

In the course of the next two years, with the help of a subsidy granted to him by the grateful council, he effectively destroyed that council, although he took no steps overtly against it. While maintaining minimal contacts, and never denying that since he had signed the formula of capitulation it was legally his own council, acting in his name, he whittled away its credibility while re-establishing his own.

After the disaster of the Roman rebellion, his first aim had to be the re-establishment of some part of his authority in central Italy, the only territory from which he could draw income that the council could not intercept. By a stroke of good fortune for him, his first for a long time, he had reached Florence at a moment of crisis in her affairs, and he chose the winning side to support. A year earlier, Cosimo de Medici had been exiled by the *Signoria* as a danger to the state. He had chosen to go to Eugene's own native Venice, and from there had watched Florence flounder against Visconti. Eugene arrived in Florence just in time to champion Medici when it would be most valuable to him. He played a large part in the negotiations which brought Medici back to Florence and to power in September 1434 and Medici paid his debt to the pope with immediate support in the Papal States. A month later, Eugene's troops entered Rome. But Eugene himself remained at Florence, as Medici's guest and friend, for the next nine years.

The retaking of Rome was the first of several major successes. By the end of 1435, Eugene had made peace with Milan, and earned such wide respect where before he had been hated that the citizens of Bologna asked him to go and live there. The tide had turned, and those cardinals who floated with it began to be washed up at the papal court again. In the worst times, only four had remained loyal: by the end of 1435, twelve were supporting Eugene, including Capranica, who had so damaged him at Basle, and Prosper Colonna, whose relations had once sought to kill him.

The final trial of strength between Eugene and the conciliarists was fought over the question of who should receive the Greeks and negotiate a reunion with them. As Eugene and his Council of Basle were now nominally at one, it was a quiet contest. Nevertheless, it was deadly, for whoever won the Greeks would win the acclaim of Europe.

The struggle began in Eugene's darkest days, when the council seemed to be speaking for most of the West when it first invited the Greeks to Basle. Eugene's invitation to the Emperor John VIII Paleologus and the patriarch went out a little later. The first victory went to the council, when in July or August 1434 a Greek delegation arrived at Basle and, in conversations interrupted by sessions of the council to pass reforming decrees limiting the powers of the pope and the Sacred College, found a good deal of common ground with the council's Deputation for the Faith. But the Greeks would not agree that Basle was a suitable place for the council of reunion. The remnants of the Eastern empire were under constant threat of attack and destruction by the Turks, and anxious though the emperor was for help from the West, he could not afford to stray far in search of it from the sea-coast and the quickest means of returning to his capital. His envoys in the West told both the Council at Basle and later the pope that the joint council would have to be held either at a sea-port, or at a city in Italy close to the sea.

To Eugene, the fact that the council had robbed him of his principal sources of income and was scheming to take away the Roman curia's rights of appointing cardinals and regulating papal elections was unimportant in comparison with Greek intransigence on this point. He knew the realities of the Greeks' grim situation at first hand, and he knew the Greek character. He made no extravagant gestures, but merely pointed out to the Greek envoys that he was willing to go anywhere for the sake of reunion. Then he waited, for a year and a half, even allowing without serious protest the princes of Europe to pay annates and other papal taxes to the Council of Basle.

Inevitably the ship of the council foundered on the rock of the Greek question. As the months passed, the Greeks let it be known that they would rather go to Italy than anywhere else. The Germans claimed that as a Western crusading army would be drawn largely from the empire, arrangements to recruit it should be made within the empire: no city had a better claim than Basle to entertain the Eastern emperor. The French proposed Avignon, which was near enough to the mouth of the Rhône to be called a port, but the whole length of Italy away from Greece and Constantinople. They said that if the disadvantage could be overlooked, they would meet all the expenses. As time passed, and no one would compromise, debates at Basle became violent, 'worse than tavern brawls' in a contemporary writer's jaundiced view. In the end, two decrees on a future meeting place were drawn up. The majority had decided on Avignon. The minority, led by Cesarini, still functioning as papal president of the council, and beginning to realize how untrustworthy popular assemblies were, had bowed to the Greeks and the pope: their decree called for a council at an Italian city, leaving the actual choice to be made later. On May 7, 1437, when the president asked for the decree on the council of reunion to be read, majority and minority leaders both started reading at once. The decree of the minority was the shorter. As soon as it was finished, all its supporters started the *Te Deum*. When the majority leader had reached the end of his text, his side began a *Te Deum* of their own. The noise was indescribable. Tempers flared and swords were drawn. Somehow, the fifty-five members of the minority escaped from the cathedral without serious injury, but they suffered one major loss: the official seal of the council, which was applied only to the majority's decree. However, the papal legates would sign only the decree of the minority. The majority-decree, with the seal appended, was carried to Sigismund. The minority-decree the papal legates carried with them when two weeks later they left Basle, with Nicholas di Cusa, to report to Eugene that in their opinion he had won. After the brawl in the cathedral, only the fanatics of Europe could continue to believe in the Council of Basle. The pope could meet the Greeks wherever it suited him.

Their judgment was confirmed by the Greek ambassadors to the council when they too left Basle and sought out Eugene, who had been living at his own city of Bologna for the past year, so demonstrating that he was master of the pacified Papal States. Within weeks he had named an ambassador to go to Constantinople and make final preparations for the council of reunion.

Sane and intelligent as the majority of the delegates at Basle must have been individually, in the following months they displayed incredible arrogance. It was not necessary for Eugene to discredit them. After the violence of the debates in the spring of 1437, they stood discredited in the eyes of Europe. Disgusted delegates began to leave Basle. The rank and quality of those who remained was not high enough to carry conviction outside the city itself. Traditionally, general councils had been assemblies of bishops, but there were now almost no prelates left at Basle, only theologians who to the faithful at large were no more than ordinary, if clever, priests. Cardinal Cesarini was in an impossible position. He believed in conciliarism, but he could no longer believe in this council. Yet he stayed at Basle, even after talk had started about a new schism in the church.

On July 13, 1437, two days before Eugene's legate sailed for Constantinople, the rump of Basle issued a *moritorium*, listing twenty-five charges against the pope, and summoning him to appear before it within sixty days. Sigismund insisted that sixty days was not long enough: the council doubled it, but would not withdraw the summons. Just as the first sixty-day period was ending, Eugene promulgated a bull transferring the Council of Basle from that city to Ferrara, thus in effect dissolving the council for a second time. The council refused to be dissolved. On December 9, it lost its most powerful and prudent supporter by the death of Sigismund, and in January 1438, when the delegates still showed no sign of a return to reason, Cardinal Cesarini left the city in the company of one of the only other two cardinals there, Cervantes of Spain, to join the pope at Ferrara. As he travelled south, he must have passed on the road the papal courier carrying a final bull from Eugene to the council, definitively ending it, and suspending any priest who persisted in supporting it against him. But, to demonstrate how reasonable he was, Eugene granted the delegates thirty days' grace after the bull was received to finish any outstanding business.

The original bull, *Doctoris gentium*, announcing the council of Ferrara, had said that it would begin with the reception of the Greeks at that city on January 8, 1438. In fact, neither Eugene nor the emperor was in Ferrara by the appointed day. Instead the council was opened by a cardinal-legate. Its first significant act was to declare that the Council of Basle had no authority. The initial reaction to this declaration came swiftly. Before Eugene reached Ferrara at the end of the month, Charles VII of France had forbidden any French prelate or priest to attend the council there. On February 14, the French Cardinal Aleman of Arles, the only remaining cardinal at Basle, a convinced and holy conciliarist, and the leader of the majority who had tried to keep the council of reunion outside Italy because he feared papal power, allowed himself to be elected president there, although he knew the possible penalties for doing so. Those penalities had in fact already been laid down at Ferrara after brief consultations between Eugene and his new council, at about the same time in the last week of January as the delegates at Basle had suspended the pope, deprived him of his spiritual and temporal powers and declared all his acts void.

The Emperor John VIII and Patriarch Joseph II of Constantinople disembarked at Venice amid great pomp on February 8, 1438. Although the emperor had been dealing through the winter with papal legates, they had spoken in the name of the pope and his council (when they had sailed for the East the break between Eugene and Basle had not been complete) and it was not quite certain whether the emperor would turn south to Ferrara or north to Basle. He seems to have been hesitant himself. Eugene's council sent him formal invitations to join it at Ferrara. The Doge explained that only the Duke of Milan and the King of Aragon, together with those most dependent on them, were still totally antagonistic to the pope. Germany was divided and France disappointed and chagrined. The emperor's decision to take the road to Ferrara was a blow from which the Council of Basle could not recover.

The Council of Ferrara, which early in 1439 became the Council of Florence when fear of Visconti and the plague drove Eugene back to Cosimo de Medici, was run on conciliarist lines but autocratic principles. The unhappy story of its ultimate failure to effect the permanent union of the churches is not relevant, except in as much as it was due to the suspicions of the lower Greek clergy towards papalism: the Greek church was always 'conciliar' in a way that the Western church was not; the accord reached between the pope and the emperor at Florence failed to find approval with the lower Greek clergy in Council, and so was ultimately rejected. The debates at Ferrara and Florence dealt with such arcane subjects as purgatory and Western additions to the creed as well as less involved points of discipline and practice, including the liturgical calendar and the right date of Easter. The atmosphere was generally cordial, especially at Florence. But the knowledge that the final Turkish assaults on Constantinople were possible at any time—they actually swept over the city in 1453—spiced the discussions with urgency: if real reunion could be achieved a vast crusade might be organized in time to save the East. Then the first accomplishment of the renascent world would be the fulfilment of the mediaeval vision of the restoration of Christendom, a single empire, subject to the Cross, from Iceland to Persia. Alas for the dream, the council's bulls of reunion were largely dead letters almost from the first. In the East, 'uniate' churches set up in Syria and Armenia entered into communion with Rome to the price of their unity with the other Orthodox Churches. In Europe, the Council of Basle, although only a splinter from the church, was large enough and irritating enough to produce a festering sore.

In the spring of 1439, while at Florence the leading theologians of the Christian world were preparing a final draft of the bull of reunion, *Laetentur coeli*, to end a schism which had lasted four hundred years, at Basle the supremacy of general councils was declared a dogma of the church and Eugene was solemnly tried and pronounced deposed.

This sentence of deposition would not have meant a great deal to anyone if Germany had been stable. But in fact the death of Sigismund and the devastating Hussite Wars had left her tottering. Albert II, the Duke of Austria, had been elected King of the Romans in March 1438, but had been compelled to accept as the price of election a ruling by the Electors that Germany was to be held neutral between the pope and the Council of Basle. Eugene's successes that year did not convert the conciliarists and reformers of Germany to him. A Diet at Frankfurt a year after Albert's election revealed that some prominent Germans were still convinced that papal powers in Germany should be reduced. Although claiming that Germany was still strictly neutral, it approved the decrees passed at Basle asserting the supremacy of general councils and suppressing most papal powers of provision, collation and taxation. The German example encouraged French resistance to the rising tide of support for the pope. In July, Charles VII called a synod of the French clergy at Bourges to seek for ways in which the king could use his influence to reconcile the pope and Cardinal Aleman's council at Basle. Instead of giving the king good advice, the synod voted overwhelmingly for the notorious 'Pragmatic Sanction' of Bourges, which again recognized the supremacy of general councils and approved the reforming decrees on appointments and taxation. Whether this decree was what the king really wanted or not, he signed it on July 7, 1438, and so renewed the bitterness first aroused by his refusal to permit French priests to attend the Council of Ferrara-Florence.

It was on the basis of this support in Germany and France, as well as in Milan, that the Council of Basle formally deposed the pope as a heretic who denied the supremacy of councils. Eugene's reply was a bull entitled *Moyses vir Dei*, debated and approved by a solemn session of the Council of Florence on September 4, and denouncing the assembly at Basle as the haunt of priests who, although properly ordained, were 'ignorant and inexperienced men', consorting there with 'vagrants, undisciplined men, fugitives, apostates, gaolbirds, gaolbreakers, rebels against their superiors and men of like sort'; whose assembly had broken its promises to the Greeks and was now trying to destroy the church. The bull quashed the definition of the dogma of the supremacy of councils, declaring all the acts of the Council of Basle of no effect, and condemned anyone who supported them.

Surrender being inconceivable to the delegates at Basle, there was only one effective reply to so complete a condemnation, the resurrection of the Great Schism. During the month of October, the council made such a move, passing a series of decrees to establish an electoral college and holding a conclave. The new college of electors was the most 'democratic' since the Romans had been excluded from the election of their bishop; consisting as it did of the one cardinal loyal to the council, Aleman of Arles, and thirty-two electors chosen by the delegates themselves, it could scarcely fail to choose the most popular man prepared to take office. In the context of Basle, he had to be a man prepared to stand against the pressure of the times and to maintain his court at his own expense, for money was tight since the council had lost support. On November 5, 1439, the college elected Amadeus VIII, Count of Savoy, to be its pope 'Felix V'. The count was a widower with several children, who after ruling Savoy successfully for many years had retired in 1431 to Ripaille, on the shores of Lake Geneva, and had since lived there as a comfortable and aristocratic hermit of means.

His rule as Felix V was not a happy one. Most of the world ignored him. Even his own council would not grant him enough power to rule those who accepted his authority. Quarrels over his rights and powers—especially his right, or lack of it, to tax the church —delayed his coronation until July 1440. His main support came from the universities, where the theory of conciliarism had originated and was still being taught. King Albert of the Romans had died, but his widow Elizabeth of Hungary gave what help she could to the council and its pope. It was not enough. Not even France, Aragon and Milan could believe in Amadeus-Felix. He managed to maintain a precarious existence at Basle until 1442 and, after he had quarrelled again with his council, at Lausanne until 1449 only because some of the Germans were unwilling to concede total victory to Eugene IV. Albert's successor as King of the Romans, Frederick III of Austria, upheld the electors' declaration of neutrality between the Roman pope and the council of Basle until 1445. By then, Eugene had made peace more or less on his own terms with France, Milan and Aragon, and the Coptic, Maronite, Syrian and Chaldaean churches. He had also, in November 1442, won the allegiance of the most able of Amadeus-Felix's advisers, the Sienese humanist Aeneas Silvius Piccolomini, and in March 1443 transfered his own council from Florence to the Lateran Palace, where it was under the immediate control of the Roman curia.

It was Piccolomini who finally persuaded Frederick to face the realities of the new world that every man of sensitivity knew had come into being. Through him, Eugene offered confirmation of Frederick's election as King of the Romans and vast concessions to the German church, if Germany would desert the Council of Basle Frederick himself accepted the terms in February 1446, but two of his electors, the Archbishops of Cologne and Triers, stood firm for conciliarism and the council. Eugene excommunicated them, and found himself within a breath of losing all Germany. A sick man now, wanting only to go on winning until he died, he hastily prepared bulls for publication in the empire, granting that councils might be supreme in certain ill-defined circumstances and promising to hold one in Germany to replace both Basle and Florence in the near future. Piccolomini argued the pope's point of view so skilfully at a Diet in Frankfurt in 1446 that German suspicion was allayed long enough to permit the pope to die, as his predecessor had done, promising a council, but not actually holding one. Almost his last

public act before his death on February 23, 1447 was formally to end
the Council of Florence, so that he died in peace, free from all legitimate councils, and acknowledged head of the whole Western church
except the excommunicate Council of Basle and its pope at Lausanne.

The only thing which had prevented total submission to him by
everyone except the most extreme conciliarists was suspicion of him
personally. His successor, Thomas Parentucelli, Pope Nicholas V,
had within a year of his election signed a concordat with Germany
that gave nothing away, reinstated the Archbishops of Cologne and
Triers and received homage from the King of France. Within two
years, he had accepted the submission of 'Felix V', whom he made
Cardinal-Bishop of S. Sabina, and in return had been elected as
pope by the remnants of the Council of Basle, meeting at Lausanne.

Except in the mind of 'Benedict XIV', the madman of Armagnac,
the Great Schism was over. In the middle of the Renaissance,
mediaeval normality had apparently been restored, and the stage set
for the pope to resume the rule of the Western world.

The irony was that in 1440 Lorenzo Valla, a Latin scholar of
international repute and a humanist who rejected Christian sexual
morality as contrary to reason, had published a treatise demonstrating conclusively that the *Donation of Constantine*, the document on
which so much of canon law relating to papal authority had been
founded, was spurious and therefore of no legal value.

The *Donation* had previously been attacked by Nicholas of Cusa
and Bishop Reginald Peacock of Chichester, but Valla's demolition
of it was so complete that none but the most obdurate of papalists
attempted to refute his arguments and conclusions. His treatise
denied that Constantine had given any temporal power whatsoever
to the pope, or any land or property except the cemeteries of Rome.
It showed that the Papal States had been founded on deception,
fraud and violence, and that the theory of the plenitude of papal
power had been constructed on a lie.

In as much as the *Donation* had been an indispensable stone in the
foundations of Western Christendom from the time of Charlemagne,
and more especially from that of Otto the Great, Valla was right to
condemn the edifice built on it. But, in fact, the *Donation* had been
only one stone among many in the edifice of canon law and mediaeval
practice, and by the time Valla pulled it out to throw at the pope—
calling it, among many other things, 'the cause of the desolation of
all Italy'—the building was able to stand without it.

The tireless endeavours of conciliarists, nationalists and humanists over more than half a century, during which the papacy was
weaker than it had been for half a millennium, had failed to destroy
the pope's spiritual authority in western Europe or his sovereign
power in the Papal States. When Pope Nicholas V was trying
to persuade Charles VII of France to renounce the Pragmatic
Sanction of Bourges and restore the ancient privileges of the papacy
in France, he was able to write and to feel secure in the knowledge
that most of Europe believed:

> It is a fact that there is one church and only one and that its faith should
> be the law by which the whole terrestrial world is governed. No one . . .
> may by his own whim withdraw himself from the governance of its laws
> . . . Anyone who thinks otherwise is denying the power of the keys given
> to the Holy See. To be silent on this matter, or to be careless about it,
> is—as it were—to lock out the Successors of Peter, to whom the
> government of the church has been entrusted . . .

Or in the briefer words of Boniface VIII in 1302: 'It is altogether
necessary for salvation for every human creature to be subject to the
Roman Pontiff.'

Chapter II

PAPAL INFALLIBILITY AND THE COLLEGE OF BISHOPS

PRACTICAL CONCILIARISM failed at Basle, but the theory did not die as a result of that failure. It was the cardinals whose position suffered most. The Council of Basle had called them 'the hinges' on which the church turns, flatteringly using the phrase in such a way as to suggest to Cardinal Cesarini and his companions that the hinges could also supply the power to move the church. It was a view that could not appeal to the popes, and had in fact little support from the lawyers. It was more usual to speak of the cardinals as the senators of the church, councillors of the sovereign pope— or even as part of the pope's body, as close to him as his own limbs, and as subservient to his will, if the body was healthy. In this view, rebel cardinals were diseased limbs, to be cured or to be cut off.

Popes after the schism and the Council of Basle continued to speak of the cardinals as parts of their own bodies, and granted them as little autonomy as the head willingly grants the hand. The later fifteenth and sixteenth centuries saw the triumph of absolute government in most parts of Europe, in church and state alike. In an absolutist regime, change can come either from the top, by the action of the ruler and his favourite advisers, or as the result of undisguised and successful rebellion. A rebellion that fails only makes an absolute ruler stronger and confirms him in his policies.

The principles of absolutism worked with text-book efficiency during the Reformation. Although the phrase *cuius regio eius religio* was coined to describe the situation in the empire after the Peace of Augsburg, it operated in practice throughout Europe. It was political power and the ability to impose a solution to problems by force that decided the future religious allegiances of regions. The Protestant Reformation was effective where rulers accepted the principles of reform, or where non-reforming princes could be ousted by an insurrection bringing reformers to power. Similarly, where Protestantism triumphed, the only way that it could be brought to an end was by a change of government, either by the peaceful succession of a 'catholic' prince (as at the death of Edward VI of England), or by the usurpation of the Protestant ruler's throne (as happened several times in Germany when principalities changed hands by war). Peaceful change through growth, by the adoption of relatively mild modifications in law and practice—that is, by what we now tend to think of as the normal processes of government—was all but impossible. Absolute government can only be carried on absolutely, or changed absolutely.

In these circumstances, mild conciliarism had no chance of modifying the government of the Western church from within. Only outright rebellion against papal theory and practice could have changed the system. When that rebellion occurred, it tended to be sporadic and coloured by nationalism: Bohemian Hussitism was different from German Protestantism, which again differed from English Protestantism. The nationalistic elements in the movements against papal absolutism made it impossible for any of them to seize control of the whole Western church. Their failure to do so left the pope stronger than ever in those areas loyal to him.

At the time of the Council of Constance, when conciliarists were a genuinely international army confronting the international papacy, they might well have been able to overthrow the papacy if that had been their united purpose. But in fact it was not. To most conciliarists the idea of doing away entirely with the papacy would have been blasphemous. Hotheads at Constance and again at Basle passed decrees reducing the powers of the popes to less than those exercised by most constitutional monarchs of later times, but the majorities which passed these decrees did not represent the overwhelming majority of the whole *congregatio fidelium* in the name of which the councils claimed to be speaking. There was no general revulsion from the concept of the papacy itself. The belief that it was the divine will that one man should rule the church was still too firmly held to be overturned easily: it is highly significant that the excommunicate conciliarists at Basle did not propose to rule the church directly, but elected a pope—Felix V—to rule, if only as a figurehead. Moreover, secular rulers would not give whole hearted support to the scholars in their struggle against the Roman curia and the general respect it still commanded despite the seventy years' captivity at Avignon and the scandal of the schism. Papal taxation was resented everywhere, but among rulers rebellion against any divinely-appointed authority was feared more deeply. A king who would deny the right of the pope to collect taxes or even to appoint bishops would hesitate to deny that Christ had given Peter and his successors authority to rule, for the canon lawyers said, and most men believed, that secular power derived from spiritual power: that God gave power to the popes who in turn gave it to kings and emperors. If the head on earth of this hierarchy of power was thrown down, where would rebellion stop?

In practice, even the councils did not deny that power and authority had been given to the popes, they tried only to define the limits within which that authority could be used. Many who would have thought it sinful to question the spiritual authority of the popes, found it difficult to believe that they also had divine authority to rule the Papal States through vicars who had previously been notorious mercenary leaders and after their appointment still found it easier to be ruthless plunderers than merciful administrators. Later conciliarists wanted all secular power taken from the papacy and the admission from the popes that they wielded their authority in the name of the whole church, which had a right to counsel them and be heard. That was all. As absolute rulers in an absolutist world, the popes could not accept these demands.

The way in which Aeneas Silvius Piccolomini's opinions changed during his lifetime provides a valuable insight into the pressures on popes during these years. As we have seen, Piccolomini began life as a conciliarist and humanist. He was 'converted' to papalism during the Council of Basle, and was himself elected pope in 1458. At his election, conciliarist forces still at work in the curia forced him to make a 'capitulation' by which he promised, among other things, to hold a council under the terms of the decree *Frequens* for the reform of the church. By this time Piccolomini's classical humanism had given way to mediaeval romanticism, and he was dreaming of a great crusade to recapture Constantinople and free the whole of the East. A year or so after his election, he did actually hold a meeting at Mantua, made to look like a reforming council but actually incapacitated by its structure from making reforms. Some of the cardinals who had been infected with conciliar ideals in youth realized what was happening and threatened rebellion. A few months later, Piccolomini promulgated a bull against conciliarists that would not have shamed

Benedict XIII. The bull, known from its opening sentence as *Execrabilis*, described as 'a pestilential poison' the recent 'execrable and formerly unheard-of abuse' of appealing to general councils against the rulings of 'the Roman Pontiff the Vicar of Jesus Christ'. Anyone who made such an appeal in future would be treated as a rebel liable to the penalties of both heresy and treason.

Popes continued to teach that conciliarism was a heresy through the whole period of the Reformation and Counter-reformation until modern times. Within the first half-century of the issue of *Execrabilis* its condemnation of appeals from popes to councils had been renewed by Paul II, Sixtus IV and Julius II. In the same period, on the other hand, minor councils were held in Italy at approximately the ten-year intervals required by *Frequens*: in Padua in 1459, and at Rome in 1481, 1490 and 1500 (a council was called for 1471, but Paul II died before it could meet and his successor Sixtus IV allowed the proposal to lapse).

The kind of appeal forbidden by *Execrabilis* was actually made twice more before the Reformation, in 1482 against Pope Sixtus IV and again in 1511 against Julius II.

The appeal against Sixtus IV, Francesco della Rovere, was made by a Dominican archbishop named Zamometic, who, in calling for a council to hear his protests against the pope and his rapacious curia, appealed to old loyalties by declaring that such a council would be a continuation of the Council of Basle, for the reform of the church in its head and in its members. When he made his proposal, the archbishop believed that many would welcome it, for it was openly said that 'the Holy Father rules as he pleases' enriching his family at the expense of the church. But in the event, none of Sixtus's most vociferous opponents—France, Austria and the anti-papal League of Florence, Milan and Naples—was willing to send delegates to the council and the project died for lack of support.

The appeal against Julius II was much more serious. Julius had been Juliano della Rovere, the nephew of Sixtus IV, and according to his contemporaries 'a terrible man'. The proposal that action should be taken against him came from Louis XII of France, in opposition to whom he was negotiating the formation of an anti-French League; but five cardinals were found to sign the manifesto summoning a council of reform to meet at Pisa in 1511. Maximilian of Austria promised his support. The pope countered by publishing a bull announcing that he himself would hold a real council at the

Lateran in 1512 and by winning a great victory over French forces then in Italy.

The cardinals' council actually met at Pisa in November 1511, but owning to the hostility of the local people had to be transferred to Milan. Eight sessions were held, at one of which the superiority of councils was reaffirmed, but there were never more than thirty prelates at the meetings and most of them were French. Maximilian, having made his peace with the pope, stayed away, and the rebel cardinals did not succeed in winning other members of the Sacred College to their cause. At its eighth session, the council declared Julius suspended. Then it simply melted away as French forces retreated out of Italy.

Pope Julius's council, the Fifth Lateran Council of 1512–17, did valuable work, especially under his successor Leo X, but devoted little time to reform of the kind that conciliarists wanted. At its eleventh session, on December 19, 1516, a little over ten months before Martin Luther posted his ninety-five theses against indulgences on the door of the castle church at Wittenberg, it approved a statement entitled *Pastor Eternus* which left no doubts about the curial attitude to conciliarism as it had been practised at Basle:

> The ordinance published [against the papacy] at the Council of Basle, and everything contained in it . . . and all the proceedings of that Council of Basle after it had left . . . Basle . . . can have no force, for that the Roman Pontiff of the time has authority over every council . . . is manifest not only from the testimony of Holy Scripture, the statements of the Holy Fathers and other Roman Pontiffs our predecessors, and from the decrees of the holy canons, but also from the admissions of the councils themselves.

That the pope holds the plenitude of power over councils has been the official teaching of the Roman church ever since, and has never been formally challenged by orthodox members of the Roman communion. It was, of course, rejected utterly by those who protested; their groups formed churches in which conciliarist-type consultative bodies have played a variety of roles, their importance —or lack of it—frequently reflecting, and sometimes even adumbrating, the political structure of the state or states from which they have drawn their members. It is instructive in this regard to compare, for instance, the changing importance of laymen in the Church of England in England with the growth of the political franchise, or the structure of the Calvinist Church in Switzerland with the political formation of that state.

The Reformation shocked the Roman curia and the continuing Catholic states into a close alliance against protest and 'reform'— although, of course, protest against the political influence of the popes continued in all parts of Europe as nationalism continued to grow. One of the first fruits of the alliance between the curia and the Catholic states was the Council of Trent, which was fundamentally a council-of-war to ensure a common front against the common enemy. Yet even so necessary a consultation had to be forced on the popes of the time, Clement VII and Paul III. It was called chiefly to prevent the summoning of a German National Council by the Emperor Charles V in imitation of the Councils of Constance and Basle, where his predecessor Sigismund had played so prominent a role and had found so much support against the early Hussites.

When it did meet, in 1545, it was run on lines laid down by a commission of cardinals supervised by the pope. Yet its character as perhaps the most reactionary assembly in history did not emerge clearly until a later reign, when it had become obvious that religious peace was unattainable without total surrender of papal authority. Protestants were admitted until 1552, and the council became wholly introverted only under the austere Paul IV, after the Peace of Augsburg in 1556 had proclaimed religious toleration throughout the empire, and the emperor had been forced to abdicate the following year. Paul IV actually effected many of the reforms regarding provisions and taxation which had been demanded over the centuries, forcing bishops to return to their own sees and monks and friars to their monasteries; but it was too late to restore the unity of the Christian West, and his successors found themselves continually at war, not with conciliarists attempting to limit the powers of the papacy, but first with religious reformers then with rationalists determined to deny them completely. The papal reaction is a familiar story.

In the period of the Counter-reformation, even the local synods which had played so important a part in the development of mediaeval Europe from the time of Pope Gregory I onwards came to be eyed with suspicion. In many places they were no longer held in recognizable form. Where synods of local clergy were held, they not infrequently turned out to be as dangerous as Rome feared that they would be. In France in particular, from the time of Jansen to that of

Napoleon, it seemed impossible for the clergy to meet without someone plotting what from Rome looked like rebellion; but in those years, fighting first Protestantism, then royalist nationalism, then secularism, Rome tended to see threats everywhere, and may even perhaps have created them by her suspicious probing of movements not originally dangerous. But this was not always true. In both France and Italy, the 'nationalist' pretentions of absolute monarchs in the seventeenth and eighteenth centuries led local synods to threaten long-established Roman privileges. So, for instance, in 1682, Louis XIV made a determined attempt to Gallicise the church in France through a National Synod, persuading it to adopt four propositions—known as the Four Articles—denying papal authority over the French church. The royal claims were all familiar ones: that the fullness of papal power did not extend over kings, that the decrees of the fourth and fifth sessions of the Council of Constance were still valid, that papal primacy should respect local customs, and that papal decrees on matters of faith are valid only if the whole church has ratified them. When copies of the Four Articles reached Pope Alexander VIII, he condemned them all. In a *Syllabus of Errors* dated 1690, the Holy Office defined papal authority and claimed infallibility in matters of faith, by the customary device of denying the reverse proposition 'that it is a vain and wholly exploded theory that the pope has authority over oecumenical councils and infallibility in deciding questions relating to the faith', and in the same year an Apostolic Constitution condemned all the Gallican propositions in terms asserting the plenitude of papal authority over the church, forbidding seminarians to study the Four Articles, or anyone to take action in support of them. At that point, popular pressure forced the king to withdraw the Articles, but Gallicanism survived in a variety of forms in France, and briefly triumphed at the Revolution when the National Assembly reorganized the dioceses of France, appointed bishops by popular vote and forbade any contacts with Rome.

Although Gallicanism was a French movement, its principles were applicable anywhere. In the eighteenth century, a German bishop named John von Hondheim introduced them into Germany when he became personally convinced that it was only the claims of personal power for the popes that was keeping Protestants and Catholics apart in his country. Writing under the pseudonym Febronius, he set out in the year 1763 to prove that papal privileges had grown over the centuries, and ended by re-asserting all the principles of conciliarism, quoting the Gallican Articles of 1682, and even going beyond them. Within thirty years, Febronius's theories had brought Catholic Europe to the point of dissolution. In Austria, his arguments met with especially warm support from the Emperor Joseph II, who was preparing a 'Gallican' reform of the church in his realm with the aim of making it thoroughly Austrian. But the damage was not limited to Austria. In Germany, the electors, led by Joseph's brother the Archbishop of Cologne, protested against papal usurpation of ancient German rights, and demanded freedom from papal interference. Their example was followed in Spain, Sardinia, Venice, the Kingdom of the Two Sicilies and finally in Tuscany, where the Bishop of Pistoia called a synod in 1786 at the instigation of the Grand-Duke Leopold, another close relative of Joseph II, to reform the church in the Grand-Duchy along Febronian lines. At the synod, approving references were made to the Gallican movement and the Four Articles condemned a hundred years earlier. It was claimed that the pope had no divine authority apart from the license given to him by the church to administer its organization. But to say this was to claim more power for the church at large than Catholics of the time were prepared to accept. Febronius's main support came not from the mass of the faithful in Catholic countries but from absolutist rulers. To the faithful, the absolute monarch in spiritual affairs was the pope, and the Synod of Pistoia, like all the Febronian movements, could make little impression on their convictions. Gallicanism and parallel movements in other countries were most attractive to those who wielded some power and believed that they were entitled to more, and was most dangerous to the papacy on the international level. It destroyed the Jesuits in 1773, but could not destroy the faith of the peasantry.

In fact, among traditional 'Roman Catholics', the terms used to express the primacy of Peter and his successors grew richer as the actual physical power of the popes to enforce their authority grew less. It was significant that the pope personally defined the dogma of the Immaculate Conception of the Blessed Virgin after most of the Papal States had been lost in the mid-nineteenth century. Recently, argument has revived among churchmen as to what precise effect such a dogmatic pronouncement has and by what authority it is made, but among the majority of Catholics in the nineteenth and early twentieth centuries there was no doubt that the pope, Pius IX, who made the pronouncement did so on his own authority as supreme head of the church—the authority he claimed for himself in the 1854 bull *Ineffabilis Deus* promulgating the dogma: 'with the authority of our Lord Jesus Christ, the blessed Apostles Peter and Paul, and our own'. Nineteenth-century liberalism provoked a reciprocal reaction among the religiously minded. The result was that after proclaiming the dogma of the Immaculate Conception on his own authority (although after consultation with the bishops), Pius IX was himself proclaimed the infallible teacher of the church at a council he had called to meet the challenge of rationalism and liberalism in the philosophical sphere: the First Vatican Council of 1870.

The dogma of papal infallibility was thus a product of its age. The concept itself was not new. Personal infallibility in teaching had been claimed for Pope Alexander VIII in 1690, and even then no one had complained that the doctrine was entirely new. But the definition of it as a dogma of the faith binding on all Catholics was an innovation in 1870 and had been condemned as such by many theologians before the council met.

The First Council of the Vatican was the pope's council from the outset. He first spoke of the need for it in 1864, the year when he published his renowned *Syllabus of the Errors of the Modernists* and the bull *Quanta cura*, bringing together the piecemeal condemnations of naturalism, communism and socialism he had made in allocutions and encyclical letters issued from 1846 onwards. As so often in papal history the spiritual force of these pronouncements had been somewhat blunted by the pope's obvious concern for his temporal authority and his income, but nonetheless the dangers to the church he ruled were very real. At the end of the year 1864, secret consultations between the pope and his cardinals resulted in the announcement that four commissions had been set up to prepare for a general council and the bull formally convoking it was promulgated in July 1868 and followed by appeals in October to the Eastern and Protestant churches to return to Catholic unity at this moment of crisis. Between the promulgation of this bull and the meeting of the council, it slowly and somewhat mysteriously became known throughout Europe that the council would be asked to promulgate the dogma of papal infallibility. The rumour aroused a good deal of opposition, but the arguments of Manning of Westminster, Deschamps of Malines, Senestrey of Ratisbon and Martin of Paderborn, to the effect that a clear statement of loyalty to and respect for the pope would strengthen the church, ultimately carried the day against those who argued either that such a definition was inopportune, or that it was simply not true. At the First Council of the Vatican itself, when the time came early in 1870 for the delegates to begin consideration of the proposed constitution 'On the Church' presented by the cardinals' commission, a petition was presented, signed by more than four hundred of the seven hundred delegates present in Rome, asking that only Chapter Eleven of the document 'On the Roman Pontiff' should be debated. The petition led to some acrimonious discussion but at last, in July 1870, after so much argument that some kind of statement had to be made for dignity's sake, the council was asked to consider a constitution entitled *Pastor Bonus*, setting out in four chapters the doctrine of Roman and papal primacy and leading up to a definition of papal infallibility. At the first count, on July 16, it was approved by 451 votes to 88, with 62 requests for modifications; after changes had been made, it was presented again on July 18 and passed by 535 votes to 2.

The constitution in its final form consists of some two thousand words of Latin text, but its essence—and in fact the essence of papalist theory—was contained in three canons and a brief definition. The first and second canons asserted that primacy had been given to Peter and that primacy had passed from him to his successors, the popes of Rome; the third declared it sinful to teach that 'the Roman Pontiff has some kind of office of inspection or direction, and not full and supreme power of jurisdiction over the universal church not only in those things pertaining to faith and morals but also in those concerning discipline and organization throughout the whole world, or that he has some measure of power and not the total plenitude of supreme power . . .'

The definition of the dogma itself was preceded by a lengthy historical statement on papal powers as defined by previous councils and ended:

> We teach and declare it to be a dogma divinely revealed [that] the Holy Roman Pontiff, when he speaks *ex cathedra*, that is, when acting as pastor and teacher of all Christians he defines by his supreme pontifical authority a doctrine concerning faith or morals to be held by the universal church, is endowed by the divine assistance promised to him in the blessed Peter with that infallibility which the divine Redeemer has willed that his church should have in defining teaching concerning

faith or morals; and therefore [that] the definitions of the Roman Pontiff are by their own nature (*ex sese*)—and not by virtue of the church's consent—irreformable.

When this definition is read with the accompanying text and canons, it is plain that its purpose was definitively to put an end to the debate about the source and centre of authority in the church, a debate which had been chronic since the Great Schism. In fact, it produced a scandal (the excommunication of its chief opponent, Professor Döllinger of Munich), a minor schism (leading to the foundation of the 'Old Catholic' Church) and a great cloud of confusion which time has done little to dispel. It is obvious that the decree was intended to have the effect of putting the pope permanently above criticism by any group of persons within the communion he ruled: as he is the inspired voice of truth when defining faith or morals, there can be no appeal from his official decisions to a general council or general opinion. Speaking privately, as a theologian or even a teacher, the pope is still liable to charges of heresy, in theory at least, but pronouncing a definition as pope, he cannot err.

Between 1870 and the Second Vatican Council, the decree on infallibility was read and approved in its plain sense by millions of Roman Catholics throughout the world. Theologians sometimes asked how we know when a pope is speaking *ex cathedra*, and whether a pope has ever done so. But the mass of Catholics believed, and the popes themselves acted as though they knew, that the successors of Peter had total plenitude of supreme power over the faith, morals, discipline and organization of the church. Papal exercise of this personal jurisdiction reached its highest point in 1950, with the declaration of the Dogma of the Assumption by Pope Pius XII, after consultations, but without a council, and in the face of some opposition, in the same way, that is, as his predecessor Pius IX had defined the Dogma of the Immaculate Conception in 1854.

The promulgation of the Dogma of the Assumption by the pope's authority did not provoke a schism but was one of the earliest stimuli to the revival of the debate about authority which has been so marked a characteristic of the church's life since the death of Pius XII. Authority was one of the main points at issue at the Second Vatican Council which began in 1962.

The *Dogmatic Constitutions* of the Second Vatican Council were not cast in the usual mould of definitions and canons. They discuss and expound doctrine, rather than define it. Although not actually self-contradictory, they are long, discursive and sometimes obscure. The Constitution *On the Church* reasserted the teaching of the First Vatican Council on the supremacy and infallibility of the pope, but with modifications that many have found significant. As well as papal infallibility, it also spoke of infallibility 'in matters of belief' as belonging to the body of the faithful as a whole—Cardinal Zarbarela's *Universitas fidelium*—and identified the Roman Pontiff as 'the head of the college of bishops' which is also infallible, so that 'when either the Roman Pontiff or the college of bishops together with him defines a judgment, they pronounce it in accord with revelation itself'.

The real significance of these statements has not yet become clear, and there has been a good deal of confused debate about them. The Second Vatican Council was certainly not a council to satisfy a fifteenth-century conciliarist. It came nowhere near conceding the main principle of conciliarism, that a general council, representing the congregation of the faithful, wields power superior to that of the pope and independent of his authority.

Societies exercising spiritual authority distrust both intellectualism and democracy; and the experience of the Roman Church at the Great Schism suggests that they may be right to do so. At the Councils of Pisa, Constance and Basle, university and national voters rocked the barque of Peter and all but wrecked it. They claimed to speak and vote as representatives of the congregation of the faithful, but the consensus of opinion within the Roman communion throughout history—and confirmed now at the Second Vatican Council in its constitution *On the Church*—has been that without its supreme head, designated by the Holy Spirit, the congregation of the faithful is incomplete and so cannot pass judgments or define doctrine.

Both the constitution *On the Church* and that *On Bishops* ascribed 'full and supreme' power over the church to the college of bishops, but both added that it could not act without 'its head' or his agreement. The Roman Church remains a hierarchical society under the pope. Having made that clear, the council went on to re-establish local synods, in the form of local episcopal conferences, and to announce the formation of a perpetual Synod of Bishops 'to render especially helpful assistance to the Supreme Pastor of the church'.

After the council had ended, Pope Paul VI established this central synod with a *motu proprio*—a personal act of the pontiff's—entitled

Apostolica sollicitudo, a distant descendant in the true Roman line from the decree *Frequens* passed at Constance five hundred and fifty years earlier.

Although the Synod of Bishops established by this document is not a general council, it is instructive to compare the two documents. *Frequens* ordered popes to hold councils every ten years at places fixed by delegates to the previous council in the series. It allowed the pope to shorten the interval between councils or change the place fixed for a council only 'on the advice of his brothers the cardinals' and 'with the written consent' of delegates. Paul VI's *motu proprio* of 1965 leaves the initiative in fixing the date and place of the meeting of the Synod entirely in the pope's hands and leaves him to decide what shall be discussed. *Frequens* took it for granted that experts of all kinds—canon lawyers, national delegates and so on—would attend its councils and vote there. The Synod of Bishops may be attended by a proportion of 'expert' delegates not exceeding fifteen percent of the total number of those attending. There is no provision anywhere in the constitutions of the Second Vatican Council or in any document since for the regular summoning of Oecumenical Councils. Regarding such councils, the Constitution *On the Church* rules that 'a council is never oecumenical unless it is confirmed as such . . . by the successor of Peter. It is the Roman Pontiff's prerogative to convoke these councils, to preside over them, and to confirm them'.

It is a pity that John XXIII did not live to sign it, as a fitting memorial to that other Pope John, Cardinal Cossa, and his contemporaries.

THE ROMAN SUCCESSION

The names of popes mentioned in the text are printed in Roman *type.*
(N.B. The names and regnal years of early popes are often uncertain)

1.	Peter the Apostle	martyred ?64 ?67
	Paul the Apostle	martyred ?64 ?67
2.	Linus	?67–76
3.	Cletus (*or* Anacletus)	?78–88
4.	Clement I	?88–97
5.	Evaristus	?97–105
6.	Alexander I	?105–115
7.	Xystus I (*or* Sixtus I)	115–125
8.	Telesphoros	125–136
9.	Hyginus	136–140
10.	Pius I	140–155
11.	Anicetus	155–166
12.	Soter	166–175
13.	Eleutherius	175–189
14.	*Victor*	189–199
15.	*Zephyrinus*	199–217
16.	Calixtus I (*or* Callistus)	217–222
17.	*Urban I*	222–230
18.	*Pontian*	230–235
19.	*Anteros*	235–236
20.	*Fabian*	236–250
21.	*Cornelius*	251–253
22.	*Lucius I*	253–254
23.	*Stephen I*	254–257
24.	*Xystus II* (*or* *Sixtus II*)	257–258
25.	*Dionysius* (*or* *Denis*)	259–268
26.	*Felix I*	269–274
27.	*Eutychian(us)*	275–283

28.	*Caius*	283–296	
29.	*Marcellinus*	296–304	
30.	*Marcellus I*	?308–309	
31.	*Eusebius*	309–310	
32.	Melitiades (*or* Melchiades)	311–314	Constantine's Edict of Toleration, Donatus
33.	Silvester I	314–335	Council of Nicaea, 325
34.	*Mark*	336	
35.	Julius I	337–352	
36.	*Liberius*	352–366	
37.	Damasus I	366–384	I Council of Constantinople, 381
38.	*Siricius*	384–399	
39.	*Anastatius I*	399–401	
40.	Innocent I	401–417	Pelagius Gothic Invasions
41.	Zozimus	417–418	
42.	*Boniface I*	418–422	
43.	Celestine I	422–432	The Vandal Invasions
44.	*Xystus III* (*or Sixtus III*)	432–440	
45.	Leo I (the Great)	440–461	Invasion of Attila, 450 Council of Chalcedon. 451
46.	*Hilarius* (*or Hilary*)	461–468	
47.	*Simplicius*	468–483	Romulus Augustulus, abdicated 476
48.	Felix III	483–492	Zeno's *Henotikon*, 482 Clovis, King of the Franks, 481–507

(*Felix II*, who reigned briefly in 335, was a false pope)

49.	Gelasius I	492–495	First Decretals
50.	*Anastasius II*	496–498	
51.	*Symmachus*	498–514	
52.	Hormisdas	514–523	
53.	*John I*	523–526	
54.	*Felix IV*	526–530	Justinian, 527–565
55.	*Dioscuros* (perhaps not a lawful pope)	530	
56.	*Boniface II*	530–532	

57. *John II*	532–535	
58. *Agapitus I*	535–536	
59. *Silverius*	536–537	
60. Vigilius	537–555	'The Three Chapters'
61. *Pelagius I*	556–561	
62. *John II*	561–574	
63. *Benedict I*	575–579	
64. *Pelagius II*	579–590	
65. Gregory I (the Great)	590–604	Mission to the English
66. *Sabinian*	604–606	
67. *Boniface III*	607	
68. *Boniface IV*	608–615	
69. *Deusdedit I*	615–618	
70. *Boniface V*	619–625	Mahommed's Flight from Mecca, 622
71. Honorius I	625–638	
(posthumously condemned for heresy)		
72. *Severinus*	640	
73. *John IV*	640–642	
74. *Theodore I*	642–649	
75. Martin I	649–655	
76. *Eugene I*	655–657	
77. *Vitalian*	657–672	
78. *Deusdedit II*	672–676	
79. *Donus I*	676–678	
80. Agatho	678–681	
81. *Leo II*	682–683	
82. *Benedict II*	684–685	
83. *John V*	685–686	
84. *Conon*	686–687	
85. *Sergius I*	687–701	
86. *John VI*	701–705	
87. *John VII*	705–707	
88. *Sisinnius*	708	
89. *Constantine*	708–715	
90. Gregory II	715–731	Iconoclasm Conversion of the Lombards
91. *Gregory III*	731–741	
92. *Zachary (or Zacharius)*	741–752	

93. *Stephen II*	752	
94. Stephen III	752–757	The Donation of Pepin, 756

(There may only have been one Stephen at this time, Stephen II; the evidence is ambiguous)

95. Paul I	757–767	
'Constantine of Nepi'	767–768	
96. Stephen IV	768–772	
97. Hadrian I	772–795	
98. Leo III	795–816	Coronation of Charlemagne, 800
99. *Stephen V*	816–817	
100. *Paschal I*	817–824	
101. *Eugene II*	824–827	
102. *Valentine*	827	
103. *Gregory IV*	827–844	
104. *Sergius II*	844–847	
105. *Leo IV*	847–855	
106. *Benedict III*	855–858	
107. Nicholas I (the Great)	858–867	
108. *Hadrian II*	867–872	
109. John VIII	872–882	
110. *Marinus I*	882–884	
111. *Hadrian III*	884–885	
112. *Stephen VI*	885–891	

(Tradition gave 885 as the year of the reign of Pope Joan)

113. *Formosus*	891–896	
114. *Boniface VI*	896	
115. *Stephen VII*	896–897	
116. *Romanus*	897	
117. *Theodore II*	897	
118. *John IX*	898–900	
119. *Benedict IV*	900–903	
120. *Leo V*	903	
121. *Sergius III*	904–911	Foundation of Cluny, 910
122. *Anastasius III*	911–913	
123. *Lando*	913–914	
124. *John X*	914–928	
125. *Leo VI*	928	

126. *Stephen VIII*   928–931
127. *John XI*   931–935
128. *Leo VII*   936–939
129. *Stephen IX*   939–942
130. *Martin III*   942–946
     (*Marinus I was also called Martin II*)
131. *Agapitus II*   946–955
132. John XII   955–964   Coronation of Otto,
                                             962
133. *Leo VIII*   963–965
     (probably a false pope)
134. *Benedict V*   964–966
     (probably a false pope)
135. *John XIII*   965–972
136. *Benedict VI*   973–974
137. *Benedict VII*   974–984
138. *John XIV*   983–984
139. *John XV*   985–996
140. *Gregory V*   996–999
141. *Silvester II*   999–1003
142. *John XVII*   1003
     (There was no legitimate John XVI)
143. *John XVIII*   1004–1009
144. *Sergius IV*   1009–1012
145. Benedict VIII   1012–1024
146. John XIX   1024–1032
147. *Benedict IX*   1032–1044
148. Gregory VI   1045–1046 ⎫ Deposed or resigned at
     Silvester III   1045   ⎬ the Synod of Sutri
     Clement II   1046–1047 ⎭
149. *Damasus II*   1048
150. Leo IX   1049–1054 The Eastern Schism,
                                             1054
151. *Victor II*   1055–1057
152. Stephen X   1057–1058
153. Nicholas II   1059–1061
     Antipope: Benedict X
154. *Alexander II*   1061–1073
155. Gregory VII   1073–1085 The Hildebrandine
                                             Reform

Antipope: Clement III   The Investiture Con-
                                        troversy
156. *Victor III*   1087
157. Urban II   1088–1099   The First Crusade
158. *Paschal II*   1099–1118
159. *Gelasius II*   1118–1119
160. Calixtus II   1119–1124   Diet of Worms, 1122
161. Honorius II   1124–1130
162. Innocent II   1130–1143   Bernard of Clairvaux
     Antipope: Anacletus II
163. *Celestine II*   1143–1144
164. *Lucius II*   1144–1145
165. *Eugene III*   1145–1153
166. Anastasius IV   1153–1154
167. Hadrian IV   1154–1159   Frederick Barbarossa,
                                           1152–1190
168. Alexander III   1159–1181
     Four Antipopes, including Paschal III
169. *Lucius III*   1181–1185
170. *Urban III*   1185–1187
171. *Gregory VIII*   1187
172. *Clement III*   1187–1191
173. Celestine III   1191–1198
174. Innocent III   1198–1216   The Sack of Constan-
                                           tinople, 1204
                                        The Albigensian
                                           Crusade
175. Honorius III   1216–1227   Frederick II, 1212–1250
176. Gregory IX   1227–1241   The Holy Inquisition
177. *Celestine IV*   1241
178. Innocent IV   1243–1254
179. Alexander IV   1254–1261
180. *Urban IV*   1261–1264
181. *Clement IV*   1265–1268
182. Gregory X   1271–1276
183. *Innocent V*   1276
184. *Hadrian V*   1276
185. *John XXI*   1276–1277
     (*there was no John XX*)
186. Nicholas III   1277–1280

187. *Martin IV*	1281–1285	
188. *Honorius IV*	1285–1287	
189. *Nicholas IV*	1288–1292	
190. Celestine V (resigned)	1294	Philip the Fair, King of France, 1285–1314
191. Boniface VIII	1294–1303	
192. Benedict XI	1303–1304	
193. Clement V	1305–1314	The Avignon Papacy
194. John XXII	1316–1334	
195. Benedict XII	1334–1342	
196. Clement VI	1342–1352	
197. Innocent VI	1352–1362	
198. Urban V	1362–1370	
199. Gregory XI	1370–1378	The Return from Avignon
200. *Either*		*or*
Urban VI	1378–1389	Clement VII 1378–1394
201. Boniface IX	1389–1404	Benedict XIII
		1394–1423
202. Innocent VII	1404–1406	Clement VIII
		1423–1429
203. Gregory XII	1406–1415	(Antipope: Benedict XIV)
Popes of the Council of Pisa		
Alexander V	1409–1410	
John XXIII	1410–1415	
204. Martin V	1417–1431	

Appendix II

CARDINALS OF THE GREAT SCHISM

Italian Cardinals
Peter Tebaldeschi, C.-Priest of S. Sabina, Archpriest of St. Peter's, 'The Cardinal of St. Peter' (died September 7, 1378).
Peter Corsini, C.-Bishop of Porto, 'The Cardinal of Florence'.
Simon of Bursano (or Brossano), C.-Priest of SS. John and Paul, 'The Cardinal of Milan'.
Jacomo Orsini, C.-Deacon of S. Giorgio-in-Velabro.

French Cardinals
The Limousin Party
Jean de Cros, C.-Priest of S. Palestrina, 'The Cardinal of Limoges'.
Guy de Malesset, C.-Priest of S. Croce, 'The Cardinal of Poitiers'.
Gérard de Puy, C.-Priest of S. Clemente, 'The Cardinal of Marmoutiers'.
Pierre de Vergne, C.-Deacon of S. Maria-in-Via-Lata.
Guillaume d'Aigrefeuille, C.-Priest of St. Stephen.

The Gallican Party
Robert of Geneva, C.-Priest of SS. Twelve Apostles, 'The Cardinal of Geneva', 'Clement VII'.
Bertrand de Lagery, C.-Priest of S. Cecilia, 'The Cardinal of Glandève'.
Hugh de Montelais, C.-Priest of SS. Quattuor Coronati, 'The Cardinal of Brittany'.
Pierre Flandrin, C.-Deacon of S. Eustatius.
Peter de Luna (Spanish), C.-Deacon of S. Martin, 'The Cardinal of Pamplona', 'Benedict XIII'.
Jean Lagrange, C.-Priest of S. Marcellus, 'The Cardinal of Amiens' (absent from the conclave, attending the Conference of Sarzena).

Independent

Peter de Sortenac, C.-Priest of S. Lawrence, 'The Cardinal of Viviers'.

William Noellet, C.-Deacon of S. Angelo, former *Vicarius* of Gregory XI in Italy.

A SHORT BIBLIOGRAPHY

General
General histories of the Papacy are too numerous to list here. They almost all contain accounts of the Great Schism and the Conciliar Movement.

HUGHES, P., *A Short History of the Catholic Church*, Burns and Oates, 1967, provides a good general introduction to papal history.

Also still valuable are the *Cambridge Mediaeval History*, vols. VII and VIII, and HUIZINGA, J., *The Waning of the Middle Ages*, Penguin Books, 1955.

HALE, HIGHFIELD and SMALLEY (Eds.), *Europe in the Late Middle Ages*, Faber, 1965, contains much interesting material, especially on late mediaeval universities.

Particular
CREIGHTON, M., *A History of the Papacy from the Great Schism to the Sack of Rome*, vols. II and III, London, 1882.

GILL, J., *Constance et Bâle-Florence*, Editions l'Orante, Paris, 1965.

HEFELE, C. J., ed. H. LECLERCQ, *Histoire des Conciles*, vols. VI and VII.

JACOB, E. F., *Essays in the Conciliar Epoch*, Manchester, 1963.

LOOMIS, L. R., *The Council of Constance*, London, 1962.

MANSI, *Sacrorum conciliorum . . . collectio*, vols. XXVII and XXVIII, Venice, 1794 etc.

MOLLAT, G., trans. LOVE, J., *The Popes at Avignon*, Nelson, 1963.

PASTOR, L., *Geschichte der Päpste* or, with additional material, *Storia dei Papi*, an Italian translation by A. MERCATI, Rome, 1910.

POWERS, G. C., *Nationalism at the Council of Constance*, Washington, 1927.

TIERNEY, B., *Foundations of Conciliar Thought*, Cambridge University Press, 1965, (invaluable for its references and bibliography).

ULLMANN, W., *Mediaeval Papalism*, Methuen, 1949.

— *Origins of the Great Schism*, Burns and Oates, 1948.

INDEX